Crime of the Century
Classic Rock and True Crime

Crime of the Century

Classic Rock and True Crime

Angie Moon

Troubador Publishing Ltd
Unit E2 Airfield Business Park
Harrison Road, Market Harborough
Leicestershire LE16 7UL
Tel: 0116 279 2299
Email: books@troubador.co.uk
Web: www.troubador.co.uk

ISBN 9781805143925

British Library Cataloguing in Publication Data.
A catalogue record for this book is available from the British Library.

Typeset in 11pt Adobe Garamond Pro by Troubador Publishing Ltd, Leicester, UK

Dedicated to my dad, James, who got me into true crime, and my husband, Eoin, who encouraged me to not just write a blog post about true crime and rock and roll, but to make it a whole book.

CONTENTS

WHY I WROTE CRIME OF THE CENTURY

The best ideas always seem to come into your head in these places: the kitchen, the shower and the toilet. This book is no exception – it was born in my kitchen. I wasn't even planning on making this a book originally, but because I tell my husband everything, he said classic rock and true crime shouldn't just be a little blog post, it should be a whole book! He saw that I was sad and feeling hopeless during the nearly year-long – although feeling more like an eternity – lockdown. So, he gave me a challenge and a reason to keep living – become a published author. That was one of my dreams. There was nothing to do but write, so why not take the writing a step further and write a book? Time keeps ticking away. Let's come out of this storm with a book!

In doing my research, I never saw a comprehensive blog post on true crime *and* classic rock, and I had so many topics to cover that a blog post wouldn't do it justice. The popularity of true crime has exploded in recent years with many books, documentaries and podcasts on it. I couldn't find a book specifically on the classic rock angle of true crime, so why not me? I love classic rock more than anything and I have an interest in true crime too. I've spent years of my life listening to classic rock and reading all I can about it to gain a better understanding and pass my knowledge on to other classic rock fans. I've written *The Diversity of Classic Rock* since

2015 and have paid my dues and learnt so much about classic rock, why not make this my first book?

While my family travelled a lot during my childhood, we did spend a lot of downtime when not travelling watching TV. My dad briefly worked as a cop in California in the '80s and had an interest in true crime and unsolved mysteries and so he'd watch true crime TV shows, before I even knew that was the genre's name. He loves 'based on a true story' movies and documentaries, and I love watching them too. Growing up, I would spend weekends and evenings watching true crime shows with my dad. We were fascinated with the psychology. Why would someone commit a murder? My mum wasn't a fan of that, because she felt like true crime programmes were not the best thing for a pre-teen to watch. Sometimes I'd watch true crime shows by myself, but whenever my mum would walk in the room, I'd change the channel straight away. I guess she'll have a better understanding now that true crime is much more mainstream.

TRUE CRIME & CLASSIC ROCK

Every book needs an introduction. My approach on *The Diversity of Classic Rock* is to never take anything for granted and my mission is to make learning about classic rock accessible and fun. It's always better to explain everything than to assume that people know everything. That approach applies to other topics I write about and have an interest in. You might be new to true crime or classic rock, so I'm writing an introduction on what these topics are. You can skip this if you already know what these topics are all about.

TRUE CRIME

True crime is self-explanatory. It's a genre of books, movies, podcasts, any media about actual crimes that happened. No fictional murder mysteries here. This is real life. For the most part, true crime is about murder, but it's not limited to that. The most popular true crime stories are about high-profile cases like the Manson Family, Ted Bundy, O.J. Simpson, Ted Kaczynski, Jeffrey Dahmer, Casey Anthony, etc. However, there are also many true crime aficionados who like to break up the routine and learn about more obscure true crime cases because there's more mystery and that can make the story more interesting.

There's some stigma and controversy around true crime and talking about violent criminals. One of the biggest criticisms is that some people see true crime as being disrespectful to the families of the victims. It can be if done the wrong way, which is why it's important to write about true crime in a responsible and respectful way by not glorifying the criminals.

Many people stereotype people who have an interest in true crime as glorifying and glamourising criminals. Yes, some people who like true crime romanticise killers like Eric Harris and Dylan Klebold, Richard Ramirez and Ted Bundy, but most of the true crime fandom are people with an interest in psychology and the legal and justice system and want to understand why people do evil things. They want to understand how criminal investigations work, they want to share their theories, solve mysteries and crack codes, and people just like dark and macabre stories to distract from a humdrum life.

CLASSIC ROCK

Classic rock is really a radio format that plays popular rock music from the '60s, '70s, '80s, and I guess the '90s, because it is the 2020s now and that music is approaching thirty years old. Typically, this is thought of as music your grandparents or parents listened to in their youth, depending on how old you are. Classic rock on the radio ranges from mid-late '60s stuff like The Beatles, The Rolling Stones, The Who, Cream, and Jimi Hendrix. The '70s on classic rock stations includes some glam rock by David Bowie and T. Rex, soft rock by Fleetwood Mac and Elton John, and hard rock by Led Zeppelin and Van Halen. The '80s is usually represented by bands like U2, Guns N' Roses, Bon Jovi, Journey, and Mötley Crüe.

On my blog, though, I have expanded the definition to mean anything rock or 'rock adjacent' released from the '50s to the '80s. What is 'rock adjacent' exactly? Any music that has similar roots to rock and roll and has crossover with rock music with rock stars covering songs from those genres and musicians from these genres covering rock songs. It includes genres like R&B, soul, ska, reggae and disco, but I don't limit it to those genres. I also don't limit it to music in English and I'll sometimes talk about music in other languages. You're missing out if you only listen to music in English. *Parasite* director Bong Joon-ho said it best at the Golden Globes, 'Once you overcome the one-inch-tall barrier of subtitles, you will be introduced to so many more amazing films.' Always keep an open mind – that's another one of my core values! Growing up with a Venezuelan mother who grew up listening to music in English but not knowing what it meant, she just liked the vibes of the music. Use your imagination and come up with meanings that are different. It's art: for all to enjoy and to be creative with.

Classic rock stations don't play the full range of music from those decades. The radio is now very commercial and homogenous thanks to concentrated media ownership. Once upon a time when there were limits on how many stations a corporation could own, music was much more regional and travelling across America you could hear a wider variety of music; well, those times are gone. Or are they? Thanks to the internet, we have more knowledge about classic rock than ever before. Some bands that didn't get the airtime and appreciation at the time finally have found appreciation thanks to real life and online 'crate diggers' who find the underrated and overlooked gems. I'll regularly have conversations with my dad and I'll talk about British groups from the classic rock era that he doesn't know about even though he's a bit of an Anglophile himself: The Shadows (even if you don't know them, you'll know 'Apache' when you hear it), The Small Faces (pint-sized Cockney mods – Steve Marriott had a voice that other classic rockers envied), and The Jam (The Clash-like punk, but more British). Sure, I didn't get to see these bands in their prime – I was born too late for that – but I think the younger, outsider perspective is a valuable one and with the internet, there are so many possibilities, and everything is at your fingertips.

WHAT DO THESE EVEN HAVE TO DO WITH EACH OTHER?

Why write this book? Is there even much overlap? Do true crime enthusiasts like classic rock? Do classic rock fans like true crime? Do you have to like classic rock to appreciate this book? As someone who is passionate about classic rock and tries to make everything in their life about classic rock, I find the connections between classic rock and literally everything I can. Makes my life more fun. That's the point of my blog and why my tagline is 'Classic Rock: more than meets the eye… and ear!' It started off as talking about musicians from different ethnic backgrounds and walks of life and evolved from that to telling stories about classic rock. I'd run out of ideas pretty quickly if I just stopped at identity. At the end of the day, my blog isn't about musicians' identities, it's telling stories about interesting, talented people. There's way more to a person than identity labels that apply to them. Every person on this planet has an interesting story, yes you too, the one reading this book. It's just up to you to ask the right questions and get to know your fellow human beings.

I think of myself as a classic rock storyteller and someone who tries to make connections and relate seemingly unrelated, random things to each other. Come, grab a cup of tea and your favourite snacks and enjoy the stories and learn a bit about the best music ever made (in my biased opinion that is). It's all about connectedness and togetherness here.

While doing research, I found more connections than I expected between these two topics that I have an interest in and I thought this would be a unique and interesting read for anyone who loves classic rock and true crime, or who has an interest in one or the other.

In short, you don't have to be obsessed with classic rock like I am to love this book, but you might end up loving it. This book tells stories about people. I don't have much interest in sports, but

I've found movies about athletes, like *42* or *I, Tonya*, interesting because they're not really about sports, they're about people. The fact that they play sports is often secondary to the movie. The narrative focuses on the human elements and who they are as a person: growing up, conflicts, challenges, struggles, overcoming adversity, successes. Similarly, you don't have to be a physicist to enjoy movies like *Oppenheimer* or *The Theory of Everything*. These movies are about life! If you have an interest in other people, you'll love this book and any media that's based on a true story or about true events.

WHY *CRIME OF THE CENTURY*?

If you know your classic rock, you'll know the reference, but in case you haven't figured it out, *Crime of the Century* is the title of an album by prog/soft rock band Supertramp. It's a fitting title since I love to make classic rock references and incorporate them in everything I do. When writing this book and searching for 'true crime' and 'classic rock' on the internet, Supertramp's *Crime of the Century* was one of the things that showed up first. Makes sense! Might as well give a little history since this is a book and you're paying for this (or borrowing it from the library – fair play to you!) and I'm gonna ensure you're well fed because I'm the mum friend. The goal here is learning all about classic rock so you can wow your friends at pub quizzes when classic rock is one of the topics and you ace it! A rare event, yes, but I'm sure it's more common than Halley's Comet.

Crime of the Century, as in the album, was Supertramp's commercial breakthrough and a pretty well-loved art rock album. Their previous two albums, *Supertramp* and *Indelibly Stamped* were commercial flops. There were a few line-up changes between albums and some new faces were brought in for *Crime of the Century*: drummer Bob Siebenberg, saxophone/clarinet player John Helliwell, and bassist Dougie Thomson. The album cover is of a field of stars and the text of the band's name is styled as a constellation. Floating in the stars are jail cell bars and two hands holding the bars, a prisoner wanting to get out, but they're floating in the void. An appropriate sentence for a *Crime of the Century*. When you're stuck in an institution, you feel like you're in the void – disconnected from society – yet time keeps ticking by and you're waiting for it all to be over.

The album appropriately opens with a harmonica; you know the film trope where the lonely prisoner is sitting in a cell bored out of his mind, playing the harmonica? The first track is called 'School,' and it's about how conformist school is, five years before Pink Floyd sang 'Another Brick in the Wall, Part 2'. Boomers had a lot more reasons to hate school than us millennials do. Back then it was legal for teachers to beat students! The negative effects of traditional schooling to your mental health though? The same whether it's the 1960s or 2020s.

The album moves onto other themes like mental health, which is very much linked to the capitalist system for sure, at least in my left libertarian, class-conscious view of the world. You spend a good portion of your life in school, then you go to work for a company that doesn't care about you for around half a century, and then you retire when you're old, grey, and not feeling well enough to enjoy life. With the rising cost of living and all these recessions, retirement is becoming a pipe dream for millennials and Gen Z. It's no wonder a lot of young people feel depressed, undervalued, and like they have no purpose.

Crime of the Century isn't a concept album, even though the songs have similar themes. 'Bloody Well Right' continues on that theme of rebelling against schools and the system and the man in general – that's rock and roll! 'Hide in Your Shell' is a relatable therapy 'sesh' of a song all about anxiety and fear of the real world. Supertramp basically said 'adulting is hard' before the slang term 'adulting' was coined (apparently adulting isn't just silly millennial slang since as I'm writing this, there's no red squiggle underneath, props to Apple for being hip, and it's in the Cambridge Dictionary). Continuing on that mental health theme, we have 'Asylum'. The people around the narrator want to get him help and send him to an asylum where he'd lose his freedom; he's trying to convince them he is fine, but in reality, he's a wreck inside. 'Dreamer' is another relatable song; everyone has their dreams and wants them to come true, but for one reason or another, a lot of dreams never come true, no matter how hard you try. The negative self-talk in the song hit too close to home.

'Rudy' is the longest song on the album about the titular protagonist of the album and is sort of an autobiographical song about Rick Davies. This song about trains wouldn't be complete without some sounds from the train station to add some realism and to take the listener to where Rudy is.

'If Everyone Was Listening' is a philosophical, even Shakespearean song that makes you think about life. Is it real? What's the point? 'All the world's a stage', as the monologue from Shakespeare's *As You Like It* goes. This being my book, I see all the classic rock connections and I'll talk about them. You might be doing the Leonardo DiCaprio meme thing from *Once Upon a Time in Hollywood*, pointing at the book (or screen, if you're reading this on a computer or tablet). That famous line, 'All the world's a stage' was referenced by Rush a couple times. That's the title of their 1976 live album and you might be Leonardo DiCaprio-ing when you hear that line in Rush's 1981 song 'Limelight', from the album *Moving Pictures* – a classic.

The album closes with the title track, considered one of Supertramp's best songs. In 1974, there was an economic recession and now in 2023, we're in an economic depression and cost of living crisis. I think of these criminals referenced in the song as being the billionaire leeches who get rich off the backs of the common people. Bookending the album is the same harmonica.

Besides *Crime of the Century* being a great album by Supertramp, it's a popular phrase that describes sensational criminal cases and isn't true crime full of those? It's a crime that only happens once or a few times a century and will go down in the history books and be talked about for many years to come, inspiring books, songs, poems, movies, plays, you name it.

A variation of the idiom 'crime of the century' is 'trial of the century'. You've definitely heard this expression used to describe televised trials, or in the pre-broadcast television era, highly publicised trials. Some examples could include the Lizzie Borden trial, Lindbergh kidnapping trial, Nuremberg trials, Julius and Ethel Rosenberg trial, the Chicago Seven Trial, Charles Manson trial, Ted Bundy trial, O.J. Simpson trial, Yolanda Saldívar trial, Michael Jackson trial, Casey Anthony trial, and the Phil Spector trial. These trials were all discussed widely in the press with sensationalist headlines and in some cases, memorable video clips that were broadcast on television.

There are some pros and cons to televising court cases. Americans reading this book are familiar with trials being televised on *CNN* or *Court TV*, but readers from Europe may find this idea odd because there are a lot more privacy laws and there's no tradition of broadcasting trials.

If you're of the pro-transparency persuasion, you might say televised trials are good because the whole world is watching and having more eyeballs on court proceedings is a good thing. Everyone has the right to a fair trial and transparency is a big part of fairness. Because there's public interest in the crime, people want to follow the case every step of the way from the police investigations to the arrest to the indictment to the trial to the sentencing and interviews with the convict in prison (and in the case of America, execution if they're sentenced to the death penalty). Not only established journalists get to see it first-hand, but also bloggers and independent media too and you can hear more perspectives and opinions, and isn't that what democracy is all about?

The broadcasting of trials has its faults though. The first one has to do with the legal principle of 'innocent until proven guilty'. Being accused of a serious crime can ruin your life even if in the end you're found to be not guilty; note that this doesn't mean innocent. The accused has their face plastered all over the place and associated with a crime. With crimes and trials being covered all over the media, there's a trial by media of sorts held in the court of public opinion. If you're accused of a serious crime, your life is never going to be the same again even if you're found not guilty or the charges are dropped, that's for sure. There's always going to be people who will think, 'What if they did do it?'. Doesn't someone who isn't convicted yet deserve privacy since they haven't been proven guilty?

Trial by media can also disrupt due process and lead to an unfair trial. In jury selection they ask potential jurors if they have been following the case. Those who have been avidly following it are going to have a bias going in. Juries need to be unbiased. In some high-profile cases, they'll even move the court proceedings to a different city or county to ensure a fair trial because the case has been talked about so much on the local TV news, radio, and in newspapers. But nowadays word gets out a lot quicker, more easily and further, thanks to the internet.

It's also important to remember that false accusations and wrongful convictions happen more than you would expect. Groups like The Innocence Project focus on getting wrongfully convicted people exonerated and freed from prison. According to their website, they have freed more than 200 people who have spent 3,555 total years incarcerated. On average, these prisoners have lost sixteen years of their life and often it's their youth and best years of their lives: their twenties, thirties, and forties. Years they'll never get back and now they're dealing with psychological trauma from being incarcerated for so long. Many of these convictions were overturned thanks to the marvels of science and technology, like DNA evidence, finally properly being used.

Is seeing trials live necessary though? If you've ever taken a law class, you'll know that law is often boring! Long words that you don't know the meaning of. Lots of formalities and rituals that you don't know the point of. If we take a step away from the sensationalism of the news, most criminal trials are boring. Most crimes aren't true-crime-book-worthy material. Who wants to watch a televised shoplifting trial or a livestream of traffic court? No one. And that's a good thing.

THE FORMAT OF THIS BOOK

We'll end this introduction with how this book is going to work so you'll know what to expect. You've seen the table of contents, but I find those so dry anyway. Introductions have a lot more character.

I have divided this book into two sections. The first section is about murderers and attempted murderers and their connection to classic rockers and the second section is about musicians who have killed people.

Each chapter will focus on a different true crime–classic rock connection. They will each have sections giving background information on the various people involved so you have the context before going into the connection. They will be in chronological order for the most part since that makes the most sense. In the chapters about musicians who have committed murders, there will be background information about the musician before talking about the crime itself.

Classic Rockers & Killers

(and Attempted Murderers)

The first section will be looking at all the connections between classic rockers, convicted murderers, and a couple of attempted murderers and a couple who were acquitted. This is where my research on true crime and classic rock began. I noticed how many close calls and encounters classic rockers had with murderers, attempted murderers, and otherwise dangerous people and it's scary to think about what could have happened had things gone differently. In this section you'll be reading stories from a range of classic rock eras from the early 1960s to the 1980s that cover a range of classic rock subgenres from rockabilly to British Invasion to surf rock to hard rock to new wave.

CHAPTER 1

A Nightmare on Elm Street: The Band & Jack Ruby (1963)

Our story of classic rock and true crime begins in the state of Texas just as the world was about to culturally move from the conformist '50s to the swinging '60s. Here's the connection between a '60s folk rock band from Canada and a mobster who shot Lee Harvey Oswald, the man who assassinated President John F. Kennedy.

THE BAND... OR RATHER, THE HAWKS

Since this connection happened very early on in their career, before they were known as The Band, this will just be a summary of their early years. At the time, they were known as The Hawks, but for our purposes the title of the chapter refers to them as The Band because that's what they are best known as. The Hawks were better known in Canada than in Ronnie Hawkins' birthplace, the USA.

The band that would later become known as The Band were formed in Toronto, Canada in the late '50s. They started off as The Hawks, a backing band for American-born rockabilly singer Ronnie Hawkins, AKA The Hawk, regarded by many as the 'granddaddy of Canadian rock 'n' roll' because he was one of the local musicians who introduced rock and roll to Canada. Now what's an American doing up there? Was he dodging the draft? No. While Ronnie Hawkins was playing shows with his band in Fayetteville, Arkansas, country singer Conway Twitty suggested he go to Canada because there were many Canadians who had an interest in country music. When Hawkins told his band they were going to move to Canada, everybody quit except for drummer Levon Helm. Ronnie Hawkins quickly won over the Canadian audiences, became quite successful there, and preferred playing there rather than in the south because of the much better working conditions. From there, they hired on Canadians Robbie Robertson, Rick Danko, Richard Manuel, and Garth Hudson, making up the classic line-up of The Band. Most of these musicians were poached from other bands playing on the same bill as Ronnie Hawkins. Ronnie Hawkins served as a mentor to not only The Band, but also other musicians including David Clayton-Thomas, Domenic Troiano, David Foster, King Biscuit Boy, and John Till. The skills that The Hawks honed while on the road with Ronnie Hawkins helped them impress Bob Dylan, who is often said to have discovered The Band, hiring them as his backing band when he famously adopted that new electric sound, and helped launch their career. The Band's most famous songs are 'The Weight' – which you might have heard in the 1960s road trip film *Easy Rider,* 'Up On Cripple Creek', and 'The Night They Drove Old Dixie Down' – famously covered by Joan Baez in 1971. In short, The Band are essential listening for any fan of folk or country rock.

Ronnie Hawkins was born exactly two days after Elvis Presley, on 10 January 1935 in Huntsville, Arkansas to Jasper and Flora Hawkins. His cousin, Dale Hawkins, wrote the song 'Susie Q', popularised by Creedence Clearwater Revival, and was one of the first white singers to perform at historic black venues, the Apollo Theater in Harlem and the Regal Theater in Chicago. When he was nine, his family moved to Fayetteville. His father was a barber and his mother was a schoolteacher. Unlike a lot of rock musicians, he stayed in school and didn't learn to play an instrument. During his childhood and teen years, he performed at fairs in his home state. One time, he ended up sharing the stage with Hank Williams. He was too drunk to perform and so the band asked for volunteers to sing and entertain the crowd; Ronnie Hawkins took his chance and sang some Burl Ives songs as well as the Stephen Foster compositions 'Beautiful Dreamer' and 'Camptown Races'. Later on, he got into blues music thanks to Buddy Hayes, a blues musician who shined shoes at Jasper's barbershop. Not only was Ronnie Hawkins a great singer, but he was also a great dancer. Decades before Michael Jackson blew everyone's minds with the moonwalk, Ronnie Hawkins had a similar dance called the camel walk, which he learnt from a young black street performer called Half Pint. He studied physical education at the University of Arkansas, but he dropped out just shy of a few credits to graduate and enlisted in the Army. During his six-month stint in the Army, he heard a band play music that was a cross between blues and rockabilly. He was moved by the music and found his calling.

Drummer Levon Helm was born Mark Lavon Helm in 1940 in Elaine, Arkansas, near the Mississippi River, to Diamond and Nell Helm. His parents were cotton farmers. He grew up in a diverse community with black sharecroppers and Mexican migrant farm workers, and his family got along well with their multicultural neighbours. This region is also the birthplace of R&B music. Many black musicians from this region migrated up north and, in some cases, west for better opportunities, bringing with them the music that would lead to rock and roll. While there was (and still is) a lot of racism in the south, the music was something that both black and white people loved. Levon's mother and maternal grandfather were anti-racists and hated the Ku Klux Klan. He was always taught that all people are equal, no matter their race, colour, or religion and it's wrong to look down upon people because it's very un-Christian. His family were a musical family. The parents both sang and father Diamond would teach his children songs. Diamond knew so many songs that he would keep teaching Levon the songs up until he died at the age of eighty-two. The family would always tune into the radio, listening to programmes like the *Grand Ole Opry*. Being surrounded by music, naturally he got into it, getting his first guitar at the age of nine. When going to live shows, he was most fascinated by the drummer and so naturally he took up drumming. As a teenager, he started travelling to Memphis to see the rock and roll there. Elvis Presley, of course, was a huge inspiration to him. While still in secondary school, Levon Helm got an offer to join Ronnie Hawkins' band, becoming his right-hand man. Because his parents insisted on him staying in school, he didn't play full-time with him until 1958. Shortly after graduating from high school, Helm and Hawkins left for Canada and little by little put together a new line-up there. This band split from Ronnie Hawkins after 1963 because they found him to be too restrictive professionally, creatively, and even in the band members' personal lives. Even then, Levon Helm had kind words to say about The Hawk in his autobiography, saying that he was a good friend, great leader, likeable, trustworthy, funny, and educated. Levon Helm died on 19 April 2012.

Lead guitarist Robbie Robertson was born Jaime Royal Robertson on 5 July 1943 in Toronto to an indigenous (Mohawk and Cayuga) mother named Rosemarie Dolly Chrysler. His biological father, Alexander Klegerman, was Jewish, but his mother was married to a man named James Patrick Robertson, which is where Robbie got his last name from. Rosemarie met both of these men while working at the Coro Jewellery – a gold- and silver-plating factory. He grew up on the Six Nations Reserve, not far from the US border, and in Toronto, in a diverse, vibrant neighbourhood with a lot of immigrants. As a child on the Six Nations Reserve, he was surrounded by music, with his relatives playing guitar and singing songs. He found that it resonated with him and so he learnt to play guitar too. As a teenager, he was in a band called The Suedes and they opened for Ronnie Hawkins.

Robbie was a fan of Ronnie Hawkins and at just sixteen years old he travelled from Toronto to Arkansas to try out for The Hawks. He lied to the border guards about the purpose of his trip because he would have been turned away if he had mentioned work. He was so dedicated to this goal that he sold his prized 1958 sunburst Fender Stratocaster, and the rest is history. Robbie Robertson died on 9 August 2023.

Bassist Rick Danko was born on 29 December 1943 in a farming community near the town of Simcoe, Ontario. His father, Maurice, was of Eastern European (Ukrainian and Romanian) and Mongolian descent and his mother, Leola, was of Welsh descent. Growing up, he dealt with a lot of health problems: allergies, asthma, and eczema, and so he had to be indoors a lot. Back in those days, there were no video games and in rural areas, TVs were not common; much of the fun stuff to do was outdoors and Rick Danko spent much of his childhood without electricity. Any kid would go stir-crazy in those conditions, but what kept Rick going and gave him an escape was music, all thanks to a humble little battery-powered radio that transported him to a whole new world south of the border – Nashville, Tennessee, famous for the *Grand Ole Opry*. Inspired by the music he heard, he decided to learn to play banjo, and from there he learnt other string instruments like guitar, violin, and later bass guitar. While country music was his first love, he got into other types of music, his other favourite being R&B. Like many other rock stars, he dropped out of school to follow his dreams of being a musician. One day, he saw Ronnie Hawkins in concert and was in awe. He started a band called The Starlights, who opened for Ronnie Hawkins and he noticed the young musician and wanted him to be in his band, and so he joined The Hawks, which later became known as The Band. Rick Danko died on 10 December 1999.

Next to join The Hawks was pianist/singer Richard Manuel. Everyone thinks of Robbie Robertson and Levon Helm as the singers of the band, but Richard Manuel also contributed lead vocals and he had a great voice too. He was born in Stratford, Ontario on 3 April 1943 to James Edwin and Gladys Manuel. As a child, he sang in church choir and took piano lessons. His biggest influences were Ray Charles, Bobby Bland, Jimmy Reed, and Otis Rush. As a teenager, he played piano in a band called The Revols with John Till, who would go on to be in Janis Joplin's backup band, the Full Tilt Boogie Band. They were fans of Ronnie Hawkins and they honed their skills so they could open for him. Like other members of The Hawks, one day Ronnie Hawkins noticed him and hired him for his band and it changed his life. The moment that Hawkins knew he had found talent was when he sang a cover of Ray Charles's 'Georgia On My Mind'. But he didn't hire him at first; instead, he managed The Revols before poaching Manuel for his band. Richard Manuel died on 4 March 1986.

Finally, multi-instrumentalist Garth Hudson, the oldest of the bunch, only two years younger than Ronnie Hawkins. He was born Eric Garth Hudson on 2 August 1937 in the border town of Windsor, Ontario to Fred and Olive Hudson. He was an only child. At five years old, his family moved to London, Ontario. He took piano lessons from a young age and was classically trained in piano. He also learnt how to play accordion and saxophone. A child prodigy, he started writing songs at just eleven years old. He briefly studied music at the University of Western Ontario before dropping out to play music professionally. Often playing organ at church, he brought gospel influences to the table, but he was a really versatile player. He also loved jazz music and played in local dance bands before Ronnie Hawkins hired him in 1961. There were some conditions though. He asked for a Lowrey Organ (which he had been jonesing for since he saw a musician play one at a concert in Detroit) and extra pay so he could give his bandmates music lessons, so his parents would be happy and not feel like he was throwing his education away to play rock music. Levon Helm said that Hudson was a very important part of the band because his organ playing helped complete the sound, truly turning them into a rock and roll orchestra with sounds coming out of that organ that no other group had.

JACK RUBY

Jack Ruby was born Jacob Rubenstein sometime in the spring of 1911 in Chicago, Illinois – many different birthdates were given between March and April. His family were a large Jewish family of ten children. His parents, Joseph Rubenstein and Fannie Rutkowski were Orthodox Jewish immigrants from Sokołów, a town fifty miles east of Warsaw. True to tradition, their marriage was arranged. His childhood was a difficult one with his veteran father being an alcoholic and his illiterate mother having anger-management problems, and the family moving around a lot between different Jewish neighbourhoods in Chicago. After years of fighting, the Rubenstein parents got a divorce and Fannie was checked into a mental hospital.

A difficult home life is not a good foundation for a child growing up and Jack got in trouble a lot as a child starting with little things like skipping school and later escalating to him joining street gangs. His truancy problem was so bad that he was sent to the Institute for Juvenile Research at University of Illinois at Chicago when he was just eleven years old. Psychologists there described him as quick-tempered and disobedient in their reports. They also noted that his mother's temperament and argumentative nature could have caused Jack to develop these traits, which led him to being nicknamed 'Sparky'. However, there are some people, such as Ruby's idol Barney Ross, who was a boxer, who said that Jack Ruby wasn't a troublemaker growing up and was well behaved. Other friends said he tended to avoid confrontation. He and some of his siblings were removed from their parents' home and sent to live in foster care for a few years. He left school at the age of sixteen, with only an eighth-grade education, as a result of years of being held back. Instead of school, his main focus was making money to support himself and his working-class family by working various odd jobs such as scalping tickets and selling various novelties.

In 1933, during the Great Depression, Jack Ruby moved to California for better opportunities. He worked various odd jobs in LA and San Francisco such as selling horse-racing tip sheets, working as a singing waiter, and as a door-to-door salesman. He didn't have a reputation for being violent or having a temper over there, but rather as a clean-cut, honest person. He would mostly hang out with other Jewish people. A few years later, he went back to Chicago, but struggled to find work until he found a job with a garbage collectors' union. He left the union after his friend Leon Cooke, who was a lawyer and the union's financial secretary, was shot and killed by the president of the union, John Martin. The union later got in trouble with the AFL-CIO, the largest US federation of unions. After that, he went back to selling novelties with friends, mostly gambling punchboards, a type of game board used for lottery games. He wasn't involved in the most above-the-board business ventures, but there is not much evidence that he had significant connections to organised crime in Chicago, according to friends and even mobsters themselves. Sure, mobsters were familiar and even friendly with him, but that was about it. There wasn't anything remarkable about Jack Ruby as a mobster. Had he not shot Lee Harvey Oswald, no one would be talking about him today. That's what gave him his notoriety.

Like many young men in America, Jack Ruby was drafted in WWII. He was one of the oldest ones, with him being in his early thirties. There is no indication that he was anti-American, but rather that he had a lot of respect for President Roosevelt. He didn't let being drafted stop him from selling punchboards and novelties; he continued selling these things on the Army base to make extra cash. He was discharged in 1946. The following year, he changed his name to Jack Ruby and moved to Dallas, Texas to start nightclubs with his sister, Eva Grant, who had experience owning and operating restaurants on the West Coast. These nightclubs were not very classy. There were strippers and he would invite cops and journalists to the clubs to get on their good side. Musicians would also play at these clubs and this is where we get the connection, but first, here's a bit of background information on Jack Ruby shooting and killing Lee Harvey Oswald. First, we'll go into the telling of the events, according to findings from the Warren Commission that Oswald acted alone. Many people have questions about this, and that will be addressed afterwards.

On 22 November 1963 at 12:30 PM Central Standard Time, the world was shaken when President John F. Kennedy was shot in Dallas, Texas while riding in a motorcade through Dealey Plaza. Not only was JFK killed, but also police officer J.D. Tippit. Texas Governor John Connally, who was in the same car as President Kennedy and his wife, suffered severe injuries: a fractured rib, punctured lung, a shattered wrist, and a bullet in his leg, and car salesman James Tague suffered minor wounds. Everyone knows where they were when they heard the news. What 9/11 was to the millennials, the JFK assassination was for the boomers.

What was the president doing in Dallas? Texas is a big state and a very conservative one and with the presidential election being the next year, President Kennedy knew he needed to win Texas if he wanted to have a hope of winning another term. He had barely won Texas in 1960, so he couldn't take chances for 1964. His goal was to get more donations and support from voters and get Texas Democrats united and supporting him. First Lady Jackie Kennedy came along to help win voters over with her sophisticated style. The image of the President riding through Dallas with large crowds cheering him on was a powerful one and would be useful for the campaign. Not even an hour before the assassination, the President, First Lady, and their party arrived at Love Field (which was then Dallas's major airport) and from there they left in a motorcade that rode through Dallas, which had been publicised the week before.

A twenty-four-year-old Marine veteran and former Soviet

Union defector named Lee Harvey Oswald shot and killed President Kennedy from the sixth floor of the Texas School Book Depository hidden behind a wall of boxes. This wasn't the first time he tried to shoot a politician. On 10 April 1963, he tried to kill a far-right ex-Army general named Edwin Walker. The bullet ricocheted off a windowsill, just missing Walker's head by an inch! Oswald fled the scene and wasn't caught or even considered a suspect. Walker died thirty years later of lung cancer. In between the Walker assassination attempt and the JFK assassination, Lee Harvey Oswald lived in New Orleans and Mexico, returning to Dallas on 2 October 1963. Two weeks later, he was hired at the Texas School Book Depository making minimum wage.

The President's 1961 Lincoln Continental convertible limousine turned left onto Elm Street and passed by Dealey Plaza and as the car passed the Texas School Book Depository, there were gunshots; the President and Governor had been shot. The President's limousine sped to Parkland Memorial Hospital in an attempt to save his life, arriving just minutes later. Surprisingly, he was still alive when he arrived at the hospital. At 1pm, President Kennedy was pronounced dead. Talk about *A Nightmare On Elm Street*!

Meanwhile, the police zeroed in on the Texas School Book Depository as the source of the shots. Building superintendent Roy Truly cooperated with the Dallas Police and he and Patrolman Marrion Baker ran into Oswald in the building, but they didn't arrest him straight away and Oswald left the building. He boarded a bus and later shot patrolman J.D. Tippit. Witnesses saw Oswald run into the Texas Theater and the cops surrounded the cinema. He was arrested and brought to police headquarters at 2pm. He famously shouted, 'I didn't shoot anybody,' and 'I'm a patsy!'

Within forty-eight hours of the assassination of President Kennedy, Lee Harvey Oswald was shot dead as well. On 24 November, Oswald was set to be transferred via an unmarked police car from city jail to county jail. Journalists were crowded around there to get film footage and photos of the presidential assassin in handcuffs, flanked by police officers escorting him through the basement to the car, when all of a sudden, a fifty-two-year-old nightclub owner named Jack Ruby approached Oswald with a gun in his hand and shot him live on national television. Ruby was arrested straight away. On 14 March 1964, he was found guilty of the murder of Lee Harvey Oswald and was sentenced to death.

In 1992, the President John F. Kennedy Assassination Records Collection Act was passed. It was supposed to provide for an expeditious disclosure of records relevant to the JFK assassination to quell speculation. All documents were supposed to be released twenty-five years later, in 2017, but time after time, the can kept getting kicked down the road. It's not a good look for the US government and it's no surprise that people have their theories and think the whole lone gunman theory is fishy. The government always tells us, 'If you have nothing you hide, you have nothing to fear', but why doesn't that apply to the government? Some possible theories of who was behind it include the Russians, the Cubans, the Mafia, LBJ, and last but not least, the CIA. The last one makes a lot of sense if you know your history and you know what the Feds have done to leftists and to leftist movements in Latin America. So, it doesn't sound that far-fetched that the CIA would 'off' the president if they saw him as a threat or too far left. And this isn't some crazy InfoWars-level tinfoil hat business. Many normies don't buy that Oswald acted alone. Here's some statistics from some polls done by JFK assassination history expert Fernand Amandi: around 70% said they want President Biden to release the records; support for releasing the records is bipartisan with 66% of Democrats and 76% of Republicans saying yes; 50% said they think others were involved besides Lee Harvey Oswald, and 31% believed the CIA planned the JFK assassination.

It is important to note that recently, some documents related to the JFK assassination have been declassified under President Biden. However, there are still thousands of documents that contain redactions. These documents give new clues to Lee Harvey Oswald being linked to the CIA and finally we had mainstream media questioning the government narrative as you'll see. Ryan Grim of *The Intercept* wrote a great article summarising some of these new finds. In the late '50s, Atsugi, the naval base that Oswald was stationed at in Japan, also had a lot of CIA research into psychedelic drugs going on and U-2 jets took off from there to spy on the Soviet Union. Allegedly, Oswald was one of those who was experimented on, taking LSD. After being discharged from the military for made-up reasons (faking his mother being ill) with only $203 dollars to his name, he took a boat to England, flew on a military transport flight to Helsinki – where he stayed in fancy hotels – and from there took a train to Moscow where he defected and stayed for 2.5 years before coming back to America like nothing happened. If someone's broke, how do they afford that? How does one just come back to America after defecting to 'the enemy' and not get arrested? That's where the CIA theory comes in, because before that he was studying Russian at a base in Monterey, California. While the CIA claimed that they didn't keep in contact with Lee Harvey Oswald, he was close friends with Russian-born CIA asset George de Mohrenschildt and that friendship grew stronger in the months before the assassination. De Mohrenschildt travelled across the north-east of the US and the Domestic Operations Division of the CIA ran a check on him for 'unknown reasons'. At the time, E. Howard Hunt (who later was one of the ringleaders behind Watergate and who *Rolling Stone* called 'the ultimate keeper of secrets regarding who killed JFK') was in charge of that division and the usually tight-lipped man right before his death later confessed to his son, Saint, in a cryptic way, that there was a conspiracy to assassinate President Kennedy involving some high-up people in the CIA and the government. He wrote down the following names on a sheet of paper with lines connecting the names: LBJ; three CIA agents: Cord Meyer, Bill Harvey, and David Morales; and then in a box he wrote 'French

Gunman Grassy Knoll'. Saint told *Rolling Stone* in 2007 that his father wouldn't implicate his own country like that if it were not true. He went into further detail telling him that CIA agents met with Oswald in Mexico City. As for de Mohrenschildt, shortly before his mysterious death (ruled a suicide), he wrote a manuscript for a book and confessed to a Dutch journalist named Willem Oltmans that he knew Oswald was going to kill the President.

On the other side of the political spectrum, when former Fox News host Tucker Carlson asked an anonymous source who had direct knowledge of documents related to the JFK assassination if the CIA had a hand in the assassination of President Kennedy, they responded, 'The answer is yes. I believe they were involved. It's a whole different country from what we thought it was. It's all fake,' and, 'Yes, I believe the CIA was involved in the Kennedy assassination.' Tucker Carlson asked former director of the CIA under Trump, Mike Pompeo, if he'd like to come on his show to talk about the Kennedy assassination, and he refused to come on the show, which is unusual because in Tucker's words, he 'rarely turns down a televised interview'. How convenient.

THE CONNECTION

Gangsters and mobsters are all over the music industry and The Hawks' encounter with Jack Ruby was not the first time they experienced this. In the late '50s, Ronnie Hawkins signed to the notorious Morris Levy's label, Roulette Records, an independent label founded in 1956, as rock and roll was starting to take over the charts. Don't be fooled by the fact that the label was independent; Levy still had a lot of reach in the music industry, leading to him being called 'The Octopus'. Morris Levy (born Moishe Levy), dubbed the godfather of the American music business, had connections to the Genovese crime family (even though he was never a member, he did business with them a lot) and is now known for his dodgy record deals that screwed over a lot of musicians of the late '50s and through the '60s. These dodgy individuals behind the scenes in the music industry had the toughness of gangsters and the shrewdness of businessmen. Levy used his knowledge of the law to make as much money as possible by taking advantage of copyright law by making sure he owned the publishing rights to songs, which is where the profits were. He would often give himself songwriting credits when he didn't have any involvement in writing lyrics or composing the music, such as giving himself songwriting credits on Frankie Lymon's hit 'Why Do Fools Fall In Love?'. Musicians wouldn't stand up to him because they knew he was connected to the Mafia and if they spoke up, their lives would be in danger. Eventually though, the law caught up with Morris Levy and in 1988 he was sentenced to ten years in prison and a $200,000 fine for conspiring to commit extortion. However, he was on bail during the appeal and never served a day in jail. He was supposed to report to jail on 16 July 1990, but he died of cancer just two months before he was supposed to turn himself in. Levon Helm wrote in his autobiography, *This Wheel's On Fire*, that he was told to always be polite to Morris Levy because 'he's Mafia up to his eyeballs'. He described Levy as a 'tough cat' who 'practically owned Broadway back then'. He knew everyone and you didn't mess with him. He also took part in an illegal practice called payola, basically owning the radio DJs and giving them cash in exchange for airplay of his musicians' songs.

While The Hawks were very popular in Canada, it was still important for them to tour in the US because it's the world's largest music market. As you would expect, The Hawks played gigs in the southern US, where country music originated. The Hawks played frat parties, college dances, on Native American reservations (fun fact: guitarist Jesse Ed Davis would sit in the front row and would pay very close attention to Robbie Robertson's playing), and roadhouses in Arkansas, Oklahoma, and Texas. Touring life was far from glamorous with many of the venues being dodgy. There was a risk of equipment being stolen, or even worse, the musicians themselves getting hurt or even being murdered – Robbie Robertson said in an interview with CBC's George Stroumboulopoulos that when playing in a lot of these sketchy venues, they were lucky to get out alive. Sometimes the band wouldn't even get paid, so they had to steal food to survive. They even had to carry guns and other weapons to defend themselves.

Months before the JFK assassination, The Hawks played a week's worth of shows at a nightclub Jack Ruby owned in Fort Worth, Texas, called the Skyline Lounge. Robbie Robertson said of that club that 'you could smell danger in the air' and that the owner seemed like a strange guy who always seemed to be on pills and would often startle them by checking on them in the middle of the night. The nightclub being owned by Jack Ruby wasn't the only dodgy thing about it; the nightclub's roof burnt down and rather than fix it up or demolish it, they just carried on operating it with no roof and no security. And because there was no security, The Hawks would have to stay there overnight to guard their equipment and so they would do so in pairs.

One night, Robbie Robertson and Rick Danko stayed overnight at the Skyline Lounge and for most of the night Rick entertained Robbie with stories about his life prior to joining The Hawks and the two played cards. Suddenly, at 4am, some police and their dogs showed up and Rick went over there with his gun. The police said to Rick that he was lucky he didn't let the dogs run and attack him because he and his bandmate would have been mauled. Rick countered that it was more likely that the two dogs would be dead. The cops had a laugh and told Rick and Robbie that they were just checking on the venue because it's a strange place and they wanted to make sure whoever was there overnight was safe.

Robbie Robertson shared some stories of the Skyline Lounge in his autobiography, *Testimony*. The shows were poorly attended with one show having fewer than five people in the audience with one of them being a one-armed go-go dancer. Two couples got up and danced to the music and then a fight broke out in the club; one thing led to another and suddenly one guy shot tear gas at another guy. As the wind blew the tear gas around the venue, everyone dispersed in tears and the show was over. The gigs had slightly larger crowds later in the week and they got paid at the end of the week. Months later when they saw the murder of Lee Harvey Oswald on the news and heard that the murderer was Jack Ruby, they made the connection. That was the strange guy who owned the sketchy nightclub they had played at!

CHAPTER 2

Death of a Clown:
The Kinks & John Wayne Gacy (1965)

By the middle of the decade, the '60s had culturally begun and it was all thanks to a bunch of young men with English accents and a classy dress sense. The British Invasion changed everything and the music scene would never be the same again thanks to The Beatles, The Rolling Stones, The Animals, The Who, The Zombies, and The Kinks. Everyone tried to copy The Beatles and even sixty years later, The Beatles and the rest of the British Invasion are still relevant and influential. But what is the craziest connection of the British Invasion? Read ahead to find out how four young guys from London came into contact with a soon-to-be serial killer:

THE KINKS

The Kinks are a band made up of two brothers from Muswell Hill in North London, Ray and Dave Davies (pronounced like Davis), the youngest of eight kids and the only two boys in the family. Their father, Fred, was a socialist slaughterhouse worker who was exempted from military conscription because his occupation was deemed essential, and their mother, Annie, was a housewife who occasionally worked part-time jobs outside the house. Ray, born Raymond Douglas Davies on 21 June 1944, was the more introverted one who went to art school. Dave, born David Russell Gordon Davies on 3 February 1947, was the charismatic life of the party and grew up with all the attention on him, being the baby of the family. Both brothers excelled in sports such as track and field, boxing and football and, of course, music, what you know them for. The Davies family loved having parties in their home in Muswell Hill and at these parties the children would play music and records. Ray and Dave's older sisters introduced them to music, playing everything from pop to jazz to classical to show tunes. Like other kids their age, they got into rock and roll and from there, both learned to play guitar and piano. Ray's older sister Rene got him his first guitar as a thirteenth birthday present. Sadly, that day, she died and Ray became very depressed and withdrawn, but music and art helped him express himself and get out of his shell. Before forming The Kinks, Ray was in the Dave Hunt Rhythm & Blues Band. Meanwhile, rebellious younger brother Dave was expelled from school after being caught skipping class to have sex with his then-girlfriend, Sue Sheehan, in the park. It wasn't long until the girlfriend was pregnant. Unfortunately for the young couple, both sets of parents conspired to break them up by forbidding them from seeing each other and claiming that one didn't want to see the other again. The breakup had such an impact on him that years later, he wrote the song 'Susannah's Still Alive' about Sue.

The band's line-up changed a bit over the nearly thirty years they were together, but since the true crime connection is only in their early years with the original line-up, only that part of their history will be covered in this chapter. The other two members in the original line-up are bassist Pete Quaife, an artist and school friend of the Davies brothers who loved the mod subculture, and drummer Mick Avory, a former delivery driver who almost joined The Rolling Stones and was initially described by Pete Quaife as a 'beautiful butch beast'.

Pete Quaife was the only member of the group not born in London. He was born Peter Alexander Greenlaw Kinnes on 31 December 1943 in Tavistock, Devon, in South West England, to a young single mother named Joan Kilby. His biological father, whose identity is unknown, was an American serviceman stationed in England. His mother was originally from London, but because of the Blitz and gossip from her neighbours, she briefly moved away to give birth in safety. He was raised in Muswell Hill by his mother Joan and stepfather Stanley Quaife. He started playing guitar as a sort of physical therapy after an accident sustained while playing in a rubbish dump. He met Ray Davies in secondary school and the two bonded over common interests: guitar, rock and roll, art, and sports, and so they started The Kinks together and Ray invited his younger brother Dave to join the band. Like Ray, Pete also went to art school, and for a short time before The Kinks made it, he worked at a fashion magazine. The puzzle was almost complete. They just needed a drummer. Enter Mick Avory.

Mick Avory was born Michael Charles Avory on 15 February 1944 in London to Charles and Marjorie Avory. His Italian-born father, Charles (born Carlo Avogadri), designed The Kinks' original logo, which the classic '60s logo with the boots was based on, according to an interview with Avory on the blog *Band Logo Jukebox*. Mick got into music during the skiffle craze thanks to the Sea Scouts, where he met other kids his age and formed a band with them. From there, he joined Bobby Angelo & The Tuxedos, and later The Kinks. He became especially close to Ray Davies, who calls Mick his best friend.

Originally called The Ravens, they changed their name to The Kinks because The Ravens sounded too generic. The Kinks? Now that's what I call edgy and attention-grabbing! It's the swinging '60s after all, sexual liberation and all that.

It would seem like The Kinks were an overnight success story. They formed in 1963 and by the following year, they had two big hits: 'You Really Got Me' and the similar-sounding 'All Day and

All of the Night' and shortly after that, they were overseas, touring Australia and the US within less than a year. What an adventure! These brief band bios you read online are like a highlight reel, you don't see the *kinks* that had to be worked out. The reality was that their first two singles flopped. They may have written 'I'm Not Like Everybody Else', but they were indeed like everybody else around them in the way that they started off playing R&B covers and had similar influences: American rock and roll and R&B music. Their first single was a cover of Little Richard's 'Long Tall Sally' and their second single was a Ray Davies original, 'You Still Want Me', which sounded like a Beatles song. It was missing some magic though. Where's the aggressive, fuzzy guitar that was a signature part of their early sound? They weren't bad at R&B and Merseybeat, but they weren't The Yardbirds or The Rolling Stones, who were better at R&B, or The Beatles, who made that Merseybeat sound. I guess the typical advice about being yourself applies in this case because once they had original material, they had found themselves, just like their contemporaries. And great original material they had! They had one of the best singer-songwriters in pop music, Ray Davies, who is thought of as a rock and roll poet. He rhymed vernacular with Dracula in 'The Village Green Preservation Society'! But let's not ignore Dave Davies, lead guitarist, who came up with that fuzzy sound on 'You Really Got Me' and wrote great songs like 'Strangers' and 'Living on a Thin Line'. He also wrote the song referenced in the title of this chapter, 'Death of a Clown', a very strange coincidence. He did say in his first autobiography, *Kink*, that he has communicated with aliens and had encounters with UFOs. Could he have been on to something? Did he know something we didn't know at the time?

JOHN WAYNE GACY

Known as the Killer Clown, John Wayne Gacy was born in Chicago about half past midnight on 17 March 1942, in the middle of

World War II. His father, John Stanley Gacy, was a machinist and his mother, Marion Elaine Robinson, was a housewife. As a kid, he was well behaved and worked casual jobs delivering newspapers and working at a grocery store. All in all, a typical kid. Like any boy, he suffered from injuries. He fell and hit his head on a swing and suffered from blackouts for a few years due to a blood clot in his brain. He had some heart problems, but injuries and heart problems don't automatically make a killer. He was overweight, but that didn't stop him from being smartly dressed. He dropped out of secondary school and moved to Las Vegas and worked as a janitor at a mortuary, only to save money to come home. He went to business college and got a job as a salesman, a good job for a chatty guy.

He did so well that he got promoted and moved from Chicago to Springfield, the capital of Illinois. He got married and had a seemingly happy life, getting involved with his community as part of the Junior Chamber of Commerce, or the Jaycees. He quickly rose up the ranks in the Jaycees and became their VP in 1965, a great role for an extrovert who loved attention. After that, he moved to Iowa with his wife to manage the KFC restaurants, being paid a decent salary, and the couple started a family and he even had time to be a Jaycee there too.

He developed a habit of lying and that got people around him to not like him, but overall, he still had a good reputation. He became promiscuous, got into drugs, and started creeping on employees at the KFC he managed. And that's when his first run-ins with the law happened. He assaulted a fifteen-year-old boy who was the son of a Jaycee. He pleaded guilty to sodomy and was sentenced to ten years in prison but was paroled after only eighteen months on the condition he return to live with his family in Chicago. His wife divorced him the day he was convicted. While in prison, he used his charm and worked hard to become a model prisoner and worked as a prison cook to appear reformed, a surprise considering he had assaulted a teenager and prisoners do not take kindly to paedophiles. He ignored other homosexuals in prison and said homophobic things as a cover for his bisexuality. When he got out of prison, there were still people who doubted that he had assaulted a teenage boy. Some friends stood by him and bought his claims that someone in the Jaycees had framed him.

Back in the '60s, prison sentences were more lenient even for violent crimes and Gacy's last few months incarcerated were spent at a prison release centre, where he would be released for a couple of hours for lunch on family day.

When he moved back to Chicago, he got a job and his own place, but it wouldn't be long until he was back to creeping on underage boys. He would hang out around the bus station and prey on teenage boys. He picked up one gay teenage boy and allegedly tried to force him into sexual acts. Gacy was never convicted since the boy didn't show up to court. It could have been because it was hard being out as gay at that time and on top of that, it would have been hard having to relive the trauma in a trial, telling the jury in detail what happened. This being the early '70s, there was no internet or centralised databases and states weren't all connected like they are now, so the Iowa parole board had no idea what was going on and even released him from parole. It didn't take long for him to find a woman to marry. He also got involved in the community where he lived in Norridge, a suburb of Chicago, hosting summer parties for a time in the mid '70s. Around that same time, he started dressing up as a clown and created his own clown characters, Pogo the Clown and Patches the Clown. He would perform as these characters at parties and fundraisers. Living a double life, he was a seemingly friendly guy in the community, but there were dark things going on that people were not aware of. He was killing young boys and men as early as 1972 until he was apprehended in 1978. In total, he killed thirty-three males between the ages of fourteen and twenty-one. He was sentenced to death in 1980 and was executed in 1994. Illinois abolished the death penalty in 2011.

Some background information on the city where the crimes took place: Chicago is the biggest city in the Midwest and is known as a city of immigrants, industry, and sadly a lot of crime. Some people call Chicago 'Chi-Raq' because of how many murders there are, but locals will tell you the whole city isn't all dangerous. Violent crime is mostly seen in certain pockets of the city, one of the most notable being Englewood, on the South Side. It doesn't help that America's first serial killer, H.H. Holmes, murdered anywhere from twenty to 200 people there, in his Murder Castle as the World's Fair was going on in 1893. No one knows the exact number. Chicago, or rather Illinois as a whole, also has a reputation for being corrupt. There's a joke that only in Illinois do the governors make the licence plates. Chicago's nickname, The Windy City, has nothing to do with weather; its corrupt, greedy politicians were historically called windbags. Journalists deemed them to be full of hot air, hence the term windbag. Chicago isn't really all bad though. Great food, beautiful architecture, interesting culture, and rich music history.

THE CONNECTION: A CLOSE BRUSH WITH A SOON-TO-BE SERIAL KILLER

The Kinks' connection with John Wayne Gacy is only a brief one during their notorious 1965 US tour, the one where they earned themselves a four-year ban from touring the US. They are the only rock band to have ever received a ban from touring the US. Financially? A disaster. Artistically? One of the most punk rock things ever and The Kinks now wear it as a badge of honour. Definitely inspired them to be more aggressively British with their music and you can hear that on their albums from *Face to Face* to *Arthur*. They're a band that do things on their own terms and don't care about following trends or being hip and that's a good thing. Being stuck in your teenybopper/teen idol phase makes it harder to be taken seriously and no one wants to look like an ageing try-hard.

Let's start with a little background on The Kinks' US tour to set the scene. After The Beatles, The Dave Clark Five, The Animals, The Rolling Stones, and The Hollies toured the US in 1964 and early 1965, the next group to come were The Kinks, and let's just say America had no idea what was coming. The other British Invasion groups knew how to behave themselves or at least were too big to be cancelled (The Beatles and The Rolling Stones). Meanwhile, in this case, The Kinks were *not like everybody else*. Everything seemed to go wrong. Were they one of the unluckiest bands? Sure, plenty of other bands had it worse, but I'd say among the big British Invasion groups, they'd probably be the unluckiest of the bunch.

It's possible that they could have been way bigger had they not been banned from America, the world's biggest music market. When you can't tour, your ability to promote your music is shot down. I wonder why they never tried going around the ban by playing in Canada instead. Most big Canadian cities like Montreal, Toronto, and Vancouver aren't too far from the American border, and at that time travelling between the US and Canada was a cinch; you didn't even need a passport then. Perhaps not enough money to be made in Canada? I mean, what overseas act even does a Canada-only tour?

Ray had back problems even in his childhood from injuries playing sports, so bad that he was told he'd grow up to be disabled. These problems continued on into his twenties, and on top of that his ankle was bitten by an insect during a stopover in Hong Kong and by the time they reached America, his ankle was swollen and he was in pain trying to walk or stand, hence why, on their *Hullabaloo* appearance, The Kinks were all seated for their performance of 'You Really Got Me', while other bands that performed were all standing, probably because Ray was in so much pain that he couldn't stand. During 'All Day and All of the Night', a woman was lying down in front of Ray's feet. Their whole appearance on *Hullabaloo* was camp. When they were being introduced, bassist Pete Quaife and Dave Davies had their arms around each other almost like boyfriends. Mick Avory was trying to slow-dance with Ray Davies. I'm sure that might have upset some conservative viewers, and even the most liberal people at the time may not have been too accepting of anything that looked remotely homoerotic.

Dave had the longest hair of the bunch, with it nearly touching his shoulders, pretty long for 1965. Having an androgynous appearance as a man in this day and age can make you the target of homophobic comments, but it was even worse in the '60s, especially in conservative America. Because of his hair and softer facial features, he would often get mistaken for a girl and mocked for it. Dave had just turned eighteen a few months back and this was the peak of his partying days – he was living it up. If you read his autobiography, appropriately titled *Kink*, you'll see many tales of him in his teens and early twenties having lots of sex, not just with women, but men, too, and doing drugs.

It's also important to note that Ray and Dave had a reputation for fighting (verbally and physically) and sometimes Mick would get involved, like one time in Cardiff in 1965 when Dave made fun of his drumming and said it would sound better if he played the drums with his cock and Mick hit Dave with his cymbal stand (some stories say he threw a cymbal at Dave's head), knocking him out, and ran out of the theatre and hid away, fearing the police would come for him. Did he think he would be inconspicuous in a red Victorian-style riding jacket and a ruffled shirt? Pete stayed out of all the drama and was the mediator and the glue that held the band together; what are bassists for? But even he had enough and by 1969, he had left The Kinks and the music industry altogether, never playing music professionally again, instead working as an artist in Canada and Denmark.

No one really knows the true reason why The Kinks got banned from America for four years. But it's often chalked up to, as Ray said it, bad behaviour, bad management, and bad luck. Not only did they party hard and act crazy, their regular managers, Robert Wace and Grenville Collins, decided to stay back in England, so they had one-time 1950s rock singer Larry Page managing them on tour, but he was distracted and left them behind, first chasing after Sonny and Cher and then going back to England, leaving three men in their early twenties and one eighteen-year-old to fend for themselves. That's a recipe for disaster! Having good management who actually see you as a priority makes all the difference. That might explain why The Who, who acted even crazier on their first American tour, didn't get a ban. I'm guessing the union wanted to make an example of The Kinks, telling other British groups: don't behave like this or you'll end up like them.

Right before The Kinks were to play their American tour, the cymbal (stand) incident in Cardiff happened. Dave ended up needing stitches and as a result, their American tour dates were pushed back or changed, and some dates had to be cut.

There are stories of The Kinks not being paid as promised, the venues being small and unsuitable, and the shows being poorly promoted, the band's pay reflecting that. On one date, the promoter didn't pay the band in cash as promised because the ticket sales weren't high enough, so the band protested and acted unprofessionally during their show. Rumour has it that the promoter reported The Kinks to the American Federation of Musicians. One other possible straw that broke the camel's back happened backstage when The Kinks performed on Dick Clark's *Where The Action Is*. Someone who worked for the station scolded The Kinks for being late and then proceeded to insult their appearances and age, made xenophobic, anti-British remarks, and insulted Ray's wife for being Lithuanian, accusing her of being a communist. Ray had it and threw a punch and next thing he knew, The Kinks were banned from touring the US, so the legend goes. Realistically, what happened was that a lot of complaints about The Kinks' unprofessional behaviour reached the Musicians' Union and as a result they were banned from touring America.

Throughout their first tour in America, Americans seemed to be triggered by them, showing bitterness about how British musicians were becoming dominant and a threat to America's music scene. Ray Davies said in his autobiography, *X-Ray*, that The Beach Boys didn't treat him or Dave gracefully, saying that Mike Love acted aloof towards him and another band member snubbed Dave, although he didn't name who.

The Kinks began their Summer 1965 US tour in New York City opening for the Dave Clark Five, then going to Philadelphia, before getting to Illinois. They played in Chicago, Decatur, and then Springfield before driving 900 miles to Denver. Not only did they run into John Wayne Gacy, but they also had a crazy driver in Illinois who had a gun and would pull it out. Ray Davies said in his autobiography, *X-Ray*, that the driver bragged about having Elvis's phone number and had a car phone. The driver kept his pistol in the glove compartment of his Thunderbird and would wave it around while driving. He even said to the band 'Kinks? What kind of motherfucking name is that?'

The Springfield show was at the Armoury and the promoter was the local chapter of the Jaycees. At that time, John Wayne Gacy was the VP of the Springfield Jaycees. He was still working a day job and concert promotion wasn't his main job, contrary to what some stories about the Kinks and John Wayne Gacy might say. John Wayne Gacy didn't appear to promote any other concerts and the reason he promoted this concert was because of its connection to the local Jaycees chapter.

Now this is where the narrative diverts. Allegedly, according to Rob Jovanovich's book *God Save The Kinks*, not only was Gacy the concert organiser, but he also drove the band around Springfield and asked Dave to stay the night at his house, which isn't surprising considering Dave was the youngest in the band, having just turned eighteen, so it would have been especially scary for him. Not sure how true this story is.

According to Ray's second autobiography, *Americana*, they

nearly ended up at John Wayne Gacy's house after the concert. Pete Quaife, however, said in an interview with *Mojo* Magazine in September 2000 that The Kinks actually were at John Wayne Gacy's house and they were drinking with him. Mind you, Pete had a reputation for stretching the truth and telling tall tales, kind of like Jay from *The Inbetweeners* or Keith Moon, as you'll see in chapter 21. One time, Mick Jagger told Pete that he wasn't buying any of his stories. Take this with a grain of salt, but in that interview, Pete Quaife claimed that they were at John Wayne Gacy's house until 3am, they had some drinks, but felt awkward about it the entire time and left. Dave Davies wrote in his 2022 autobiography *Living on a Thin Line* that John Wayne Gacy threw the band a party after the gig and he thought he was a 'really nice guy', which didn't turn out to be the case and he said '… shows what a good judge of character I was in those days.' He did not elaborate any further about what happened at the party. So it seems like The Kinks and John Wayne Gacy did come into contact with each other, but The Kinks had no idea what that portly man would become.

John Wayne Gacy didn't kill anyone in the '60s and had just got married, but The Kinks' already disastrous American tour could have ended up even worse had they got drunk and stayed the night at his place.

CHAPTER 3

When Brothers (Nearly) Collide:
The Kinks, The Kemps, and The Kray Twins
(1965–1990)

This chapter is brought to you by the letter K (Get it? It's a *Sesame Street* reference). Since the previous chapter talked about The Kinks, there's no need to explain any background information about them. Before explaining the connection, let's give some context on the two other sets of brothers in this chapter.

SPANDAU BALLET – THE KEMP BROTHERS

Spandau Ballet are another band made up of brothers from London: Gary and Martin Kemp. Older brother Gary was born within the sound of the St Mary-le-Bow's bells and younger brother Martin was born two years later at the family home in Islington, in North London. The family were working class. Both brothers loved to act and were in a drama club and acted in some Children's Film Foundation productions.

Gary plays guitar and synthesiser and Martin plays bass. The classic line-up also includes Tony Hadley on vocals, Steve Norman on saxophone, and John Keeble on drums. Gary Kemp and Steve

Norman formed the band in 1976 after seeing punk rock band The Sex Pistols perform. Besides punk rock, they were inspired by bands of the '60s like The Rolling Stones, The Beatles, The Kinks, and The Animals – playing sped-up covers of their songs in the early days. Power pop, glam rock, and progressive rock were other influences as well. Gary's brother, Martin, joined in 1978 when the band were called The Gentry and by that point, they had a new sound, more electronic-inspired. He learnt the bass in three months and left his job to become a musician.

Like a lot of classic rock bands, they went through a name change. They later changed their name to Spandau Ballet because the band's original name sounded too old-fashioned, 'like sixties hair models', as Gary Kemp wrote in his book, *I Know This Much*. A friend of the band and DJ, Robert Elms, suggested Spandau Ballet because he thought it sounded cool. He had just come back from Berlin. Spandau is the westernmost borough of Berlin, and the least populated one too. The new name gave the band new life and they went on to be successful.

Spandau Ballet's sound can be described as new wave and synth pop, with a bit of blue-eyed soul, popular among the New Romantic subculture of the '80s. New Romantic was a movement and subculture that started in London in the late '70s with a flamboyant, androgynous look that is a mix of late '60s dandy with the frilly shirts and early '70s glam rock with the make-up and bright colours. Before the name 'New Romantic' was settled on, they were called new dandies, romantic rebels or peacock punks. In a way, the New Romantics were a Second British Invasion thanks to MTV playing lots of synth pop from British musicians. Every decade has its music craze. The '60s was beat music, '70s was glam or disco, and the '80s was synth pop and new wave.

Spandau Ballet were underground at first, playing secret gigs and word of mouth spread about them. In 1981, they made it to the US and got a top-ten hit with the funky 'Chant No. 1 (I

Don't Need This Pressure On)'. From there, they went to Ibiza and were the first British act to play the Ku Club (the world's largest nightclub), now called Privilege Ibiza. The band really took off in 1983 with their poppier album, *True*. 'Gold', from that album, was a big hit, reaching number two in the UK and the top five in multiple European countries. Throughout the '80s, they had a lot of successes, but after ten years as a band, they wanted to take a break. Being in a band is hard work, okay! The Kemps decided to take up acting, something they've loved since they were young, and that's where the Kray connection comes in, but that will be talked about later in the chapter.

THE KRAY TWINS – RONNIE & REGGIE KRAY

Everyone talks about the glamour and the music and all the pretty things about the Swinging Sixties, but under that beautiful veneer, there was an ugly underworld going on.

Identical twins Ronnie and Reggie Kray were Britain's most notorious gangsters and most famous criminals. In the Swinging Sixties, as Ronnie Kray put it, 'The Beatles and The Rolling Stones were the rulers of pop music, Carnaby Street ruled the fashion world… and me and my brother ruled London. We were fucking untouchable.' No gangster came close to having the swagger and sophistication of the Kray twins, but it is important to remember that they were violent men. One does not simply mess with the Krays. They would demand loyalty and respect and get it.

For years they got away with their crimes because they were celebrities and friends with people in the government and they would intimidate any witnesses or people in the government who dared to speak against them. Prime Minister Harold Wilson and his government tried everything to stop the Krays – Scotland Yard, tax men – but they were more slippery than the mobsters in America. Members of the Royal Family would go to their nightclubs. However, they weren't invincible and even having those powerful connections, they were powerful to a fault.

Before we briefly discuss their crimes and what landed them in prison, let's talk about their background and upbringing to better understand them. The identical twins were from East London. There's this cliché or stereotype about those from the East End, that if you're from there you're either going to end up a villain, a thief, or a fighter. Well, we all know what the Krays became.

They had a close relationship, but their personalities were quite different. Ronnie was the shy one, while Reggie was the more outgoing one. Their family were poor and life was difficult, but their childhood was mostly happy. They had an older brother, Charlie, and a sister, Violet, who died in infancy – they were both named after their parents. Their father made money by reselling gold, silver, and clothing for a profit. During WWII, he was absent from his children's lives because he was called for military service and didn't want to serve so he went into hiding. The war had a big impact on the twins, who would go outside like any curious kids and would look for bombers, explosions, and fires. They were athletic and good at fighting and before becoming gangsters, they tried to break into a boxing career and did all sorts of odd jobs. Their mother got them a room that they turned into a gym for training and singer Kenny Lynch would go there before he was famous. Kenny Lynch was the first singer to release a cover of a Beatles song, 'Misery'. The Kray Twins were quite successful at boxing in their teen years, with both of them winning multiple titles and being in the newspapers, one saying they had a lot of promise, they could be 'as famous as another pair of sporting twins, the cricketers Alec and Eric Bedser'. They were even professionals for a while, but they were called up for the Army to join the Royal Fusiliers. They would often try to run away and hide so they wouldn't have to serve.

By the age of sixteen, they started their own gang. Their first big run-in with the law was being charged with grievous bodily harm against three men when they were sixteen. Once again, they were arrested at seventeen and charged with assault. While in the Army, they were sentenced to a month in jail for assaulting a police officer and after that they were sent to Army barracks, and they escaped and later got court-martialled. Eventually, they were discharged from the Army and that's when they decided that they would become 'villains'. They quickly gained a reputation for being tough and smart and always armed and not afraid to use their weapons. Other gangs may have used empty threats, but not the Krays.

They did various illegal activities to get the funds to own a nightclub. Some of them were typical ones like gambling, but one interesting one they had was a service where they would work with a doctor to write notes exempting young men from National Service. A high cost, but worth it, because who wants to be conscripted? National Service would not end until 1960. The Krays would also commit fraud by buying warehouses under fictitious names and gaining the trust of suppliers by being honest customers at first, but then not paying and going ghost and then selling the whole lot and disappearing.

The other big thing they ran were protection rackets, an operation where criminals guarantee protection to people or properties, but for a high price… and they're paying the people that they need protection from. Basically, 'Pay us and we won't destroy your business or kill you'. And if you don't pay up? You might be swimming with the fishes or things might start breaking. In fact, protection rackets are where we got the term 'blackmail' from. In the late medieval times in the Anglo-Scottish border area, farmers would pay the Border Reivers for protection and the agreements were called 'Black mal', with 'mal' being an Old Norse word that means agreement. Why would someone pay for protection? Because the police are corrupt and can't be easily trusted.

While Ronnie was in jail for grievous bodily harm, Reggie was hard at work buying clubs and making money and that's when they started their gang, The Firm, and they were a strong gang, but in the end they all testified against the Krays because everyone is out for themselves and who would want to go to jail for such a long time when you can get a good deal or immunity by testifying?

Owning nightclubs proved to be a good investment for the Krays because it made them celebrities.

One other thing that brought them into the public attention was that Ronnie was bisexual and had an affair with a bisexual conservative member of the House of Lords, Lord Boothby, a big scandal back in 1964. Back in the '60s, male homosexual acts were still a criminal offence and few were openly gay. A tabloid called the *Sunday Mirror* published a story about a homosexual affair between an unnamed person in the government and someone from the criminal underworld. No one was named, but The Krays and Lord Boothby knew it was about them and they sued the paper. They won and Lord Boothby was paid £40,000.

In summary, the Krays were very violent and got away with it, but not for long. Their secret was that they would intimidate witnesses to ensure no snitches. As the popular saying goes, 'snitches get stitches'. But it was when they killed George Cornell – a member of rival South London gang the Richardsons – and Jack 'The Hat' McVitie – an enforcer and hitman – that their streak of getting away with crime ended. Frank Mitchell was murdered at the twins' behest by one of their associates, Freddie Foreman, but no one was convicted of that killing. In *My Story*, Ronnie Kray said the twins' biggest mistake was killing people themselves, and that led to them being caught by the authorities less than two years later. He said, '… we never learned one good lesson from the Americans, and that was this. In America, a Mafia boss doesn't kill his enemies himself, he gets someone else to do it.' The other big mistake was their hunger for fame. Renowned Swinging Sixties photographer David Bailey took photos of them. He told the BBC, 'I did everyone a favour by making them famous. If you are a real gangster nobody knows who you are, so their big mistake was posing for me.'

In March 1969, after a thirty-nine-day-long trial – at the time the longest murder trial in English history, the Kray twins were found guilty of the McVitie murder and received life sentences, with a recommendation that they serve at least thirty years in prison, the longest sentence given at the Old Bailey. The trial was a spectacle, a media circus, celebrities were there to see what was going on and the twins were escorted from jail to the courthouse in a cavalcade of cop cars. It was noisy, with sirens wailing.

A lot of books have been written about the Kray twins and two movies have been made. Next, you'll see how two bands made up of brothers crossed, or nearly crossed, paths with the notorious Kray twins.

KINKS AND KRAYS

Chrissie Hynde, ex-girlfriend of Ray Davies and lead singer of The Pretenders, once jokingly called the Davies brothers the Krays of rock 'n' roll (for the most part, Ray and Dave's fighting was only within the band though, except for the time Ray punched a union guy in America getting The Kinks banned from touring the US, but let's not think too much about that one). Did she know about the connection? The Krays were fans of The Kinks, they had good taste, and they tried to get into contact with them multiple times.

The first connection between The Kinks and the Krays was when the Krays wanted to manage them. They were rubbing shoulders with celebrities and running nightclubs that celebrities would go to, so why not manage a rock band? They couldn't get The Beatles or The Stones, for obvious reasons, but they thought they had a chance of managing The Kinks. The Kinks have had many issues with their management, so many issues that they wrote an entire concept album about the how the music industry rips off musicians, *Lola Versus Powerman and the Moneygoround: Part One* (there is no part two, despite the title implying the existence of it), and it's pretty much based on a true story. Great album, you gotta give it a listen! The musical *Sunny Afternoon* even tells the same sort of story.

The band's managers, Robert Wace and Grenville Collins, were business-y stockbroker types who would get as much money as they could from the musicians and didn't care about the art. They had a third manager, Larry Page, who tried his hand at being a pop star, but failed. They signed a bad deal, but rock was still in its infancy and when you're a teenage boy with dreams of being a rock star, you care more about girls, being all over magazines and on marquees, and jet-setting than you do about finances. Things could have been worse had The Kinks said yes to being managed by the Krays. According to Ray, the twins contacted the band's managers and asked if the band's drummer, Mick Avory, was available to chat with them. Dave said in his autobiography, *Kink*, that Robert Wace briefly ran a clothing boutique because it was the hip thing to do and one day a visitor showed up at his office and said that he knew that he had a boutique and that he could provide protection for a fee. Robert rejected the offer, and the man left a business card that read 'Kray Enterprises'. It wasn't long until the shop was destroyed: broken windows and looking like it'd been hit by a tornado.

Some decades passed before the Krays contacted them again. Sometime in the '80s, the Krays contacted Ray and Dave's sister Gwen about them possibly playing them in a biopic. Dave isn't much of an actor, but Ray starred in two made-for-TV movies – *The Long Distance Piano Player* in 1970 and *Starmaker* in 1974; he is a film buff, and had an interest in making films, even going as far as to buy a fancy camera to make music videos. He was the one who came up with the idea for the very influential 'Dead End Street' music video (it was banned from the BBC for its depiction of poverty), often considered one of the earliest rock and roll music videos that told a story. Decades later, Oasis made a music video heavily inspired by it for their song 'The Importance of Being Idle'. When you're best known for music, it's a risk taking a break from it to work on another project and Dave had reservations about acting in a movie that could be seen as glamourising crime. Depending on the film's budget, you may not get as much money being in a film as you would from recording albums and going on tour (although by the '80s, The Kinks were way past their peak). Years later, Dave regretted that decision and said that even though the Kemp brothers did a great job acting, he and Ray would have been better suited to the roles. In my opinion, had the movie been made in the mid-to-late '70s or early '80s, I think the Davies brothers would have been the right age and a good fit.

One last time in 1998, while imprisoned, Reggie Kray called Ray Davies's agent to say how much he loved 'London Song', which mentions him.

KEMPS AND KRAYS

In 1990, *The Krays* biopic starring Gary and Martin Kemp of Spandau Ballet was released, with Gary playing Ronnie and Martin playing Reggie. Originally, Roger Daltrey was going to produce a film about the Krays based on the John Pearson book *The Profession of Violence*, but that fell through and instead the film was produced by Dominic Anciano and Ray Burdis and directed by Peter Medak.

When you're in a rock band and have to take time off to shoot a movie and do all the promo stuff that goes along with it, that takes away time from the band and if you're the leader of a band, everyone else is waiting on you to come back and they might feel like they're being put on the back burner. That's kind of how it was for Spandau Ballet; two-fifths of the band were gone to work on *The Krays*, and that led to the breakup of the band. Another reason a musician may not want to be in a movie is that sometimes the role you're playing requires you to change your appearance: cut your hair, dye your hair, work out, gain weight, or lose weight. Rock stars can be really particular about their looks and be reluctant to cut their hair or change their body unless the pay is right.

In order to prepare for their role as the Krays, the two brothers met the twins, as well as their brother Charlie and their aunt May. Martin Kemp said in his autobiography, *True*, that Charlie was nice to both him and Gary and was happy to answer any questions they had about Reggie and Ronnie. Martin also described May as a 'remarkable character' who provided a 'fantastic insight' into the twins. Both Gary and Martin Kemp met Ronnie Kray at the infamous Broadmoor Hospital, where he was incarcerated, or rather, where he was a patient. Being locked up at Broadmoor, he didn't have to wear a prison uniform. Like on the outside, he was well dressed. Looking fashionable was very important to Ronnie. Gary asked Ronnie some questions and noticed how well dressed he was: sky-blue seersucker suit, personalised gold and diamond-encrusted cufflinks, and a shirt with his initials embroidered on it. Martin noticed how much smaller and thinner Ronnie looked than the photos of him in his heyday. While he was a recognisable person in the Swinging Sixties underworld, don't get it twisted, he was no hippie. Gary Kemp described him in his autobiography as being from a 'theatrical version of the past' because of his old-fashioned style, ethics, and morals. When Gary asked how Ronnie felt when he killed George Cornell, he said he felt nothing and he'd do it again. At the end of the meeting, the Kemp brothers were billed for tea, some beers, plus some cigarettes for Ronnie. Martin said they were billed £20, while Gary said it was £100. Martin said that meeting Ronnie was an experience, but not one that he thought helped him and Gary portray the twins in the movie. Martin opted not to meet Reggie, as Reggie had limited visitation hours, and he wouldn't have found meeting him to be helpful or productive in portraying him.

The film tells the story of the Kray twins' lives starting from growing up in working-class East London, falling ill with diphtheria and growing up during World War II. It follows their rise to becoming gangsters running London and intimidating everyone, and their fall, including the murders of George Cornell and Jack 'The Hat' McVitie. The final scene is the twins mourning at their mother's funeral, which they were allowed to attend, while handcuffed to prison guards.

This being a movie, and not a book, there are going to be certain things missing. It doesn't show their previous run-ins with the law and them being locked up in the '50s, but that was before their infamy so it's understandable why that was left out. While the movie shows Ronnie Kray having a boyfriend, it doesn't talk about the Boothby affair. That would have made for an even more interesting movie but given that the '90s was not the most gay-friendly era (the film was released in 1990, at the height of the AIDS crisis at that!), it would have been even more controversial to talk even more about Ronnie's attraction to men in a Hollywood movie.

The real controversy though was that the Krays made six figures from this movie. The twins weren't happy with the fact that their mother swore in the movie because their mother didn't swear in real life. While Roger Daltrey panned the film as glorifying violence and said the story didn't live up to its potential of being the British *Godfather*, Gary Kemp said that Quentin Tarantino loved it and the aesthetic was a big influence on his 1992 debut, *Reservoir Dogs*. In fact, he gave each of the crew a copy of the film and told them it was his vision for the aesthetic. Generally speaking, British gangster films are a big influence on Quentin Tarantino, as well as spaghetti westerns, grindhouse, Hong Kong martial arts films, Blaxploitation, and many other film genres.

CHAPTER 4

Other Kray Twins Connections: Cliff Richard, The Tornados, Roger Daltrey, and Frank Sinatra (1960s–1980s)

In this chapter, four more celebrity encounters with the Krays will be discussed. Since these are rather brief connections, it makes more sense to group them into one chapter and do it lightning-round style.

CLIFF RICHARD

Before there was even a British Invasion, there was Cliff Richard, commonly regarded as the first British rock star. What Elvis Presley was to the Americans, Cliff Richard was to the British. He was born Harry Webb in India in 1940. Some say he is partially of Indian ancestry, so that would make him one of the first Asian rock stars to get famous. He chose the name Cliff Richard with Cliff being a reference to the face of a cliff – rocks – and Richard coming from his idol, Little Richard. Cliff and The Shadows were a huge influence on all the British Invasion groups and before everyone started imitating The Beatles, they imitated The Shadows.

He's a big part of British musical history, the first and only musician to reach the UK top five in eight decades: the '50s, '60s, '70s, '80s, '90s, 2000s, 2010s, and 2020s – yes count it, that's eight decades! He recorded his first songs at the age of seventeen and is still going strong at eighty-three years old. If that doesn't make someone a musical legend, I don't know what does.

His backing band, originally called The Drifters (they changed their name because there's an American doo-wop/R&B group of the same name), The Shadows were an important part of his sound and on their own, they were the British answer to The Ventures, quite successful in their own right, but never achieved much fame in America. However, if you listen to 'Apache', you'll certainly recognise it, at least from it being sampled by The Incredible Bongo Band, The Sugarhill Gang, and other hip hop acts.

THE TORNADOS

The Shadows may have been Britain's best known instrumental guitar rock group, but there were other groups similar to them and one of those was The Tornados. And the Tornados had something on The Shadows: they were the first British rock band to get a number one in America and that song was 'Telstar', a Joe Meek instrumental released in 1962, the year before The Beatles released their debut and a year and a half before The Beatles arrived in America. 'Telstar' even had a Scopitone music video, almost twenty years before MTV! However, they never got another hit in the United States, but back at home they had other hits like 'Globetrotter', 'Robot', and 'The Ice Cream Man', but then a little thing called Merseybeat happened and guitar instrumentals became old-fashioned and rock and roll went in a blues/psychedelic direction later in the '60s.

The Tornados were formed in 1961 as a session band for Joe Meek and later worked as a backing band for Liverpudlian Billy Fury, an early British rock star who had just as many UK hits as

The Beatles (but none topped the charts). Because 'Telstar' and 'Globetrotter' were such a success, there was a time when people thought they were serious rivals for The Shadows, but that ended with the beat music explosion and their bleach-blonde eye-candy bassist Heinz Burt leaving the band to pursue a solo career. After that, they worked again as the backing band for Billy Fury, and in the '70s, they toured with Billy Fury and Marty Wilde, both of whom were big pre-British Invasion rock stars.

Other members had success like drummer Clem Cattini, who went on to be a session musician who worked with pretty much all the big bands of the '60s. You could say he was to drums what Nicky Hopkins was to keyboards. Rhythm guitarist George Bellamy worked as a session musician in the '70s and his son, Matt Bellamy, is the lead singer of alternative rock band Muse.

How did The Tornados get acquainted with the Kray Twins? Look later in the chapter to find out!

ROGER DALTREY

Roger Daltrey was born Roger Harry Daltrey on 1 March 1944 in West London to working-class parents Irene and Harry Daltrey. He is a firstborn, with two younger sisters. He was a very good student and was top of the class on his eleven-plus exam, so he went to grammar school, where he befriended his future bandmates Pete Townshend and John Entwistle. With his family being working class, they had a lot of hope for him and were disappointed when he dropped out of school because he wanted to be a rock star. As soon as he heard Elvis Presley, he knew that's what he wanted to be. Like Brian May, he made his own guitar since he couldn't afford to buy one.

Roger Daltrey is the lead singer of The Who. He's easily one of rock's most recognisable and most loved lead singers. There's no doubt that he is a big influence on a lot of rock stars who came after him. Don't be fooled by his short stature and slim build, his voice is very powerful, just listen to his scream in 'Won't Get Fooled Again'.

Since Roger Daltrey didn't write songs for The Who, except for 'Anyway, Anyhow, Anywhere' (cowritten with Pete Townshend) and lesser-known songs 'See My Way' from *A Quick One* and 'Early Morning Cold Taxi' from *The Who Sell Out*, he wasn't making big bucks like main songwriter Pete Townshend. When it comes to making music, the money is really in songwriting, not in performing. For Roger, his income from music depended on concerts. Luckily, The Who were one of the top live acts so playing enough concerts wasn't a problem. The real problem was that The Who were notorious partiers and everyone but Roger Daltrey did lots of drugs, and honestly, who could blame them with how often they were on the road? You'd need uppers to be able to keep the energy up from show to show. This would cause fights in the band and Roger Daltrey, who used to be the leader of The Detours, was outnumbered and would physically fight his bandmates, even though he was the shortest and skinniest. At one point, it led to him being temporarily fired, but he was let back in the band on the condition he stop fighting his bandmates and put up with their behaviour.

The Who would regularly destroy hotel rooms while on tour and with any record deal, any money spent, whether on music videos, studio time, fancy clothes, or limos, all comes out of the musician's earnings. The Who would come back broke from being on tour due to causing thousands of dollars of damage to hotel rooms.

This meant that Roger had to get creative and diversify his income streams: a very smart move. He's a man with many talents, not just a pretty face who could sing. He also acted in movies and TV shows such as *Tommy*, *Lisztomania*, *McVicar*, and *That '70s Show*; and has started businesses, such as a trout farm; and signed endorsement deals to promote Eminent Life champagne, American Express credit cards, and Kickers shoes.

He also does charity work with Teenage Cancer Trust, as a long-time patron.

Money and movies are how he ended up connected to the Krays. More on this later in the chapter.

FRANK SINATRA

Frank Sinatra was considered one of the most influential musicians of his time and important in traditional pop, jazz, and swing and was known for his flashy dress sense and blue eyes. That's why they called him Ol' Blue Eyes. He was best known as part of the Rat Pack, the name given to a group of entertainers best known for Vegas residencies in the '60s: Frank Sinatra, Dean Martin, Sammy Davis Jr, Joey Bishop, and Peter Lawford. Not only was he a musician, but he was also in sixty movies in total, some of them including *From Here to Eternity*, *The Man With The Golden Arm*, and *The Manchurian Candidate*. He is one of the bestselling music artists of all time with over 150 million records sold.

Long before progressive rock was a thing – in fact while rock and roll was in its infancy – he released one of the first concept albums, *In the Wee Small Hours*. He also had a famous daughter, Nancy Sinatra, of 'These Boots Are Made For Walkin'' fame.

THE KRAYS AND CLIFF RICHARD

The Kray twins also liked Cliff Richard. Not surprising because he is incredibly popular. Albert Donoghue, who was Reggie's right-hand man and driver, claimed that Ronnie Kray spotted Cliff in a restaurant, liked him and wanted to meet with him. Interestingly enough, Cliff Richard once told his friend, Gloria Hunniford, that he had the chance to sing on Frank Sinatra's *Duets* album, but he turned it down because he didn't think two men should be singing a love song together. There are even more scary rumours of the Krays and Cliff Richard though. In an interview with the *Daily Express*, prominent gangland figure Freddie Foreman claimed that the Krays wanted to kidnap Cliff Richard. He alleges that they sent three of their heavies to pick him up at one of his concerts and bring him to them, but that they never did it because they didn't have the heart to do so. Even though they were fans of his, if the kidnapping plot had happened, it would likely have ended really badly for Cliff. Ronnie once wrote that he was happy to receive a letter from Cliff Richard.

THE KRAYS AND THE TORNADOS

The Kray twins wanted to get involved in the entertainment industry and not only did they try to get The Kinks to hire them as their managers, but they also tried to manage The Tornados.

According to *The Legendary Joe Meek: The Telstar Man* by John Repsch, the Kray connection began in 1966 after The Tornados played a benefit concert in Cardiff after the Aberfan disaster in Wales on 21 October 1966, where a spoil tip from coal mining collapsed due to heavy rainfall and turned into slurry, sliding down the hill onto the town, killing 116 children and twenty-eight adults, with many more experiencing medical problems and PTSD from the disaster. A primary school was destroyed, as well as multiple homes and other buildings. As The Tornados retreated to their hotel after the concert, they got a phone call from the Kray twins saying they wanted to see them straight away and let's just say that's not a phone call you want to receive. So they went and met up with the Kray twins and no, this wasn't about a protection racket, they wanted to manage The Tornados and made the deal sound pretty sweet by boasting of their American connections, saying they could get them an American tour. The Tornados responded by saying they'd have a think about it and for six weeks, the Krays pestered them. They never told the police about it, nor did they tell their manager Joe Meek, but Joe Meek had fears of the Krays stealing his musicians and blackmailing him anyway. They met again at a pub called the Grave Maurice in January 1967, with the organ player showing Ronnie Kray pictures of the group and saying that Joe Meek, their manager, would never let them go, with Ronnie replying, 'Leave that to me'.

It was a good thing the Krays never managed The Tornados because in May 1968 they were arrested for murder and in March 1969, they were found guilty of murder. Then again, the Krays had ways of doing business behind bars, and where there's a will there's a way. But would you really want dodgy, dangerous gangsters managing you?

THE KRAYS AND ROGER DALTREY

Roger Daltrey had a couple encounters with the Krays. One of them was being loaned money and the other was almost producing a biopic about them.

Roger wasn't exactly rolling in the dough in the '60s, but he still wanted to have nice things. He grew up working class, got famous at a young age, and wanted to treat himself to nice things. One day in 1965, he was going out for a drive across Salisbury Plain and he crashed into another car as his car was flying over the top of the hill – not the most sensible driving. His car was crumpled. The cost of the repairs was steep, one-third the cost of his £1,200 Austin Westminster. That's a lot of money. Managers being managers, they certainly weren't going to give him an advance. Banks didn't want to loan to a young rock star. Desperate, he asked a roadie if he knew anyone who could loan him some money. The roadie didn't say who the lender was, but warned him that if he didn't pay them back on time, he'd basically get his legs broken. On the cheque was Charlie Kray's signature. Don't worry, Roger paid the loan back on time, his legs were safe, and he actually thanked them in his autobiography, *Thanks A Lot Mr Kibblewhite*, for loaning him money when no one else would, saying they stood up for him and saved the day. The Krays saved him, but it wouldn't be the last time they'd have contact with him.

In 1975, Roger Daltrey made his acting debut in the movie *Tommy*. He wasn't sure at first about being an actor because he was rejected from acting as a kid in a school play, but people around him encouraged him and said that he was Tommy and no one else could portray him as well as he could. If you watch The Who's performance at Woodstock, you'll see with his big curly blonde hair and fringed leather jacket that he came out of the cocoon and became a butterfly. Thinking about it in Pokemon terms, this was his final evolution: Rock God. Roger Daltrey was a natural as Tommy. From there, *Tommy* led to other movie roles such as him starring as Franz Liszt in *Lisztomania* and as armed robber John McVicar in *McVicar*. You could say all three of these movies were fan service because Roger Daltrey is often seen shirtless or in really tight-fitting clothes. To give a little background on John McVicar, he was one of Britain's most dangerous criminals and was once on the top of Scotland Yard's most wanted list. He was a professional at escaping from prison and did so multiple times. He was sentenced to twenty-six years in prison but was paroled in 1978 and reformed after his release, earning a university degree and working as a journalist and writer. He died on 6 September 2022 at the age of eighty-two.

Roger Daltrey believes that it was because of his performance in *McVicar* that the Kray twins were interested in having him produce a biopic about them. So Roger Daltrey went to Broadmoor, where Ronnie Kray was locked up, and they started talking business. According to Roger Daltrey, the Krays had a little grift going where they'd sell the film rights and then the deal would fall through and then rinse and repeat, but this deal was solid, thank goodness – talk about 'Won't Get Fooled Again'! The Krays were very particular about how they wanted the movie to be. At the end of the day, Roger wanted to let the project go. Too much drama and Ronnie Kray was very intimidating and confrontational even when he was behind bars. Ronnie Kray's method of convincing people was to dig his knee into the other person's thigh.

THE KRAYS AND FRANK SINATRA

Being an A-list celebrity means life isn't normal for you; you can kiss that goodbye. You can't go anywhere and live like a normal person and that's why it's important to have security. Did being convicted murderers stop the Krays from making money behind bars? No! They continued to run businesses behind bars and one of those businesses was providing security for celebrities under the company name Krayleigh Enterprises. Under that company name, they would licence out their name and sell merch. Krayleigh's bodyguard business was quite successful and celebrities like Frank Sinatra would hire bodyguards from them. Supposedly, eighteen of them in 1985.

LIGHTNING ROUND: THE KRAYS AND OTHER CELEBRITIES

At the end of *My Story* in the aptly titled chapter 'Seeing Stars', Ronnie Kray did a lot of name-dropping. Some of the rock stars he mentioned having some sort of connection to include: Roger Daltrey – whom Ronnie called genuine; the Kemp brothers – whom he incorrectly called twins; David Essex – who Ronnie says got his big singing break in the twins' club the El Morocco; Debbie Harry – Blondie singer who has visited Ronnie at Broadmoor; Marvin Gaye – who Ronnie says wrote supportive letters to him; Eric Clapton – who made one of his earliest professional appearances at the Krays' club Esmeralda's Barn; and The Walker Brothers – who also played at Esmeralda's Barn.

The Kray twins also had a connection to a band that would become a one-hit wonder, The Smoke, best known for their freakbeat hit 'My Friend Jack', which reached number two in Germany and did well in mainland Europe. Funnily enough, it was not a major chart hit in their UK because the BBC banned the song because of the 'sugar lumps' lyric, referring to LSD, the hip drug of the psychedelic late '60s. Very little is known about the band, but here's what is known. Before the 'My Friend Jack' fame, The Smoke were known as The Moonshots and they were from a city in the north of England called York. When they moved to London for the chance of better opportunities, they shortened their name to The Shots and they had the Kray twins as their managers. Sure, the Krays didn't get The Kinks, but they thought they had a shot at pop management success with The Shots. The Shots didn't go anywhere and they were frustrated with their management and so they bravely stood up to the Krays and said enough is enough, and Reggie and Ronnie retaliated with an injunction to prevent them from recording or performing. But the band were fearless young guys and didn't care about legalese or threats. They were intent on recording and pursuing their dreams of pop stardom so they continued recording anyway. Eventually, the law caught up with the Kray twins and they had more pressing things to worry about than a management contract with a fledgling rock band. The Shots became The Smoke and with the release of 'My Friend Jack' they became notorious for singing so overtly about the use of psychedelics in the counterculture.

CHAPTER 5

Helter Skelter: The Beach Boys, The Beatles, and Charles Manson (1968)

This is almost certainly the biggest classic rock true crime story of all and the Manson Family are among the most talked-about people in true crime. It's a story that has fascinated people for over fifty years because of its combination of the beautiful setting of California, the '60s peace and love era, hippie aesthetics, a bit of rock and roll, and the fact that some of the victims were famous. It's a sad story and not one to be glamourised. Many books have been written and a bunch of movies and documentaries have been made about the Manson Family. This is the first of a few chapters on the Manson Family.

THE BEACH BOYS

Yet another band of brothers in this book. The Beach Boys don't need an introduction, but just in case, here's a quick rundown on who they are. The Beach Boys were a band made up of three brothers: Brian, Dennis, and Carl Wilson, plus their cousin, Mike Love, and a friend, Al Jardine. They started off as a surf rock band, but like any legendary band, they evolved and blossomed into more than that: innovative pop music that incorporated R&B influences, psychedelia, and experimental sounds. They were one of the few American rock bands to survive the British Invasion, a real shake-up in the music scene in the mid '60s, and I think it's because they were so innovative and changed the music industry themselves. Survive is the wrong word, they thrived: hit after hit after hit in the charts and as I name them, you can probably hear them in your head: 'Surfin' USA', 'Fun, Fun, Fun', 'I Get Around', 'Help Me, Rhonda', 'California Girls', 'Barbara Ann', 'Wouldn't It Be Nice', 'Good Vibrations', and many more! They put California on the map in the music world. Before them, music was really centred around New York, but that all changed with The Beach Boys, surf rock, sunshine pop, and later on, the psychedelic rock coming out of San Francisco. The Beach Boys were competition for, but also an inspiration to, The Beatles. Without *Pet Sounds*, there would be no *Sgt Pepper*.

As you may already know, Brian Wilson was their leader and main songwriter, considered one of the biggest geniuses in popular music. The Beach Boys were a band who personified '60s idealism and optimism. But behind that feel-good music, there was darkness. There's a common trope of the genius who struggles with their mental health. That was the case with Brian Wilson. His father was abusive both physically and mentally. Brian Wilson had it pretty bad, but his younger brother Dennis was the one who was beaten most out of the three brothers.

Dennis was the member of The Beach Boys who had contact with Charles Manson, so much of this background information about the band will focus on Dennis. This might be because he was very much the outsider and misfit of the family. However, according to Mike Love's autobiography, Dennis really wanted his father's approval. He was also a rebel, who would sneak out of the house. But he had a soft side to him too. He was a free spirit, maybe a hippie in the way that he didn't care about having the most expensive, flashy things or being rich as much as his peers.

He just wanted to have a good time. His cousin, Mike Love, described him as 'generous to a fault'. Love also said that Dennis once snuck into a mortuary and pushed in the nose of a dead man and that he would drive cars fast even before he had his licence.

He was considered the cute one and the ladies' man of The Beach Boys and the only one who knew how to surf, and it was his idea to have The Beach Boys sing about surfing and he encouraged his brothers to form a band. In David Leaf's *The Beach Boys and the California Myth*, he was described as the only fighter of the three brothers and this is likely because he was beaten the most and needed to defend himself. He was the last of the three brothers to pick up an instrument. In 1965, Dennis participated more in The Beach Boys' albums and sang lead vocals on a couple of songs, a cover of Bobby Freeman's 'Do You Want To Dance' and 'In The Back of My Mind'.

In 1966, Dennis started taking LSD and that changed him in a lot of ways. With Brian Wilson taking a step back from the band due to his battle with mental illness, his brothers and his cousin were writing more songs and Dennis came into his own on the *Friends* album, contributing multiple songs, and he would go on to write more songs for later albums.

In 1968, his marriage was falling apart and he got in with a pretty bad crowd, and not just any bad crowd: the Manson Family. Besides that, he was always partying and frequenting Sunset Strip clubs. If you want an idea of how crazy his life was, he told *Record Mirror* in an interview published in December 1968 that he lived with seventeen girls in the woods near Death Valley and got into transcendental meditation (which was a big influence on the *Friends* album). A lot of American and British bands got into Eastern culture in the late '60s, it was a rite of passage. Every band seemed to dress in Indian-inspired clothes and incorporated droning sitars and tablas in their sound.

One day, though, Dennis Wilson picked up two hitchhikers who were part of a certain notorious cult. He was taken advantage of and it could have put his life in danger. More on this later in the chapter.

THE BEATLES

They're only the most famous classic rock band, and many young people's gateway into classic rock, so there's not much point in spending much time going over the background of these four lads from Liverpool: John Lennon, Paul McCartney, George Harrison, and Ringo Starr. However, what will be discussed in this section is *The Beatles* album (also known as *The White Album*) since that's the relevant part of Beatles history in this true crime story.

But here's an obligatory blurb on why I love The Beatles. While they weren't the inventors of rock, they changed it forever by putting their own spin on it and making it something unique. They constantly innovated, never stood still and were so prolific in the seven years they recorded studio albums. In my opinion, they are the most consistently good rock band. They never released a bad album. Each year of The Beatles was a different sound and era for the band. Not just any band can do what they did. Yes, their songs may sound simple, but that's the brilliance of their work. Everyone wanted to be like them. Other British groups looked at them and took notes.

The Beatles themselves didn't have any contact with Charles Manson, but Charles Manson famously misappropriated one of their songs, 'Helter Skelter', for his agenda of a race war against Black Americans. When I look up 'helter-skelter' in the Merriam-Webster dictionary, I see a few definitions: the first being 'in undue haste, confusion, or disorder,' or 'In a haphazard manner' and I see another use for the term, particularly in the UK, as 'a spiral slide around a tower at an amusement park'. With The Beatles being British, it sounds likely that they were talking about a slide, hence the opening lyrics.

First, let's get into the background of *The White Album*. It is considered one of the best known and most popular albums of 1968. It has the simplest album cover of all, as it's a plain white, but it's an album that is far from boring. Lots of fan favourites and a diversity of sounds on this double album: 'Back in the USSR' is a Beach Boys/Chuck Berry pastiche. 'Dear Prudence' was inspired by Mia Farrow's sister Prudence who was into transcendental meditation. 'Glass Onion' is a meta song with John Lennon writing about other Beatles songs. 'Ob-La-Di, Ob-La-Da' is a Caribbean-influenced song. Yoko Ono joins in on vocals on 'The Continuing Story of Bungalow Bill'. Another guest musician, Eric Clapton, plays lead guitar on George Harrison's 'While My Guitar Gently Weeps', a favourite of many Beatles fans. 'Happiness is a Warm Gun' is proto-prog with its multiple movements and time signature changes. 'Martha My Dear' has some British music hall influences and is a song for Paul's Old English sheepdog. 'Blackbird', 'I Will', and 'Mother Nature's Son' are such beautiful acoustic songs – ideal for MTV Unplugged if it had been a thing in 1968. The baroque pop 'Piggies' predates Pink Floyd's *Animals* by a decade with its *Animal Farm*-inspired commentary on class and consumerism. 'Rocky Racoon' is a country rock song and an underrated Beatles song. Ringo Starr makes a songwriting contribution with the country flavoured 'Don't Pass Me By'. 'Why Don't We Do It in the Road?' is a heavy blues song inspired by Paul seeing two monkeys having sex in India. John Lennon wrote 'Julia' for his mother, whom he lost at seventeen. 'Birthday' blows 'Happy Birthday To You' out of the water and demonstrates The Beatles' talent for making simple concepts sound amazing. 'Yer Blues' is a self-aware parody of blues music. British rock stars arguably loved and appreciated the blues more than American rock stars. 'Everybody's Got Something To Hide Except Me and My Monkey' is a crazy long song title, but an awesome hard rock song that shows The Beatles weren't just a poppy teenybopper group (just compare this with 'Love Me Do' or 'She Loves You' – so different). The psychedelic folk number 'Long Long Long' is a song that George wrote while in India and dedicating himself to studying the sitar. He knew how to play so many more instruments and one of the benefits of that is that it provided more sources of inspiration. 'Revolution 1' is not to be confused with the more familiar 'Revolution', the B-side to 'Hey Jude'. It's a slowed-down, blues-y version of the song. 'Savoy Truffle' is another great George Harrison composition. It's a common joke in The Beatles fandom that George Harrison really loved food because there are so many pictures of him eating. How did he stay thin? What were his secrets? 'Cry Baby Cry' is a beautiful John Lennon song and I can definitely see this song as one that influenced Oasis. 'Revolution 9' is an experimental song; a lot of Beatles fans don't like it. It's not my cup of tea either. The album appropriately ends with 'Good Night', with Ringo on lead vocals. To me, it sounds like something from a Disney movie; I like that.

I left out 'Helter Skelter' in this lightning-round overview/ rundown of *The White Album* because it's a key point in this story and deserves a paragraph of its own on the background and true story of it.

As for 'Helter Skelter', there was a battle of sorts between all the rock bands over who could make the hardest rocking song. Rock and roll was a competition, and all these bands brought interesting things to the table and the competitive spirit led to innovation in rock and roll. The Who put their name in the ring with 'I Can See For Miles', calling it the heaviest rock song. Paul McCartney basically went 'Hold my beer' and came out with 'Helter Skelter' to show that he could write more than just poppy love songs. Well, he more than proved himself. Music is subjective, but I think Paul won this contest between The Who and The Beatles. The Who had the edge live, but The Beatles were incredible in the studio. However, bring some other bands into the mix and I think The Beatles have some serious competition. In my opinion, after years and years of listening to classic rock, I can say that The Pretty Things' 'Defecting Grey' from 1967 gets heavy metal at one minute in; 'Balloon Burning' and 'Old Man Going' from their 1968 rock opera *S.F. Sorrow* also sound proto-metal (if that was even a thing at a time) or rather like Black Sabbath before Black Sabbath; these all give 'Helter Skelter' a run for its money. Moving onto other bands, Vanilla Fudge's 'You Keep Me Hanging On', Blue Cheer's 'Summertime Blues', The Open Mind's 'Magic Potion', MC5's 'Kick Out The Jams', The Stooges' 'I Wanna Be Your Dog', The Gun's 'Race With The Devil', King Crimson's '21st Century Schizoid Man', Pink Floyd's 'Ibiza Bar', and Led Zeppelin's 'Communication Breakdown' give 'Helter Skelter' a run for its money as most metal song of the '60s. You be the judge of what's the heaviest. And from there, the songs only get heavier, like Black Sabbath's 'Paranoid', Focus's 'Hocus Pocus', or Budgie's 'Breadfan'.

Coincidentally, both The Beach Boys and The Beatles' 1968 albums were their 'transcendental meditation albums'.

CHARLES MANSON

Charles Manson was born disadvantaged from the start because his family were poor and because of how his life went; having a hardly normal childhood and only knowing crime, it's really no wonder that he went down the path he did. This is not an excuse for his crimes or forming a cult, but an explanation. This is his backstory so you can understand where he was coming from, his background, and how the Manson Family formed.

He was born in Ohio to a teen mother, Kathleen Maddox, from Kentucky. Kathleen was from a very religious Appalachian Christian family and, like a lot of teenagers, she was rebellious. She wanted to bob her hair and go to dances, like the other girls. The man listed on his birth certificate (but not his biological father), William Manson, was not really in his life. Kathleen married William, but they divorced in 1937. She tried to get child support from his biological father, Colonel Walker Henderson Scott. She got $25 from an initial judgement but not a penny more. Kathleen, being a very young single mother and without a job, couch-surfed with her son at relatives' houses. Being penniless, she eventually turned to crime to survive, with she, her brother, and sister-in-law robbing a wealthy man named Frank Martin. She ended up in prison for unarmed robbery and Charles was placed to live with relatives in West Virginia while his mother was in prison.

As a child, he was a troublemaker, compulsive liar, and attention-seeker. Academically, he was not a good student. His reading skills were behind those expected of a kid his age. Because Kathleen was well behaved in prison, she got paroled after serving three years of a five-year sentence. Charles was so happy to be reunited with his mother that he regarded it as the happiest day of his life. Once he went back to school, he caused trouble and skipped class regularly to see his mum at her job at a grocery store. The two moved around a lot and Kathleen couldn't control her son, who was now stealing, because of her own demons she was dealing with: alcoholism. At only twelve, Charles Manson was sent to a Catholic school for male juvenile delinquents in Indiana. He didn't like it and tried to run away but was sent back. One time, instead of going back to his family, he ran away to Indianapolis and broke into shops and stole money from the tills. He didn't get caught the first time, but he did end up getting caught another time and was sent to another Catholic programme, but in Nebraska. He had been there for less than a week when he decided to escape with a friend in a stolen car, and they decided to commit armed robberies, making him an even more hardened criminal. It wasn't long until he was back in custody, this time being sent to a reform school. This being the 1940s, there was corporal punishment. It was during this stint in reform school that he started acting out, something he called the 'insane game'. He would make noises and move his arms around to convince people he was insane and not to mess with him. He still managed to escape and commit more robberies and get himself in more trouble, ending up at yet another reformatory when he was sixteen. While at the reformatory, he allegedly raped another inmate and was allegedly a rape victim himself as well.

In total, he spent seven years of his childhood at six different reform schools. He worked a job and briefly went to the Nazarene church his grandmother attended but got tired of life in Appalachia and stole a car and drove all the way to Los Angeles with his pregnant seventeen-year-old wife, Rosalie. He was sentenced to probation for stealing the car instead of being given a prison sentence because he was young and about to become a father and the judge thought that fatherhood would mellow him out and change him as a person. Later, his probation was revoked because he didn't comply and report to his probation officer, so he was arrested in Indianapolis and taken back to LA for trial. He was sentenced to three years in federal prison at Terminal Island in 1956.

He was paroled in 1958 due to overcrowding at Terminal Island, after serving almost two and a half years behind bars, and that meant he had to find a place to live and honest, gainful employment. The first one wasn't too hard because his mum lived in LA, but a stable job wasn't something he was too interested in. He only did the bare minimum, working menial, casual jobs such as food service, bartending and sales to appease the parole officer. He also was a pimp because he learnt a lot about how to control women from fellow inmates at Terminal Island. It wasn't long until he was back in jail because crime was what he knew best. He tried to cash a forged cheque and was caught red-handed. Like his mother, he wasn't the smartest criminal and was easy to catch, but he had some luck and that's how he didn't get the longest possible sentence. This time, a prostitute who worked for him named Leona (also known as Candy Stevens) did a solid for Charlie and said she was in love with him and would marry him if he were freed. She married him so she didn't have to testify against him but ended up testifying against him anyway afterwards. Charles Manson was back in jail and, by this point, he had been incarcerated for longer than he'd been free. On 23 June 1960, Charles Manson was sentenced to ten years at McNeil Island Federal Penitentiary in Washington State, but he stayed in Los Angeles County Jail until 1961 while appealing his prison sentence. Like Rosalie, Leona divorced him not too long after.

Everything in life is a learning experience and for Charles Manson, he learnt two key things in prison that are a big part of this true crime story: 'how to win friends and influence people' and how to play guitar. Being surrounded by hardened criminals who bragged about how they'd manipulate women to do what they wanted, Charles Manson wanted to be just like them. He didn't want to be the short guy being pushed around. He wanted to be in charge. But who would want to associate with a crazy-looking guy with strange ideas? Women with low self-esteem and mental health issues. The prisoners taught Charles Manson that those were the perfect marks for recruitment. While imprisoned at Terminal Island in San Pedro, he was selected to take part in a coveted Dale Carnegie course on his book *How To Win Friends and Influence People*. There, he learnt how to be charming and likeable enough to sucker people in. When he wasn't teaching himself how to be a cult leader, he was playing sports and guitar and learning about Scientology and Masonic lore. In prison, he had a lot of spare time on his hands and he read a lot.

While incarcerated at McNeil Island, he used his time to learn to play guitar better, learning from Great Depression era gangster and brains of the Barker-Karpis gang, Alvin Karpis. He also got into Scientology and hypnotism – both of which taught him even more manipulation and cult recruitment techniques – and became fascinated with The Beatles (more on this later in the chapter). While in prison he practised his manipulation tactics by broadcasting 'posthypnotic suggestions' over the radio and through all the prisoners' headphones in the middle of the night. He earned a reputation for being a user and manipulator and would befriend and turn on the charm when someone was 'useful' to him, but he would get very visibly angry if anyone 'betrayed' him.

He was transferred back to Terminal Island in 1966 thanks to help from fellow inmates familiar with the law who wanted him to have a chance at parole. He was released in 1967 with just a suitcase of clothing and $35. This time out of jail would be the last time he was free. When he got his parole date, he panicked because prison was more a home to him than the outside and he worried he would turn to crime again. Well, we all know what happened with regards to that. After a few days, he left LA for Berkeley, and later San Francisco because he had a friend from prison living there, and he walked around the UC Berkeley campus with his guitar, playing songs.

There was a stark difference between the late '50s/early '60s and 1967 and Charlie had a lot to learn about how the world had changed. The '60s was a decade of change. It was the Summer of Love, young hippies all over the place, many of them fresh out of secondary school and trying to discover who they were – exactly who Charlie Manson was looking to recruit. Hippies often had a kind, accepting, generous nature and he took advantage of that. Still, he wanted to be someone. Having an entitled personality, he saw rock and roll superstars and thought that he could do that too and finally get what he wanted: fame, adoration, and loyal groupies. He didn't care about money though.

He spent time in both San Francisco and Los Angeles, places where you'd want to be if you're a wannabe rock star or just someone who wants to be a hippie. Obviously, he couldn't approach rock stars and be taken seriously, so he needed some help. That's where the cult recruitment came in. If you read about how cults and extremists recruit, you'll know that there are some ingredients in the recipe of making a cult: you need vulnerable people to recruit (including the young, poor, unhealthy, or mentally ill), claiming to offer help or 'truth', sharing the more reasonable parts of their ideology while hiding the more dangerous parts of it, using non-threatening (even fun) small events as a foot in the door, and separating recruits from the outside by creating an 'us' and 'them' (for example: Charles Manson wouldn't allow any members of his cult to read books). Think of cult recruitment like the frog in boiling water. Throw the frog into a pot of already boiling water, it jumps out straight away, but put the frog into warm water and slowly crank up the heat and it can't escape. Cults are supposed to be like quicksand, easy to be sucked in and hard to get out of.

CHARLES MANSON AND DENNIS WILSON

While at Terminal Island, Charles Manson met record producer Phil Kaufman, who had music connections and was locked up on federal marijuana charges. Kaufman worked with The Rolling Stones, Emmylou Harris, Frank Zappa, and The Flying Burrito Brothers. He became notorious for stealing Gram Parsons' dead body and burning it at Joshua Tree National Park; he ended up getting arrested for that. While Kaufman knew that Charles Manson would take advantage of people, he thought he was amusing, even if his guitar playing wasn't very good. He saw some potential in his voice. Kaufman couldn't help Charles Manson network with people in the industry in person, but he offered something valuable: a contact – Gary Stromberg at Universal. In California, though, there were many aspiring musicians with hopes and dreams of being stars and that meant tough competition. Charles Manson wasn't interested in doing minimum-wage jobs since he saw that work as beneath him.

While in Berkeley, he found his first recruit, an assistant librarian at Berkeley named Mary Brunner. She was a transplant from the Midwest who wanted a change of scenery, and being new to California, she didn't have a lot of friends. 'Eureka!' thought Charles Manson, and so he smooth-talked his way into her home and into her becoming his personal bank machine. Brunner was so desperate that she let him stick around. He'd spend time in the Haight, a Mecca for the psychedelic sheep and misfits. He tried acid for the first time and smoked weed. He soaked up the scene like a sponge and that helped him perfect his recruitment techniques and philosophy: a mix of pop culture (Beatles mostly), The Bible, Scientology, *How To Win Friends and Influence People*, environmentalism, and free love. Seems non-threatening at first, right?

He liked to wander and he met his next recruit in Venice, Lynette 'Squeaky' Fromme, who will have her own chapter in this book. She was young and came from a dysfunctional family. Once again, another perfect target, a human being with cracks, but not completely shattered. Just how Charlie liked them. Eventually, he left the Haight, finding that it wasn't what it was all cracked up to be, and in late 1967 the Family moved to Los Angeles, in the Topanga Canyon area. They stayed at a place frequented by Satanists called the Spiral Staircase before moving into a house with Bobby Beausoleil. In the summer of 1968, the Manson Family moved to Spahn Movie Ranch.

His next recruit was Patricia Krenwinkel, an unremarkable-looking girl with long hair who had low self-esteem from being bullied for her appearance. Manson met her while he, Mary Brunner and Squeaky were visiting a jail buddy in Manhattan Beach. Charles Manson took advantage of her like the other girls, using her as a piggy bank; he had sex with her and told her she was beautiful, a common cult recruitment technique called 'love bombing' where they dote on new recruits. He also would drug the girls. He'd take drugs too, but always a much smaller dose. He may have looked like a hippie, but he wasn't feminist or socially progressive. His views were stuck in the 1950s, thinking the purpose of women was to serve men.

Other girls who joined him include Susan Atkins, Ruth Ann 'Ouisch' Moorehouse, Linda Kasabian, Dianne Lake, Sandra Good, Leslie Van Houten, and Catherine 'Gypsy' Share. Bruce Davis, Charles 'Tex' Watson, Bobby Beausoleil, Paul Watkins, and Steve 'Clem' Grogan were some men who were part of his cult.

Members of the Manson Family saw Charles Manson as Jesus, as Linda Kasabian testified on 17 August 1970 at Manson's trial. They'd all travel around California and neighbouring states in a supposedly haunted school bus that was painted black with a goat's head and the words 'Holywood Productions' (it was supposed to be spelled Hollywood, but the girl painting it made a mistake) on the outside and psychedelic designs in bright colours on the inside. It was reminiscent of The Beatles' *Magical Mystery Tour*, an album Manson was inspired by.

Charles Manson wasn't the only one in the Family who recorded music. Before Share joined the cult, she had recorded a single under the moniker Charity Shayne called 'Ain't It?, Babe' with a B-side called 'Then You Try'. Bobby Beausoleil and Clem Grogan also tried their hands at music. Most notably, Clem Grogan sang vocals on *The Family Jams*, recorded in 1969 and released in 1997. In chapter 8, you'll see Bobby Beausoleil's classic rock connections. Manson Family defectors Paul Watkins and Brooks Poston formed a group called Desert Sun after leaving the cult. Little is known about the group since they never had any mainstream success, but they released two studio albums called *Potpourri of PB&J* and *Jazzacide*. They wrote and composed the music for the 1973 Oscar-nominated documentary *Manson*.

He brainwashed them into thinking they were family and to forget about their old lives, telling them that the Manson Family were their new family. If they obeyed him, he would reinforce and reward that behaviour with praise and adoration, but if they strayed a little too far, he would abuse them. To survive, the girls would burglarise houses and steal credit cards, this scheme being called 'creepy crawling'.

The Beach Boys were still well known in 1968, but not at their peak. They went on a US tour, but it was cancelled midway through because of poor ticket sales. If you want to know how poor those ticket sales were, they only sold 200 tickets for a New York City tour date. Bands make a lot of their money from touring and the failure of a tour was a blow to The Beach Boys who wanted to finance a record label and have enough money to live lavish lifestyles. The positive though for Dennis was that he had some leisure time to socialise and hook up with girls.

Charles Manson used his cult members to do things for him and that's how he got into contact with Dennis Wilson. Music industry people would be a lot more receptive to pretty young women than a thirty-something dishevelled man. So he would send his girls to Topanga and the Sunset Strip to seek out rock star connections for Charlie. Two Manson Family members Patricia Krenwinkel and Ella 'Yeller' Bailey went hitchhiking on Sunset Strip. They were in the right place at the right time and Dennis Wilson saw them, picked them up, and took them to his mansion at 14400 Sunset Boulevard. He was renting Will Rogers' rustic, opulent hunting lodge. When they got there, they talked about Charles Manson and Dennis being a very outgoing, generous type who liked to meet all kinds of characters let him come over. The two girls didn't know who Dennis Wilson or The Beach Boys were, but Charles Manson knew and wanted to be at Dennis's place as soon as possible and so he arrived there after a recording session. Paul Watkins later said in an interview with Maureen Reagan on *Larry King Live* that when the Manson Family were friendly with Dennis Wilson, they were 'in and out of the best music studios', places that 'musicians would give their left arm to be in' and that the cult had quite a few artistically gifted and talented members and that industry people in LA could see that.

When Charles Manson arrived at Dennis Wilson's house, he acted like what is in modern days called a stan. The diminutive man startled the Beach Boy at first by getting on his knees and kissing his feet. A creepier version of the 'We're not worthy!' scene from *Wayne's World*. At first, Dennis was worried Charlie was going to hurt him, but once he showed he wasn't a threat and that he was actually quite charming at times, the party continued: loud music and sex. Dennis Wilson's house was full of transients who stayed briefly, but Charles Manson and his group of female followers stuck around a lot longer. Dennis didn't mind, as long as they eventually left. Dennis and Charlie would have deep conversations and Charlie influenced Dennis. Dennis Wilson clearly liked Charles Manson and was enthusiastic about introducing him to his industry friends who could help the aspiring singer-songwriter. Charles Manson had found the perfect mark: a good-natured, generous famous guy with good connections. Dennis had some similarities to the girls that Charlie recruited: his father abused him in his youth and he was seen as an underdog and his bandmates didn't really have much faith in him or his abilities. He just wanted to be taken seriously and appreciated. Dennis even had a nickname for Charles Manson, 'The Wizard'.

The Manson Family took and took from Dennis, freeloading, spending his money, and driving (and crashing) his cars. But Dennis hooked up with a bunch of the girls. Dennis took Charles Manson to Brother Records to record, but it didn't go well because he smelled bad and was intimidating, once pulling out a switchblade during the sessions.

The rest of The Beach Boys weren't thrilled. Mike Love said in *Good Vibrations: My Life as a Beach Boy* that Dennis essentially was a part of the Manson Family for a bit, but said in all fairness that he was just looking for answers like everyone else because right before that he was into the Maharishi Mahesh Yogi. Love knew that something was off in Charles Manson's behaviour and couldn't trust him. An employee at Brother Records did a background check on Manson and found he had a long criminal record and was on probation. The band's accountants also noticed a bunch of suspicious charges on Dennis's credit card.

After a whole summer with the Manson Family, Dennis had had enough. He was generous, but losing $100,000 on these layabout leeches was too much for him. He cut ties with them abruptly by moving out of his rented home. Once the lease was up, the Manson Family were kicked out and back to Spahn Ranch they went.

That wasn't the last contact or connection they had. While Charles Manson was hanging out with Dennis Wilson, he would play his songs for him and Dennis particularly liked one of them, 'Cease To Exist', which was later released in 1970 on Charles Manson's only album, *Lie: The Love and Terror Cult*. The song's title had its origins in Scientology sessions Charles Manson attended with Lanier Ramer. He liked it so much that he wanted to record it and The Beach Boys did, but changed around the music, lyrics, and renamed it 'Never Learn Not To Love'. In the end, Charles Manson didn't get credit for the song; the credit went to Dennis Wilson instead. The song didn't make it big when it was released as the B-side to a cover of rockabilly singer Ersel Hickey's 'Bluebirds Over The Mountain', which only reached number sixty-one in the Billboard Charts. That single did better overseas, reaching number nine in the Netherlands and number thirty-three in the UK charts.

After the Manson Family went to Spahn Ranch, Dennis Wilson went there for a visit and allegedly saw something scary. Afterwards, he rushed to his brother Brian's house and told Mike Love what he had allegedly seen: Charles Manson shooting a black man and stuffing him down a well. It was a frightening sight and very traumatising to Dennis, who feared going to the police and hoped that the Manson Family would just fade away into obscurity. He didn't want to be questioned. When Manson went to trial, Dennis was so afraid to testify – he couldn't bear the thought of Charles Manson seeing him and having to look at him.

A big part of true crime is the why. Why did Charles Manson kill? There are theories that Charles Manson masterminded these murders out of revenge, to get back at the music industry for rejecting him. Brian Wilson said in *I Am Brian Wilson* that Charles Manson was trying to work with Terry Melcher, a friend of The Beach Boys and music producer, on a music or film project. It never materialised and their friendship faded away. Terry Melcher rented Rudi Altobelli's mansion on 10050 Cielo Drive in Beverly Hills from 1966-1969, but then moved to Malibu and the house was subsequently rented out to Roman Polanski and Sharon Tate.

Tex Watson, Susan Atkins, Patricia Krenwinkel, and Linda Kasabian went there shortly after midnight on 9 August 1969. On Charles Manson's orders, they killed the people who were there. Sharon Tate was living there, but her husband Roman Polanski was in London shooting a film. The other victims were Abigail Folger, Wojciech Frykowski, Steven Parent, Jay Sebring, and Sharon's unborn baby who would have been named Paul Richard Polanski. Tex Watson shot Steven Parent when he ran into him after he was visiting the caretaker of the house, William Garretson, trying to sell him a clock radio. Patricia Krenwinkel chased and stabbed Abigail Folger twenty-eight times. Folger pleaded to her killers to stop stabbing, crying 'I give up, you got me!' and 'I'm already dead'. Wojciech Frykowski was tied up, beaten with a revolver and then stabbed before escaping outside and screaming for help. When he got outside, Tex Watson shot and stabbed him to death. Tex Watson shot Jay Sebring and kicked him as he was bleeding to death on the floor. Sharon Tate was the last one killed and spent the last moments of her life watching her friends be murdered in her home and was pleading as Tex Watson and Susan Atkins stabbed her that she didn't want to die and that she was going to have a baby. The word 'PIG' was written on the front door in Sharon Tate's blood. According to prosecutor Vincent Bugliosi, there were 169 stab wounds and seven gunshot wounds. The killers left Cielo Drive after thirty minutes, arriving back at Spahn Ranch at 2am, with Charles Manson greeting them with the words 'What're you doing home so early?'. When Charles Manson asked the girls if they felt remorseful, all said no. The Tate murder made front-page news and were described as 'ritualistic murders'.

Charles Manson wanted more murders, and so the following day, he set Watson, Atkins, Krenwinkel, Kasabian, Leslie Van Houten, and Clem Grogan to the Los Feliz neighbourhood of

LA, near Hollywood. Charles Manson tagged along to show them how it was done and so, in a packed yellow and white '59 Ford, they drove to the Leno and Rosemary LaBianca's house at 3301 Waverly Drive, chosen for its familiar location. The house was next door to one where the Manson Family partied the previous year. The LaBiancas had just returned home from a long weekend away at Lake Isabella. The LaBiancas were aware of the murders at Cielo Drive and were upset, but they were not expecting to be the next victims. Leno was an investor and owner of a chain of grocery stores and Rosemary was one of the co-owners of a dress shop. The couple were very successful businesspeople and were millionaires. The night of 10 August, they fell asleep and were woken up when the Manson Family broke into their house. Charles Manson tied the couple up and then instructed the people with him to kill them. Tex Watson stabbed Leno LaBianca and Leslie Van Houten held Rosemary LaBianca while Patricia Krenwinkel stabbed her. Rosemary's spine was broken, and she was wounded forty-one times. 'DEATH TO PIGS' and 'RISE' were written on the wall in Leno's blood, 'HEALTER (sic) SKELTER' was written on the fridge, and the word 'WAR' was carved into Leno's stomach. A knife was left in Leno's throat and a fork was left in his stomach. Leslie Van Houten tried to clean the house of fingerprints. Before leaving the house, the Family took a shower, changed clothes, and helped themselves to some food. While the house had a lot of valuables, the Manson Family didn't take anything except for one bag of rare domestic and foreign coins worth about $25. Afterwards, the group of seven split up with some of them hitchhiking back to Spahn Ranch straight away and the others going to Venice Beach, where Lebanese-born actor Saladin Nader, whom Linda Kasabian and Sandra Good had met at a party, lived. Charles Manson sent Linda Kasabian, Clem Grogan, and Susan Atkins up to Nader's flat to kill him. Kasabian didn't want to kill Nader and so she gave the wrong information to Charles Manson about which apartment he lived in. Kasabian knocked on the wrong door, told the occupant they had knocked on the wrong door, got nervous, and the three ran away, disposing of the revolver they borrowed from a biker. They then hitchhiked back to Spahn Ranch. En route, Atkins and Grogan sang 'Piggies' from The Beatles' *White Album*.

For months, no one knew who was behind the Tate–LaBianca murders and there were many theories floating around. One classic rock related theory was that Roman Polanski thought that John Phillips was responsible for the murder of Sharon Tate because he was jealous of him because he had an affair with his wife at the time, Michelle Phillips, while Sharon Tate was filming a movie in Italy. Roman Polanski went as far as to sneak into his home to try to find some sort of evidence that he killed Sharon, and later threatened John Phillips with a meat cleaver. Michelle Phillips later said that all the stars were suspicious of each other and started carrying guns. Spahn Ranch was raided during the early morning hours of 16 August, a week after the Tate murders. That day, Charles Manson and twenty-five members of his Family were arrested, but it wasn't for murder. Charles Manson was under arrest for auto theft and burglary. Within seventy-two hours, though, he was a free man, but he was arrested again within days for trespassing and possession of marijuana (when the joint was tested, it turned out that it did not actually contain any cannabis). Once again, Charles Manson was out of jail after seventy-two hours.

In late August, the Family committed another murder. The victim was a stuntman named Donald Jerome 'Shorty' Shea, whom Charles Manson believed snitched to the cops, which led to the raid. Charles Manson, Clem Grogan, and Bruce Davis were convicted of the Shea murder.

In late October and early November, while Susan Atkins was in jail for the Hinman murder, she confessed to fellow inmates that she had killed Sharon Tate (she later recanted this and said that Tex Watson was the one who stabbed Tate) and said that stabbing someone felt better than an orgasm, that she got a sexual kick out of it. She also said that the Manson Family went to Cielo

Drive to kill so they could shock the world in a gruesome way. She expressed a desire to kill other famous people like Tom Jones and Frank Sinatra and she described to her cellmates what she wanted to do to them in great detail.

From there, the others involved were arrested. Clem Grogan was arrested during the 10 October Barker Ranch raid. Two days later, Charles Manson was arrested. On 25 November, Leslie Van Houten was arrested. Days later, Tex Watson was arrested in his birthplace of Texas. In December, Patricia Krenwinkel was arrested in Mobile, Alabama, where she was living with relatives and hiding from Charles Manson. Linda Kasabian turned herself into the police in New Hampshire and was offered immunity in exchange for testifying against the Manson Family.

Manson, Watson, Atkins, Krenwinkel, and Van Houten were all sentenced to death in 1971, but all death sentences in California were commuted to life in prison with the possibility of parole after the People v. Anderson decision in 1972, which outlawed capital punishment for nine months until the passing of Proposition 17, which reinstated the death penalty. Clem Grogan was sentenced to life in prison because the judge deemed him to be 'too stupid and too hopped up on drugs to decide anything on his own'. Grogan was paroled in 1985. Leslie Van Houten was paroled on 11 July 2023 after years of parole being granted only later to be reversed by the Governor of California.

Charles Manson died in hospital of natural causes on 19 November 2017, a week after his eighty-third birthday. Before his death, he allegedly made $250,000 a year selling T-shirts, signed art, and voodoo dolls. Isn't this illegal? Surely a convicted criminal can't be making money off their crimes, right? Well, the explanation is that it's a grey area and something prisoners can easily skirt around by having friends or family on the outside run their business and mailing art and other products they're selling to their business partner on the outside. There is a high burden of proof on the prison to prove that the convict is profiting off their crimes, so it's not that simple to just shut it down without due process.

CHARLES MANSON AND 'HELTER SKELTER'

In prison, entertainment is mostly limited to books and radio. The radio was their window to the world of sorts, so they weren't completely disconnected from what was going on. If you know your music history, you'll know that in 1964 the '60s really took off with the British Invasion, an era of rock and roll that forever changed the music scape. Songs like The Kingsmen's 'Louie Louie', The Rivieras' 'California Sun', and Bobby Vinton's 'There! I've Said It Again' were the end of an era when Americans were dominant in rock and roll. All of a sudden, late '50s and early '60s American rock acts were not 'hip' or 'cool' anymore. Everyone's eyes were on these groups of young British men, but one group in particular got more attention than anyone else and everyone either wanted to be them or be with them. They are none other than The Beatles.

Charles Manson was swept off his feet when he first heard them while in prison; he was fascinated with them – it was an obsession for him: the way the people reacted to their music, the coverage and publicity they got. Everywhere you turned you could see and hear The Beatles. He wanted to be them. He had delusions of grandeur and told everyone around him that he was going to be bigger than them. He spent time writing songs – about eighty or ninety of them, practising guitar, and even performing some of his compositions in front of the prisoners. It kept him out of trouble while in jail and at least it wasn't hurting anyone even if his songs weren't mind-blowing or revolutionary. They became more notorious because of who he was and no doubt had an impact on some rock and rollers like The Beach Boys singing one of his songs, Guns N' Roses covering 'Look At Your Game Girl', and groups like Kasabian and Marilyn Manson naming themselves after Manson and people who surrounded him.

It's no secret that Charles Manson was a racist. While the Manson Family were living at Spahn Ranch, he'd ban them from listening to Jimi Hendrix. He famously tattooed a swastika on his forehead in the '70s. His racist views were seen in prison, long before that. In prison culture, people of different backgrounds are often segregated and there are cliques. Charles Manson took prison segregation and turned it to 11 by not only not interacting with Black and Hispanic prisoners, but not even looking at them or making eye contact. He bought into the debunked racist IQ theory that claims that black people have lower IQs than white people. He was against race-mixing and was repulsed by interracial sex because he thought it interfered with evolution. He feared the Black Panthers, who did good for the community by feeding poor children and giving them basic healthcare and knew their Second Amendment rights to bear arms. He saw the rising racial tensions between white people and black people, and that planted the seeds for what would become 'Helter Skelter'.

A historical, revisionist, rose-tinted view of the '60s commonly espoused by conservatives say that the '60s were a time of racial equality because the Civil Rights Movement was happening and Martin Luther King was prominent, but the truth is that MLK was not popular, with 75% of Americans disapproving of him in 1968. America was a conservative place even in the '60s and non-white and mixed Americans didn't have the same opportunities as white Americans because of the large wealth gap, perpetuated by segregation and redlining, a discriminatory real estate practice that restricted where black people could live and classified predominantly black neighbourhoods as risky and excluded them from government homeownership and lending programmes. Wealthy and middle-class white Americans see the '60s as a prosperous time because of low unemployment and union jobs, but for many young black and Hispanic people, they weren't seeing any of the riches that the supposed richest country in the world provided. Instead, there were few jobs, little hope, and opportunities were few and far between.

Racial tensions only worsened in 1968 with two major assassinations, MLK and Robert F. Kennedy, plus the war in Vietnam was ramping up and War on Drugs architect Richard Nixon was elected president. This opened the door to Charles Manson's delusional idea that there was an impending race war and that The Beatles were warning him with 'Helter Skelter', the words famously written in blood at the crime scene of the Tate–LaBianca murders. As well as that, the words 'death to pigs' were written in blood on the living room wall.

He wanted to trigger the race war by making the murder look like it was committed by the Black Panthers. He often would read things into Beatles songs and try to find alleged 'hidden meanings', believing that they were prophets speaking to him through their song lyrics. Vincent Bugliosi gave examples in his book, *Helter Skelter*, such as Charles Manson interpreting 'Happiness is a Warm Gun' as a call for black Americans to get guns and kill white people or 'Blackbird' being about black people rising up to overthrow the white man. 'Rocky Raccoon' was interpreted as a song about black men taking over (because the racial slur 'coon' can be found in the word Raccoon). When Manson listened to 'Revolution 9', he felt that The Beatles were leading him to the message in chapter 9 of *Revelations* that the establishment will be overthrown and that the bottomless pit will open and that's where the Family will run to safety. (The Family searched for the Bottomless Pit in Death Valley in late 1969.) 'Piggies' was about overthrowing the establishment and the knife in Leno LaBianca's stomach was a reference to this song. Susan Atkins went by the nickname 'Sexy Sadie', one of the songs from *The White Album*.

What did 'Helter Skelter' mean to Charles Manson though? Paul Watkins, a former member of The Manson Family and prosecution witness, told this to Vincent Bugliosi: 'And he started rapping about this Beatle album and Helter Skelter and all these meanings that I didn't get out of it… and he builds this picture up and he called it Helter Skelter, and what it meant was the Negroes were going to come down and rip the cities all apart.'

Watkins also said, 'He used to explain how it would be so simple to start out. A couple of black people – some of the spades from Watts – would come up into the Bel Air and Beverly Hills district… up in the rich piggy district and just really wipe some people out, just cutting bodies up and smearing blood and writing things on the wall in blood… all kinds of super atrocious crimes that would really make the white man mad.' Paul Watkins left the group as soon as Charles Manson became serious about unleashing his Helter Skelter plan.

Gregg Jakobson, a talent scout who introduced Charles Manson to record producer and Doris Day's son Terry Melcher, who produced for The Byrds and Paul Revere and the Raiders and knew The Beach Boys, said that Charles Manson discussed a 'black–white revolution' called 'Helter Skelter' that he believed would happen in 1969 and involving 'the black man going into white people's homes and ripping off the white people, physically destroying them, until there was open revolution in the streets, until they finally won and took over. Then black man would assume white man's karma. He would then be the establishment'.

According to Ed Sanders' book *The Family*, in early 1969 Patricia Krenwinkel bought a couple of hundred dollars' worth of topographical maps of California to plot their 'Helter Skelter' escape plans from Barker Ranch in Death Valley to Malibu. These maps were buried in Death Valley and found later.

There were even rumours of The Beatles being called to testify at the Manson Family trials, but this never happened.

What really made the Manson murders so notorious and something that true crime enthusiasts are so fascinated by is that the motives and what was said in court was like nothing people had ever seen before. The combination of elements: racism, cults, supposed secret messages in Beatles songs, an apocalypse in our midst. The antics from Susan Atkins, Patricia Krenwinkel, and

Leslie Van Houten singing in court, laughing during testimony, carving X's on their foreheads, and shaving their heads were memorable. Manson's supporters held vigils and sang songs outside. And of course, Charles Manson acted out in court, holding up a newspaper that said that Nixon believed that Manson was guilty, and threatening and trying to attack the judge. It really was a *Trial of the Century* and a rabbit hole that you can fall down and research for ages. As Ed Sanders, author of *The Family*, called it, it was a 'case that won't go away'.

CHAPTER 6

Cease to Exist: Charles Manson & Other Musicians (1967–1969)

The main classic rock connection to Charles Manson was Dennis Wilson, but there are some others who aren't as talked about, mostly because the connection is pretty superficial so for our purposes, we'll condense all these other connections here. As usual, there will be a brief background on the musicians before talking about their connections to Charles Manson. This is basically a lightning-round chapter. In these cases, there's enough information about the connection between these musicians and Charles Manson that it deserves a mention, but not enough for each have a dedicated chapter.

TERRY MELCHER

Terry Melcher was a pretty big music producer and even a musician himself in the '60s. He was the son of actress Doris Day. He got his start in music in a vocal duo with Bruce Johnston, who would later go on to join The Beach Boys in 1965. Both of them were also in a surf rock group called The Rip Chords, of 'Hey Little Cobra' fame.

With the British Invasion radically changing the music scene in the '60s, surf rock was out and other kinds of rock were in: mainly folk, psychedelic, and blues. Terry Melcher decided to turn to working behind the scenes, and that's the work he's best known for, particularly producing the music of The Byrds and Paul Revere & The Raiders, two successful American rock bands of the '60s. The '60s was a decade of change and in the music world, it was so important for music to appeal to the youth, who had more disposable income than ever before so they could buy records and cool clothes. The Byrds' label, Columbia Records, assigned Terry Melcher to work with them because he was the youngest producer and was around the same age as the band members. He worked out to be an excellent fit for the band and got them a lot of success. In the spring of 1965, The Byrds got a number-one chart hit with their version of Bob Dylan's 'Mr Tambourine Man' and Melcher produced it. He wasn't completely done performing. He also did some backing vocals on the classic Beach Boys album, *Pet Sounds*. He was also the one who introduced Brian Wilson to Van Dyke Parks. Another notable music business thing he did was being a board member of the Monterey Pop Foundation and producing the famous Monterey Pop Festival in 1967. Overall, Melcher was very successful and produced a lot of hits and this meant he was trusted to find new musicians to record and so he hired Gregg Jakobson as a talent scout.

Charles Manson thought he had a pretty good shot with Melcher because he got along well with Gregg Jakobson and Dennis Wilson. However, Melcher wasn't interested in signing Manson. A foot in the door wasn't a guarantee of stardom. Charles Manson tried to make an impression, but friendship or a business relationship never materialised. He would never be more than an acquaintance, at best. When Manson invited Melcher to his house sometime in February or March 1969 to hear him and the Family sing, Melcher promised he'd be there, but he ghosted. Melcher wasn't the only producer who wasn't interested in Manson's music,

Family member Catherine Share tried to get The Doors' producer Paul Rothschild to listen to Manson's music, but no dice.

Manson felt rejected but, instead of expressing sadness, he lashed out and got angry and went on this fake progressive rant to his cult saying that society was corrupt and unfair, but he went far-right crazy with his beliefs of an apocalypse coming and that it would culminate in a race war.

Members of the Manson Family have said that 10050 Cielo Drive was targeted because 'it represented Manson's rejection by the showbiz world and society'. Seven months before the murders, around the time that Charles Manson was asking him to listen to him and the Family perform, Terry Melcher moved out of that home and it seemed to be on purpose too. Mike Love said that Melcher told his mother, Doris Day, that he was afraid of Manson and told her a bunch of red flags: his zombie-like cult of followers and his penchant for violence. So he moved out of that home and into one that his mother owned on Malibu Beach Road. Roman Polanski and Sharon Tate moved into the Cielo Drive house on 15 February, just six months before the murders. On 23 March, Charles Manson showed up to the property asking where Terry Melcher was, but was pointed to the caretaker's guesthouse, where agent to stars like Henry Fonda and Katharine Hepburn, Rudi Altobelli, was staying. Tate and Altobelli saw Manson and Altobelli briefly spoke to Manson, telling him that he knew who he was, but he didn't know Terry Melcher's whereabouts. Shortly after that, Wojciech Frykowski and Abigail Folger moved into the property.

The Beach Boys and Terry Melcher were all worried about their safety when the bombshell came in November 1969: the Manson Family were the ones behind the Tate–LaBianca murders. Brian Wilson and his wife Marilyn wrote the police department's phone number on their arms because they were worried that they could be next because Charles Manson recorded in their home studio. Terry Melcher was startled and felt a sort of survivor's guilt because he believed Charles Manson meant to kill him and instead innocent people who hadn't wronged him ended up dying. He was a witness in the murder trial. The house at 10050 Cielo Drive where the murders took place has since been demolished. Probably because who would want to live somewhere someone has been murdered, and a *crime of the century* at that? Even the least superstitious people wouldn't want that.

NEIL YOUNG

Canadian singer-songwriter and guitarist. He was born in Toronto but his family moved around quite a bit to small towns in rural Ontario, Pickering (a suburb of Toronto), Winnipeg, and even living in Florida for a bit while he recovered from polio. Like pretty much any rock star, R&B, rockabilly, doo-wop, and guitar groups of the '50s were his biggest inspirations and so he picked up a ukulele and eventually a guitar. His first bands were Shadows/Ventures-style instrumental rock bands. After dropping out of school to focus on music, he formed his first serious band, The Squires, and they played hundreds of gigs all over Manitoba and even parts of Ontario. While in The Squires, he met future Buffalo Springfield bandmate Stephen Stills. After leaving The Squires, he met Joni Mitchell and wrote Bob Dylan-inspired folk songs. The Guess Who sang one of his songs, 'Flying on the Ground is Wrong' (originally by Buffalo Springfield), and it reached the top forty in Canada, an early success for Neil Young. While in Toronto, he joined The Mynah Birds, who got a record deal with Motown, but while recording their debut album in America their lead singer, Rick James, who was dodging the draft in Canada, was arrested, which led to the band breaking up. Later, Neil Young and Bruce Palmer drove to LA. One day, while on Sunset Boulevard, they happened to bump into Stephen Stills and Richie Furay and so they formed Buffalo Springfield. After Buffalo Springfield broke up in 1968 Neil Young formed Crazy Horse and in 1969, he joined the supergroup Crosby, Stills, Nash & Young. Until 1970 when he got his green card, Neil Young was an undocumented immigrant.

Neil Young got to know The Beach Boys when Buffalo Springfield toured the South with them. He befriended drummer Dennis Wilson and later visited him at his fancy rented one-storey mansion in Pacific Palisades that used to belong to Will Rogers. This was during the summer when the Manson Family lived with him. Neil Young described them in his book as distant and detached. While Neil Young was visiting, Charles Manson showed up, picked up his guitar and played improvised, off-the-cuff songs. Young described his songs as 'kind of like Dylan' and said that he was fascinating, but chaotic and out of control as a person. He tried to get him signed to Reprise Records, but producer Terry Melcher wasn't interested and Neil Young didn't try to pursue other record labels to sign Charles Manson.

That wasn't the last Manson connection for Neil Young. He wrote 'Revolution Blues', from his 1974 album *On The Beach*, about the Tate–La Bianca murders, referencing how the Manson Family lived – in squalor far away from the city and armed – and how Charles Manson's cult killed celebrities as a revenge for his rejection. Bassist Rick Danko and drummer Levon Helm of The Band played on this track.

JOHN PHILLIPS & CASS ELLIOT

Cass Elliot was best known for being in the Mamas and the Papas and for her successful solo career. One of the most charismatic musicians in classic rock, she was friends with everyone and threw amazing parties. She was born Ellen Naomi Cohen in Baltimore, Maryland to a Jewish family. She started going by Cass in secondary school, possibly coming from actress Peggy Cass and the last name Elliot was to honour a friend who had passed away. She was a theatre kid and acted in plays, originally planning to act, but life had other plans for her when, after touring in *The Music Man*,

Barbra Streisand was picked for the role of Miss Marmelstein in *I Can Get It For You Wholesale* over her. While studying at American University in Washington DC she got into the folk scene and sang in groups The Triumvirate and The Big 3 before she formed The Mugwumps with Canadians Zal Yanovsky and Denny Doherty. The group went their separate ways after eight months and Doherty joined John and Michelle Phillips' group The New Journeymen. He wanted Cass Elliot to join, but they were sceptical because of her appearance. She had an incredible range and voice though and so she joined the band and they needed a new name and while chatting and watching TV, Cass came up with the name by saying she wanted to be a Mama, and Michelle liked the sound of that and John and Denny said they'll be the Papas. The rest is history.

You know how Mama Cass threw wild parties? You might even remember seeing one of those crazy parties depicted in Quentin Tarantino's *Once Upon a Time in Hollywood*. Well, Charles Manson came to a couple of parties and sometimes would hang around outside John and Michelle Phillips' house and asked John multiple times if they could record together. We all know how that turned out: a resounding 'no'. That wasn't the last of Manson, though. John Phillips and Cass Elliot were supposed to appear in court during the Manson Family trial, but they never ended up showing up. Cass Elliot never showed up because she didn't want the stress of the trial to ruin her ability to host *The Tonight Show*. As for John Phillips, the subpoena was served when he was performing a poorly attended gig at the Troubadour in Hollywood. Sharon Tate's husband Roman Polanski believed that John Phillips was the killer because he wanted to get revenge on him for hooking up with Michelle.

JACKSON BROWNE

Singer-songwriter born Clyde Jackson Browne in Germany to an American serviceman father and a Minnesota-born mother. At the age of three, his family moved to LA. As a teenager, he started singing folk songs at venues like the Ash Grove and the famous Troubadour Club. In 1966, he joined the country rock band the Nitty Gritty Dirt Band, but he left to pursue songwriting in New York City, where he became a staff writer for Elektra Records. Aged only sixteen, he wrote 'These Days', which was performed by Nico, Gregg Allman, Terry Melcher, and Cher, among others. He also worked with The Eagles, co-writing their 1972 hit 'Take It Easy'. In 1972, he released his solo debut album and the '70s were a very successful decade for him with many successful albums, especially his signature work, his 1977 album *Running on Empty*, an AOR classic. He was ranked number thirty-seven on *Rolling Stone*'s '100 Greatest Songwriters of All Time' list.

Jackson Browne never met Charles Manson, but he was intrigued by his supposed free love hippie lifestyle and wanted to go to Spahn Ranch to see him and the Manson Family, but Terry Melcher warned him not to go and so he didn't go. Smart advice from Terry.

TONY VALENTINO

Tony Valentino is the guitarist of 1960s garage rock/proto-punk band The Standells, who were formed in Los Angeles in the early 1960s by Valentino, Jody Rich (later replaced by Gary Lane), Larry Tamblyn, and Benny King (later replaced by Dick Dodd). The band's name came from the Standel amplifier and the fact that they were standing around a lot trying to get gigs. They added an extra 'l' to the band's name so they wouldn't risk getting sued by the amplifier company. Tony Valentino was born in a small town called Longi in Sicily on 24 May 1941, the same exact day as Bob Dylan. Ever since he heard rock and roll, he knew he wanted to come to America and he was going to make that happen. He first moved to Cleveland, Ohio when he was seventeen years old, but later realised that he was far, far away from Hollywood and so he made his way to California, where he had family living, and so he pursued his dreams of being a rock star. Before The Standells were signed to Tower Records (a subsidiary of Capitol Records), they played some gigs in Hawaii at the Oasis Club, alternating with a Japanese floor show with comedians, musicians, dancers, and a stripper. In 1965, they appeared as themselves (in Beatle-esque costumes similar to their 1963 collarless suit) on an episode of *The Munsters* called 'Far Out Munsters'. At the end of 1965, The Standells released their biggest hit 'Dirty Water', which was inspired by songwriter Ed Cobb being mugged in Boston when he was visiting his girlfriend there. At first, they weren't impressed with the song, but after they added some of their own lyrics and Tony Valentino wrote the catchy fuzzy guitar riff, it became a hit, peaking at number eleven on the Billboard charts. Since then, the song has been played at Red Sox and Bruins games. After that, they were in the film *Riot on Sunset Strip*, a counterculture exploitation film about the Sunset Strip curfew riots, which inspired songs like Buffalo Springfield's 'For What It's Worth'. Tony Valentino wrote the titular song that The Standells performed in the film. In 1967, The Standells released 'Try It'. The album cover boasts about it being banned and 'the most talked about record of the year!'. The title track was banned from airplay on stations across the country because a conservative radio station owner in Texas named Gordon McLendon banned 'Try It' from his station as part of a crusade against indecent, raunchy song lyrics. McLendon placed ads in publications sharing his opinion. In those days, station owners were afraid of the Federal Communications Commission, and they caved and pulled 'Try It' from their playlists. This ultimately led to the break-up of the band.

In the late '60s, Tony Valentino befriended Dennis Wilson of The Beach Boys, who as you know hung out with Charles Manson. In an interview on my website, *The Diversity of Classic Rock*, Tony Valentino said he went to Spahn Ranch with Dennis Wilson and rode motorcycles there. On another occasion, he visited Dennis Wilson's house on Sunset Boulevard and the two would be skateboarding while Charles Manson was playing guitar, writing songs, and asking for feedback. His entourage of Manson girls were with him and he'd tell Tony that if he needed anything the girls would take care of him.

When he found out the news that Charles Manson had been arrested and charged with murder, he was utterly shocked and didn't expect it at all. He was living in the fashionable Laurel Canyon neighbourhood of LA and one day a guy came into his house saying, 'Tony! Tony! Oh my god! Charles Manson, the Family, all the guys, they killed all these people!' Tony said he got chills when he heard it. He said in the interview, 'I was shocked, shocked! I mean it was like I could not believe it. That we were at the Spahn Ranch and hanging out with the motorcycles. That was another part of my life, rock and roll, a big chapter of my life.'

ED SANDERS

Ed Sanders is a poet, activist, and founding member of The Fugs, an underground rock band formed in New York City in 1964. The band's name as you may have already guessed is a euphemism for 'fuck' that came from a Norman Mailer novel called *The Naked and The Dead*. As part of the '60s counterculture, they had songs with socialist and anti-establishment themes. Ed Sanders himself was involved in anti-war protests in the '60s and while he was in jail, he wrote his first notable poem, 'Poem from Jail'. His biggest writing influences are Welsh poet Dylan Thomas (whom Bob Dylan named himself after), modernist poet Ezra Pound, and Beat poet Allen Ginsberg. Before joining The Fugs, he founded a literary magazine called *Fuck You*, which was active from 1962 to 1965. In total, thirteen issues of the magazine were published.

Ed Sanders formed The Fugs with Beat poet Tuli Kupferberg after graduating from NYU with a degree in Greek. In 1964, he opened a 'vegetarian literary zone' called the Peace Eye Bookstore inside a former kosher butcher shop. Andy Warhol would hang out at the bookstore and he printed flower banners for the grand opening. Abbie Hoffman, whom Pete Townshend famously pushed off the stage during The Who's set at Woodstock, would also frequently be seen at the bookstore. At the time, Tuli Kupferberg lived nearby and he'd previously published some of his poems in Ed Sanders' publication. After one of Kupferberg's poetry readings, Ed Sanders approached him about starting a rock band and the two became songwriting partners and were quite prolific, writing fifty to sixty songs together. The Fugs made their live debut at the grand opening of the Peace Eye Bookstore in February 1965 and a couple months later they were signed to Verve/Folkways and started recording their debut album. Later that year, they started touring the US and got involved in anti-Vietnam War protests, performing at colleges and sharing bills with Allen Ginsberg, The Mothers of Invention, and Country Joe and the Fish.

Contrary to popular belief, the 1960s were not a free-spirited, liberal decade. Just because the young were dominant in the popular culture doesn't mean they were running the show; the establishment ran everything and politically it was still quite conservative. Left-wing views were not popular positions. Being anti-establishment means that the authorities have their eyes on you and once again Ed Sanders found himself arrested after his bookstore was raided and copies of his magazine were seized. Luckily, the ACLU helped Ed Sanders out and he won his case. However, it would not be the last time 'the man' went after him. After receiving a complaint letter about The Fugs, the FBI investigated them after they released their second album, but luckily the case was closed because the music was not considered to be obscene. The Fugs went on to have more fame in 1967, getting to meet fellow socialist musician Phil Ochs, meeting Janis Joplin, appearing on Les Crane's show, and opening for Eric Burdon and The Animals.

Some priceless experiences! Ed Sanders got politically active in San Francisco and continued protesting the Vietnam War with a group called The Diggers and, together with them, they attempted to 'exorcise' the Pentagon. On a scarier note, Ed Sanders got a bomb threat from someone who also sent a bomb threat to Frank Zappa.

The Fugs broke up in March 1969 after playing some final concerts with bands like The Velvet Underground, and Grateful Dead. That same year, Ed Sanders released a solo album called *Sanders' Truck Stop*, which had a country music sound, quite different from his work with The Fugs.

What else happened in 1969? The Tate–LaBianca murders. Like many others around the world, Ed Sanders was fascinated with the case because it had so many layers: you had an aspiring rock star turned cult leader in Charles Manson, the cult lived on a ranch in the middle of nowhere like a cross between hippies and Wild West cowboys, it was counterculture gone evil, there was a lot of sex, drugs, and rock and roll, and you had the dark side of Hollywood in there with a beautiful young actress and mother-to-be, Sharon Tate, being one of the murder victims – makes you wonder what could have happened had she not died. This case was much more than met the eye and as Ed Sanders did more and more research, clipping articles about the case, attending the trial and writing a weekly column on the case for the underground newspaper the *Los Angeles Free Press*, and even spending time at Spahn Ranch and interviewing various members of the Family. Through his research, he found out that the Manson Family activities didn't stop at the Tate–LaBianca murders. He was so fascinated, yet horrified, that he wrote a book about the Manson Family called *The Family*, which was published in 1971. The book is very detailed and well researched. In the late '80s, Sanders corresponded with Charles Manson, who called him 'CIA' and sent him a Christmas card with a drawing of the Devil on it.

If you're a fan of Bob Dylan, especially his early to mid '60s protest songs, you'd also like the topical singer Phil Ochs, whom Bob Dylan once considered a rival. Phil Ochs was born on 19 December 1940 in El Paso, Texas to a Jewish father, Dr Jacob Ochs, and a Scottish mother, Gertrude Phin Ochs, while Jacob was stationed at an Army base in Columbus, New Mexico. He was the middle child; he had an older sister named Sonny and a younger brother named Michael, who became a famous rock and roll photographic archivist. The family moved around the country a lot because of Jacob's job. At one point, Phil Ochs and his siblings briefly lived in Scotland with their grandparents. Eventually the family ended up in Ohio, going to school in a town where they were the only Jews. While in secondary school, he picked up the clarinet and saxophone and found that he had a knack for it, learning difficult solos quicker than his peers. In those days he didn't think much about politics. As a teenager, he loved writing and he fell in love with rock and roll when he heard Elvis on the radio. While the songs he wrote in the '60s were critical of the US government, he was still patriotic and he was fascinated with cowboys and Western films. He wanted to be like Elvis, James Dean, and John Wayne for their larger-than-life personas.

While studying journalism at Ohio State University, a roommate named Jim Glover introduced the Elvis fanatic to the music of Woody Guthrie and Pete Seeger, and so Phil Ochs was converted into a folkie. Phil Ochs got his first guitar in the most Phil Ochs way possible, betting his best friend, Jim Glover, that if JFK won the election, he would get his guitar. From there, Jim Glover taught him some guitar chords and the two formed a short-lived folk music duo called The Sundowners (aka The Singing Socialists). While spending time with Glover's family, Phil Ochs learnt more about socialism since his friend's dad was a Marxist and the two friends became even more political together: reading theory in their free time and protesting. While in university, Phil Ochs wrote for the student paper, the *Lantern,* but he was banned from writing political stories and so he started a rival paper called the *Word*. Phil Ochs came close to graduating – just a few credits shy – but he decided to drop out to pursue a career as a... in his words... 'singing journalist', after the editorial board of the *Lantern* chose another student to be the editor of the newspaper. Even though his mother wanted him to stay in Ohio to finish his studies, Phil Ochs wanted to achieve bigger and better things. You have one shot at fame, why not take that chance?

Just like Bob Dylan, he moved from the Midwest to Greenwich Village and started playing in the coffee houses there, gaining a following. In those days, any starry-eyed folk musician could go to an open mic night and play their songs. Phil Ochs was one of those who found success and was part of the same scene as Bob Dylan, Joan Baez, Dave Van Ronk, Tom Paxton, Judy Collins, Buffy Sainte-Marie, and Peter, Paul and Mary. Ochs reunited with his best friend, Jim Glover, and hit the ground running, getting his name out there and writing a repertoire of topical songs. The audiences loved these songs and some of the lyrics would be published in *Broadside* magazine. While working with *Broadside*, Phil Ochs became acquainted with Bob Dylan. In the early '60s, Phil Ochs's flat on Bleecker Street was a hangout for folk musicians, where they'd party, talk, and play music. In 1963, he played the Newport Folk Festival and although he wasn't in the best condition health wise and was advised by doctors and Pete Seeger not to perform, he did it anyway and the performance was well received, a well-deserved breakthrough for him. The following year, he got a record deal with Elektra Records and released his first three albums under that label. While he dreamed of going gold like Bob Dylan, his album sales weren't even close to his: *Bringing It All Back Home* reached the top ten on the Billboard albums charts and went gold, while *I Ain't Marching Anymore* only sold over 40,000 copies.

All was not lost. Phil Ochs played shows around the country and appeared at protests, demonstrations, rallies, and teach-ins. He would appear at pretty much any event or demonstration he was invited to. Joan Baez covered his song 'There But For Fortune' and it reached the top twenty in the UK. He sold out Carnegie Hall in 1966.

In the late '60s, Phil Ochs had his brother manage his career and left Elektra for A&M Records and tried to branch out and try new things musically. After the 1968 Democratic National Convention in Chicago, Phil Ochs felt disillusioned. It was a turbulent time. That same year, Martin Luther King Jr and Robert F. Kennedy were assassinated. It also wasn't helping that album sales were in a lull. And so, in 1970, Phil Ochs decided a new approach was needed and so he went back to his roots: country and '50s rock and roll. He thought the way to get people to listen to his socialist messages was to be a combination of Che Guevara and Elvis Presley. He commissioned Elvis's tailor, Nudie Cohn, to make him a replica of Elvis's gold lamé suit, which he wore on the cover of *Greatest Hits* (a misleading title, it was all new songs) and for a few tour dates. His setlist was a mix of his original songs and Elvis Presley, Buddy Holly, and Merle Haggard covers. He made history as the first Elvis impersonator. Fans were not happy with this new Phil Ochs and because of the rowdy, violent reception and his strange behaviour, he was banned from playing Carnegie Hall. He never recorded another studio album after *Greatest Hits* and he struggled with alcoholism and depression. His mental health spiralled the last five years of his life. He took his life in 1976, aged thirty-five.

In the late '60s and early '70s, Phil Ochs and his brother were living in LA and, like many others, he was fascinated with the Manson Family trial. His friend Ed Sanders was fascinated with the case and the two would talk about it and at one point Ochs told him he'd become engrossed in the case. Phil Ochs and Ed Sanders visited Charles Manson on multiple occasions. Ochs at first believed that Charles Manson was set up by the FBI. Sometime in 1970, Phil Ochs and Ed Sanders visited Gary Hinman's house to see what Bobby Beausoleil wrote on the walls. On 30 May 1970, Phil Ochs and Jerry Rubin visited Manson in jail. On 18 June 1970, they along with Abbie Hoffman travelled to Spahn Ranch, where Ed Sanders interviewed Manson Family members, including Squeaky Fromme. Later that day, they travelled to the Hall of Justice in Downtown LA, where Charles Manson was incarcerated during the trials. On 4 April 1971, Ed Sanders was at future Eagles singer Glenn Frey's house and he asked Phil Ochs to bring his revolver and the musicians all went to look for a film that an informant claimed to have stolen from Spahn Ranch. An informant was supposed to meet them, but they never showed up any of the times they tried to meet up and they never got the film. One of the people Sanders' book *The Family* was dedicated to was Phil Ochs, 'who knew these times, knew them well.'

CHAPTER 7

The Anti-Woodstock: The Altamont Speedway Free Festival (1969)

The 1960s, or rather the culture of the era, was essentially bookended with tragedies: one can say that the '60s truly began after the JFK assassination and Beatlemania taking over the world shortly after that, and that the '60s ended with the disaster that was Altamont. This is the story of that tragic, infamous music festival.

ALTAMONT: BACKGROUND INFORMATION

The Altamont Speedway Free Festival was a one-time festival that took place on 6 December 1969, which was supposed to be California's answer to Woodstock. The festival had a lot of San Francisco bands and the goal was to bring that Woodstock magic back to their home turf. While Woodstock was famous and went down in history as one of the most iconic music festivals ever, Altamont was infamous, historic for all the wrong reasons. Much like Woodstock, the organisers of the festival were young, but unlike Woodstock, whose founders were more business-minded types. The founders of Altamont were musicians, some of the biggest ones in San Francisco as a matter of fact: Jefferson Airplane members Spencer Dryden and Jorma Kaukonen, and The Grateful Dead. The biggest difference is that Woodstock had a much more positive legacy despite some logistical shortcomings and financial problems, while Altamont was the anti-Woodstock: a nightmare of a music festival. It was deadly, dubbed by the BBC as 'the most dangerous rock concert'. Not a great way to end the decade.

The founders of the festival wanted to stage a one-day free concert in California that would rival Woodstock with The Rolling Stones headlining. They wanted to have another Hyde Park moment by holding it at the beautiful Golden Gate Park in San Francisco, but life threw them curveballs and it didn't help that the mayor, Joe Alioto, was a total square who believed in law and order and was determined to thwart the hippies' plans. The Rolling Stones were on tour in the US that November, their first American tour since 1966 because Brian Jones' convictions prevented him from getting a visa to tour in the US. Their festival appearances were added to their itinerary while on tour – the first one was the West Palm Beach International Music and Arts Festival and the second one was Altamont – both held at racetracks. Part of the reason for The Rolling Stones playing a free concert at Altamont was because they were criticised by *San Francisco Chronicle* journalist Ralph Gleason for charging such high ticket prices ($5–7 for an hour of their music, which is about $40–60 in today's money – actually not that bad compared to what The Stones charge now, let's be real. On top of that, tickets were being scalped and sold for multiple times the cost). In those days, free concerts were huge among the hippies in San Francisco. A documentary directed by Albert and David Maysles, *Gimme Shelter*, and a live album, *Get Yer Ya-Ya's Out!*, were recorded during that famous tour. They also made it a point to have black musicians who inspired them like Chuck Berry, Ike & Tina Turner, and B.B. King open for them. It was also a year of change for the band with the death of the band's founder, Brian Jones, whom many fans say was ousted and done dirty. Brian was replaced by a young guitarist named Mick

Taylor, who was formerly in John Mayall's Bluesbreakers. Decades later, bassist Bill Wyman put respect on his bandmate's name saying in an interview with Yahoo! that The Rolling Stones weren't Mick and Keith's band, but rather Brian Jones' band. No Jones, no Stones. He died just two days before The Stones played Hyde Park. During that concert, Mick Jagger, in Brian Jones's memory, read a portion of Romantic poet Percy Bysshe Shelley's 'Adonais', which was an elegy Shelley wrote for fellow Romantic poet John Keats, who died at the age of twenty-five.

Their original plan was for the festival to be held at Golden Gate Park in San Francisco or at San Jose State University, but the former didn't work out because it was football season and the 49ers were playing the Chicago Bears at Kezar Stadium, located in the park, and the latter didn't work out either because the city didn't want to host yet another festival. They also looked at Sears Point Raceway in Sonoma County, but that didn't work out either because the owners, a film distribution company called Filmways, wanted exclusive rights to distribute the upcoming Rolling Stones documentary because a previous deal to film their LA Forum show had fallen through. Eventually, they settled on the desolate, not so idyllic-looking Altamont Speedway in Tracy, California, fifty miles east of San Francisco, thanks to a connection through a celebrity lawyer named Melvin Belli (who represented Jack Ruby during his trial for killing Lee Harvey Oswald). The use of it was offered to the festival for free by the lessee Dick Carter, who did it for publicity. A deal you can't refuse, especially when you're in a pinch and scrambling to put together an event last-minute. Everything was so last-minute that when The Rolling Stones were interviewed about the details of a rumoured free concert in California, Mick Jagger wasn't sure if it would even happen at all. Michael Lang, one of the organisers of Woodstock, and Grateful Dead manager Rock Scully flew over the site to scout it. Lang gave it the green light and everyone had reason to trust him because of how iconic Woodstock was.

Besides Jefferson Airplane, The Grateful Dead (who actually left early and didn't end up playing because they saw the scene getting violent), and The Rolling Stones, a few other big names were booked for the festival: Santana, The Flying Burrito Brothers, and Crosby, Stills, Nash & Young. With the festival's planning being rushed (the contracts were only signed the day before the festival), crew were scrambling to turn a racetrack into a rock concert so they had no time to build a bigger, higher stage. Not a good sign. With such short notice, the local government didn't have much, if any, time to prepare, and the property owners complained to the Alameda County Sheriff. As for security, The Grateful Dead's manager, Rock Scully, and The Rolling Stones' tour manager, Sam Cutler, hired some Hells Angels, paying them with $500 worth of beer. Cutler had previously hired a group that called themselves Hells Angels to do security work for The Rolling Stones' famous Hyde Park concert that he'd organised, which was considered a huge success and had 300,000 people in attendance. Well, those 'Hells Angels' in London were imitations who only mimicked the aesthetic of their American counterparts, who were much more violent and hardened. However, The Grateful Dead and Jefferson Airplane had previously used Hells Angels as security guards without an issue because they liked their 'outlaw' anti-authority vibe that wasn't so different from the counterculture, anti-establishment hippie – they were no squares, and anyone who wasn't a square was an ally, the idea being 'the enemy of my enemy is my friend'. What could possibly go wrong? Well, in those days a lot of people were naive and a little too trusting, hence why you have so many serial killer true crime stories from the era. The truth is that the Hells Angels had a history of racist attacks on black people in the Bay Area. There was also no oversight and very little police presence so the Hells Angels pretty much had free rein to do what they wanted because they outnumbered the cops and Sam Cutler's instructions to them were basically 'we don't give a fuck' and 'just keep these people away.'

The festival had a rough start, similar to what happened at rapper Travis Scott's Astroworld Festival in 2021. The festival had a large turnout thanks to it being free and widely publicised on radio and TV. With a line-up like that, there were going to be a lot of fans willing to travel and see their favourites, with some passionate fans even camping out the day before so they could get a good view of the concert. Due to the lack of professional security and poor organisation, thousands of eager concertgoers broke down the gates and flooded right onto the festival grounds. A rough start like that makes the crowd difficult to control. Like Woodstock, there was a miles-long traffic jam full of rock music fans and the crowd was pretty close in size at 300,000 people. There also were not enough medical staff so if people had bad trips, there wasn't much help for them. The Haight-Ashbury Free Clinic turned down working at Altamont because Bill Graham was opposed to The Rolling Stones holding a free concert. On top of that, the stage was rather low at only four feet off the ground and it was a difficult job for a bunch of drunken Hells Angels, with quite a few of them being prospective members who had to do something to prove their worthiness, to keep the peace and guard the stage from rowdy, stoned fans (it was really more like hitting audience members with pool cues). One big recipe for disaster if someone acts the fool: shit, meet fan.

Santana was a relatively new band from San Francisco who had made a major breakthrough thanks to their performance at Woodstock, which was a few days before the release of their self-titled debut album – a critical success and widely considered a Latin rock masterpiece, perhaps the boomer generation's gateway to world music. They were the first band to go on and lucky for them, everything went relatively okay, except a fight broke out after a fat man stripped and started dancing and the festival site manager Bert Kangeson was beaten during the set and needed sixty stitches.

Next to go on were Jefferson Airplane who, like Santana, had played Woodstock months before, and they were at Monterey in 1967 and Isle of Wight in 1968, so they were well established in the festival scene. While they had had no major chart hits at the time, their last two albums, *Crown of Creation* and *Volunteers*, did well on the Billboard albums charts, peaking at number six and number thirteen respectively and being certified Gold by the RIAA. Just before they went on stage, a woman gave birth, one of four births that day. Things started going wrong just two songs into their set when Marty Balin was knocked unconscious by a Hells Angel known as 'Animal' after Balin told him to 'fuck off' after trying to get him to leave a black guy in the audience alone. Balin had to be dragged backstage. According to an interview that his bandmate Paul Kantner gave to *Music-Illuminati* in 2010, the Hells Angel who beat Balin up punched Balin in the face after he apologised and Balin didn't accept his apology, telling him 'fuck you'. Kantner defended Balin saying 'don't let it happen again' to the Hells Angel. Still, the band got through their set. Grace Slick later said of the festival that 'the vibes were bad' and that 'something was very peculiar' about the atmosphere. She admitted in an interview with *Rolling Stone* that hiring Hells Angels to do security was her idea because they hadn't had problems with them working at their previous free concerts. Jefferson Airplane left the festival early in a helicopter during The Rolling Stones' set. Jefferson Airplane cut ties with the Hells Angels after Altamont.

The next group to go on were up-and-coming country rock band The Flying Burrito Brothers, founded by two former members of The Byrds, Chris Hillman and Gram Parsons – Parsons was also in the International Submarine Band along with bandmate Chris Ethridge, who left the band before Altamont due to creative differences. Earlier that year, they released their debut album, *The Gilded Palace of Sin*, not a commercial success, but decades later it was recognised for its influence on country rock. The previous year, Gram Parsons left The Byrds because he didn't want to play in Apartheid South Africa and so he stayed behind in England to hang out with his new friend Keith Richards, who later wrote the song 'Wild Horses' with Mick Jagger for The Flying Burrito Brothers (The Stones later recorded their version for their 1971 album *Sticky Fingers*). Overall, a decent performance from the band and you can find bootleg recordings of the performance online, and there wasn't very much violence relatively speaking during their set.

Afterwards came the folk rock supergroup Crosby, Stills, Nash & Young made up of David Crosby of The Byrds, Stephen Stills and Neil Young of Buffalo Springfield, and Graham Nash of The Hollies. Earlier that year, Crosby, Stills & Nash had released their self-titled debut album, which had two top-thirty hits: 'Marrakesh Express' and 'Suite: Judy Blue Eyes' and they had played Woodstock. Their second live performance as a band was a breakthrough for them, even with Stephen Stills saying the group were 'scared shitless'. Their performance was reluctant because they saw how violent the scene was and how much of a disaster the much-hyped festival was turning out to be, and so David Crosby coaxed his bandmates into performing and fulfilling that commitment they had made. They had to choose the lesser of two evils: flee and don't go on and the crowd riot because you don't perform or try your best to perform and pacify the crowd. Once again, another musician was injured, this time Stephen Stills was stabbed multiple times in the leg with a bicycle spoke by a member of the Hells Angels. By the end of the set, the blood was soaking through his trousers. They only played for half an hour, leaving early amid all the chaos. David Crosby later told the *Washington Post*, 'Hells Angels don't do security. Hells Angels fight.' In another interview, he called the festival a nightmare, and 'the exact 180 degrees out antithesis of Woodstock' because of the bad vibes. Things only got worse after that.

After The Grateful Dead made a game-time decision to not play the festival, there was an awkward gap until The Rolling Stones' set and tensions increased in the crowd. An hour or two is a long time to wait in between bands and with the day turning to night, it got chilly, so the wait was even more uncomfortable for those who didn't plan ahead with their outfits. When The Rolling Stones arrived at Altamont, Mick Jagger was punched in the mouth by an angry member of the audience who screamed 'I hate you!' at him. This altercation plus the fact that they were waiting on bassist Bill Wyman to make it to Altamont delayed their performance by a bit, making it a nearly two-hour gap between CSNY's and The Stones' performances. In the meantime, fans were sitting on the stage, a defeated Sam Cutler telling them to get off the stage so the Rolling Stones can start their performance. What was intended to be a great show to cap off the '60s and a gift to the loyal Stones fans turned out to be far from that.

In total, four people died at Altamont: two twenty-two-year-old transplants from New Jersey named Mark Feiger and Richard Salov who died in a hit-and-run accident, a man from Buffalo named Leonard Kryszak who flipped off the cops and jumped into and drowned in the South Bay Aqueduct during a bad trip, and an eighteen-year-old mixed black/Native American man from Berkeley named Meredith Hunter, whose death made Altamont notorious. There were also four births, hundreds of bad trips and LSD freak outs, and multiple arrests.

Meredith Hunter attended the festival with his girlfriend, Patti Bredehoft. He came from a family who originated from Texas and had moved west for better opportunities, part of the early-mid 20th century Great Migration, in which millions of African Americans moved from the South to the Northeast, Midwest, and West Coast, in the hopes of better opportunities and to escape the racism, segregation, and disenfranchisement in the South.

During WWII, Meredith Hunter's mother, Altha Anderson, and his older siblings, Dixie and Donald, moved from San Angelo to Berkeley, seeing California as a land of opportunity, a fresh start. They already had family in the area, Altha's sisters, Tommie and Claudia. The family were poor, with Altha not being able to hold down a job because of her schizophrenia and alcoholism and no father in the picture and her often turning to the world's oldest profession to make money. Meredith, born in 1951, was mostly raised by his sister, Dixie, who was eight years older than him. Their living conditions were so poor they had to dumpster-dive for food and their home was so cramped and overcrowded. He turned to stealing to survive. Definitely far from a picture-perfect 1950s suburban sitcom upbringing; it was not a prosperous time for everyone. Between the ages of eleven and seventeen, Meredith spent a significant amount of time in juvie on burglary charges and during this time he got the nickname Murdock. He liked spending time outdoors, smoking weed, listening to soul and rock music, and fashion, like a lot of other people his age. California nowadays, especially the Bay Area, has a reputation for being the most progressive part of America, but in the 1960s, the government was still very much establishment and not very 'swinging' or 'hip' and there was still a lot of racism. California was not an egalitarian paradise and in the Bay Area there were huge differences between the different cities and suburbs and it was still very much segregated: there were predominantly white areas and predominantly black areas. Still, he loved the counterculture of Haight-Ashbury and the escapism and pleasure it offered. He could lose himself in psychedelic drugs and music. He had been to concerts and festivals before and when he heard about Altamont and how it was supposed to be California's answer to Woodstock, he was excited and really wanted to go. So naturally, he talked to his older sister Dixie about it and she warned him not to go because in the outer fringes of Alameda County it was very conservative and very white and he shouldn't go because it was not safe for black people, especially black men who had white girlfriends. Dixie's worries weren't unfounded; this was a time of sundown towns and just because the Civil Rights movement happened in the '60s, it didn't mean that racism was over.

Meredith ignored his sister's concerns and went to the concert anyway with his girlfriend Patti, his friend Ronnie Brown, and his girlfriend Judy, but he made sure to bring his gun with him for protection. As we all know from all those news stories, America is very much a country where people 'pack heat' and it's protected by the Second Amendment, in theory anyway. There's one set of rules for the white and wealthy and another set of rules for everyone else. When you're being discriminated against and oppressed and the system that's supposed to protect you fails to do so, all you can do is defend yourself, which is why, in the 1960s, the Black Panthers encouraged black people in America to arm themselves as it's a constitutional right. The government was afraid and passed laws to restrict open carrying only after that happened.

As you have already read, the tensions were growing and things were growing more violent and chaotic as time went by, so Meredith decided to go back to the car before The Rolling Stones played to get his gun so he could protect himself and his girlfriend Patti, who was very nervous after a whole day of seeing the Hells Angels rough up concertgoers left and right. Not a good idea. The Rolling Stones finally got on stage and just three songs into their set, during 'Sympathy for the Devil', a fight broke out and they stopped performing while the Hells Angels tried to calm down the crowd. Clearly that didn't work because the violence escalated throughout the day and the Hells Angels were extremely drunk because they'd been drinking all day long. While The Rolling Stones performed 'Under My Thumb' (a common myth is that Hunter was killed during 'Sympathy For The Devil' – not true), Meredith Hunter moved forward to get a better view and was stabbed by one of the Hells Angels, Alan Passaro, after he saw him pull out a gun, even though he said, 'I wasn't going to shoot you'. A Hells Angel yanked on Meredith's hair and another one punched him in the mouth after he tried to climb onto a speaker box to get a better view, like many members of the audience did. After that he pulled out his gun from his waistband, escalating the situation, and he was stabbed as a 'last resort'. However, an eyewitness named Paul Cox, who was quoted in that landmark *Rolling Stone* article about Altamont, said that he saw someone stab Meredith Hunter before he pulled out his gun, although this claim was scrutinised and disputed. He was brutally beaten as well, Hells Angels stomping him with their boots and kicking him in the face. Hells Angels didn't allow anyone to help Meredith, saying it was pointless because he was going to die. He was stabbed in the neck, head, and back and bleeding heavily and beaten with a rubbish bin. His gun was taken too.

Even after Meredith Hunter was stabbed and was bleeding to death, The Rolling Stones did not end their performance (probably out of fear for their own safety), only briefly stopping when the Hells Angels dropped Meredith's body on the stage and a startled Mick Jagger called for a doctor. They performed eight more songs, including their live debut of 'Brown Sugar' (a controversial one, with the lyrics referring to slavery) and hits like '(I Can't Get No) Satisfaction', 'Gimme Shelter', 'Honky Tonk Women', and 'Street Fighting Man' (you can say ending the concert with that song was tasteless, to say the least). Meredith's body was taken backstage, where his blood was washed away with hot coffee. Meanwhile, his girlfriend, Patti, was pleading 'Don't let him die', 'I don't want him to die'. Because of the racetrack's remote location, medical help couldn't get to him in time and he was pronounced dead on site. The family had no idea until the following morning when a friend called them to tell them he was dead. Hours later, family members went to the morgue in Oakland to identify Meredith's body.

As heard in *Gimme Shelter*, the Stones' tour manager Sam Cutler said, 'The Angels did as they saw best in the difficult situation. As far as I'm concerned, they were people who were here who tried to help in their own way.' A very cold, unsympathetic statement. Mick Taylor told *Rolling Stone* in 1970, 'I got the impression that because they were a security force they were using it as an excuse. They're just very, very violent people.' On the other hand, Keith Richards at the time called the show 'basically well-handled' but said that people were tired and 'a few tempers got frayed'; that last part is an understatement. The following day, Mick Jagger told the press, 'If Jesus had been there, he would have been crucified.' In a *Rolling Stone* interview decades after the concert, Mick Jagger said that he felt 'just awful' and felt 'a responsibility' after he found out someone was killed at Altamont and that the Hells Angels behaved 'dreadfully'. The Hells Angels tried to kill Mick Jagger twice because they were upset that The Rolling Stones didn't pay the five-figure legal fees for Alan Passaro's defence. In the mid '70s, Hells Angels in NYC staked out outside a hotel that they thought Mick Jagger was staying at. In 1979, a group of Hells Angels in New York allegedly plotted to kill Mick Jagger while he was at his holiday home in the Hamptons by getting on a boat and trying to blow up his home; thankfully there was a storm that sank their boat.

The newspapers and the documentary *Gimme Shelter* ran with this narrative of Meredith Hunter being some crazy, angry black guy with a gun who was going to kill one of The Rolling Stones or someone in the audience, and of course this upset his family, with his sister Dixie Ward saying she's never seen the documentary and never will because it's too painful. Vincent Camby wrote in his review of the film in the *New York Times* that the film was opportunistic, exploiting the events that unfolded in the film as well as the people involved. In *Gimme Shelter*, you can see footage of the band looking saddened hearing the news of the Altamont murder on the radio. Much of the film is concert footage, but there's behind-the-scenes stuff and crowd footage too. You can see Mick Jagger getting punched in the face at about forty-eight minutes into the film; the fight during Jefferson Airplane's set with

Grace Slick repeatedly saying 'easy' to calm down the situation and Marty Balin getting knocked out at about one hour and four minutes in; the fight breaking out during 'Sympathy For The Devil' and Mick's reaction to the footage at one hour and nine minutes in and one hour and seventeen minutes in with Mick pleading to the audience 'Who's fighting and what for?' and 'Why are we fighting?'; and at one hour and twenty minutes in, The Rolling Stones perform 'Under My Thumb' and three minutes later Meredith Hunter is being pushed and beaten by the Hells Angels after being stabbed and there's talk of him having a gun and it cuts to Mick Jagger looking at the footage in slo-mo where they see him holding a gun and the Hells Angel stabbing him when they see him pull out his gun. There is also footage in the documentary of Meredith Hunter's body on a stretcher and you can see under the body bag his green blazer covered in blood – his girlfriend was distraught.

In the newspaper coverage, for the most part he wasn't humanised, there were not really any photos, no way to put a face to a name. An award-winning 20,000-word article about Altamont in *Rolling Stone* put the magazine on the map and provided honest, balanced coverage about the irresponsibility and poor planning that led to the tragic loss of life. The article summed up Altamont as 'the product of diabolical egotism, hype, ineptitude, money manipulation, and, at base, a fundamental lack of concern for humanity'. In an interview with *Rolling Stone*, Meredith's younger sister Gwen said that no one contacted them and it would have been the right thing for The Rolling Stones to do so, but she didn't expect anything because she knows they don't genuinely care and they'll go off and play another rock festival. She also defended her brother and his character, calling him 'highly educated', a quiet guy who had just got a job at the post office, and that the gun was something he always had for his own protection and that 'he pulled it out and showed it to them only to make them stop and think when they were beating him.'

After months of investigation, Alan Passaro, the Hells Angel who fatally stabbed Meredith Hunter, was arrested after careful examination of the footage. Passaro was the son of an Italian immigrant who owned a barbershop in San Jose. Alan wanted to be a lawyer, but because he didn't apply himself in school, he followed in his father's footsteps, working a day job as a barber. He got interested in motorcycles, drinking, and drugs because he didn't feel fulfilled and wanted some excitement in his life. He joined a motorcycle gang called the Gypsy Jokers before joining the Hells Angels. He had a rap sheet with automobile theft charges and marijuana possession charges and was back in trouble with the law again when he was arrested four days after Altamont on charges of burglary and armed robbery and serving time in Vacaville Prison.

When Alan Passaro was tried for murder, he was acquitted on the grounds of self-defence because of the film footage that showed Meredith pulling out a gun before he stabbed him. Even though Alan Passaro wasn't a free man after that – because he had an unrelated prison sentence to serve – it still brought no closure to Meredith's family. His mother sued The Rolling Stones for $500,000. She only ended up getting $10,000 as a settlement (of which a significant amount went to her lawyer), no apologies or contact with any of The Rolling Stones themselves. No amount of money could bring her son back. She hoped for Altamont Speedway to become a public park and for there to be a memorial marker for her son. That did not happen, but concerts were banned there and they put a 3,000-person limit on future gatherings there. The speedway shut down in 2008.

In 1985, Alan Passaro, the Hells Angel who killed Meredith Hunter, was found dead in the Anderson Reservoir with $10,000 in his pockets. He had just got out of prison the year before after serving two years on an unrelated weapons charge and a federal racketeering charge. A coincidence, because that's the same amount of money The Rolling Stones paid as a settlement to Hunter's family. For decades, Meredith Hunter's grave was unmarked and it was only after a documentary directed by Sam Green called *Lot 63, Grave C* came out in the 2000s that people became aware of the aftermath and raised money for his family to put a headstone there.

The Alameda County Sheriff's Office reopened the Meredith Hunter case in 2009, but it was determined there was no other person who stabbed Hunter and he was a 'contributing factor to his own death' by bringing a gun with him to the concert.

CHAPTER 8

Stupid Cupid: Bobby Beausoleil and Arthur Lee, Frank Zappa, and Kenneth Anger (1965–1980)

Charles Manson wasn't the only member of the Manson Family to have connections to classic rockers; his associate Bobby Beausoleil also tried his hand at music before turning to crime. Even behind bars, he still pursued music and visual art. In this chapter, his various classic rock connections will be explored. As Bobby Beausoleil met Arthur Lee and Frank Zappa in the '60s, the background information on those musicians will only cover up until the '60s.

ARTHUR LEE

Singer-songwriter and leader of rock band Love, who were best known for their 1967 classic album *Forever Changes*. He was born Arthur Porter Taylor in Memphis to a schoolteacher mum and a jazz musician father, who fostered in him a love of music. In his childhood, he loved listening to blues music and performed in church. When his parents divorced, he and his mother moved to California and she remarried there, and her new husband, Clinton

Lee, adopted her son, giving him his last name. While in school, he met future bandmate Johnny Echols. While in middle school, he focussed more on music, first learning how to play accordion and mimicking musicians just from hearing their records. He later learnt how to play organ and guitar.

He first started recording music in 1963, with his first band being a Booker T. & the M.G.'s-style instrumental R&B band. He also wrote surf rock songs during his pre-Love years. Some early Arthur Lee recordings can be found on bootleg CDs.

The British Invasion forever changed music and America had to have a response to it. One of the most influential American '60s post-British Invasion bands were The Byrds and they changed Arthur Lee's life. The Byrds created their own type of sound that hadn't really been heard before: a combination of psychedelia, folk, and later country and they were one of the first jangle pop bands, paving the way for the revival of it in the '80s. When Arthur Lee heard The Byrds, he was already writing folk rock songs of his own and wasn't sure if that would resonate with people, but given The Byrds' popularity in the '60s, it validated him. And so he started a band called The Grass Roots, but they couldn't keep that name because there was already a band with that name.

FRANK ZAPPA

One of the most prolific and unique classic rockers, he was well known for being non-conformist, using free-form improvisation, writing satirical lyrics, and experimenting with sound. His discography is one of the most diverse out there in terms of how many genres he played: everything from rock to pop to jazz (fusion), you name it. As intimidating as his discography is, there's bound to be something you'll like in it. He had a reputation for being 'weird', but he began his autobiography with a quote from an interview with *The Baltimore Sun*, 'I never set out to be weird. It was always other people who called me weird'.

He was born Frank Vincent Zappa (not Francis!) on 21 December 1940 in Baltimore, Maryland to a family of mixed Sicilian, Greek, Arab, and French ancestry. His family were all recent immigrants to the US with his French-Sicilian mother being the first generation of her family born in the US and his Greek-Arab-Sicilian father having been born in a Sicilian village called Partinico and immigrating to the US as a child. His parents both spoke Italian, but they never taught their children so they could speak without them understanding and so the children could better integrate into American society (a very old school attitude). The family left Maryland when Frank Zappa was a pre-teen, first moving to Florida before going back to Maryland and eventually settling down in California. They left Maryland because Frank got sick all the time and for a change of scenery.

As a kid, Zappa had an interest in science and his father wanted him to be an engineer, but because he wasn't good at maths, that wasn't a feasible career path. At the age of twelve, he started playing drums, but rock and roll wasn't a thing yet so he didn't have goals of being a rock drummer. His parents rented a snare drum for him and when they couldn't afford to pay to rent it anymore, Zappa would drum on the furniture and pots and pans, but it was challenging because practising drums in a flat is a nightmare for the neighbours. While in secondary school, he befriended Captain Beefheart and they bonded over R&B. In the early '60s, he played R&B music. He started his own studio called Studio Z in 1964. That same year he formed The Mothers of Invention, who released their debut album, *Freak Out!*, in 1966. They broke up in 1969, but they got back together in 1970 and in 1973–1975. Besides music, Frank Zappa even made some films like *200 Motels* and *Baby Snakes*.

KENNETH ANGER

Kenneth Anger was an underground experimental filmmaker and

is widely considered to be a music video pioneer because of his use of music in place of dialogue in his films, even if he didn't see himself that way. Kenneth Anger had some connections with classic rockers: Mick Jagger was in *Invocation of My Demon Brother* (and also composed the music for it) and Jimmy Page was in *Lucifer Rising*.

He was best known for a collection of his short films which are shown together as part of the *Magick Lantern Cycle: Fireworks* (1947), *Rabbit's Moon* (1950), *Eaux d'Artifice* (1953), *Inauguration of the Pleasure Dome* (1954), *Scorpio Rising* (1963), *Kustom Kar Kommandos* (1965), *Invocation of My Demon Brother* (1969), and *Lucifer Rising* (1981, but completed in the early '70s).

He was born Kenneth Anglemyer in Santa Monica to a middle-class family. His parents met while studying at Ohio State University and moved to California in 1921. His father was an electrical engineer at Douglas Aircraft and his mother stayed at home, as she was disabled. Kenneth Anger was the youngest of his siblings and had a difficult relationship with his family. Early on he had an interest in film and he went to the Santa Monica Cotillion dance as a child and met Shirley Temple and danced with her once. At the age of ten, he made his first film called *Ferdinand the Bull*. He dressed up as a matador and two friends played the bull. The film was never released. In 1941, he made a more serious film, a music video of sorts called *Who Has Been Rocking My Dreamboat* (named after an Ink Spots song), which is footage of kids playing while popular songs play in the background. His early work is considered lost, as he burnt most of it in the '60s. While in secondary school, he had an interest in the occult and that can be seen in his films in the '60s and '70s and his friendship with Anton LaVey, founder of the Church of Satan. That said, he was not a Satanist, he was a pagan.

As a teenager, he realised he was gay and he got into the underground gay scene, something very dangerous during the homophobic time that was the 1940s. A couple of times he was arrested because of this, once in a 'homosexual entrapment' and another time when he was arrested on obscenity charges for his earliest surviving work, the 1947 homoerotic film *Fireworks*. Sexologist and creator of the Kinsey Scale, Dr Alfred Kinsey was one of the first to buy a copy of *Fireworks* and they became friends.

In the '50s, he moved to Paris and befriended director Jean Cocteau, who loved *Fireworks*. He travelled to Rome, where he filmed *Eaux d'Artifice*, which was supposed to be a longer film with four scenes, but only one scene was shot. He returned to America for a moment in 1953 after his mum died and the following year he released the Aleister Crowley and Thelema inspired *Inauguration of the Pleasure Dome*. To earn money to make more films, he wrote a celebrity gossip book called *Hollywood Babylon*.

In the '60s, he released one of his best-known films, *Scorpio Rising*, which some consider to be an early music video. It showed the biker subculture while exploring themes of homosexuality and the occult and showing Nazi imagery and nudity. The soundtrack was all popular music of the time with songs by musicians like Ricky Nelson, The Angels, Bobby Vinton, Elvis Presley, Ray Charles, Martha & The Vandellas, The Crystals, and The Surfaris. He followed it up with the erotic, experimental *Kustom Kar Kommandos,* which was funded by a grant from the Ford Foundation, who were giving grants to filmmakers. In the late '60s and early '70s, the hippie subculture took off and so Anger returned to making more occult films like *Invocation of My Demon Brother* and *Lucifer Rising*, which were very ambitious.

Kenneth Anger died at the age of ninety-six on 11 May 2023.

BOBBY BEAUSOLEIL

Bobby Beausoleil was born in Santa Barbara, California on 6 November 1947, the firstborn of five children. He was bored with his surroundings and as a teenager, he left home and went to LA. While in LA, he made music, something that he really enjoyed doing. In 1965, he went to San Francisco and got into the counterculture music and film scenes. He moved to Topanga Canyon – near LA – in the late '60s and lived with Gary Hinman, a music teacher and PhD student at UCLA, originally from Colorado. He worked at a music shop and taught people how to play bagpipes, piano, trombone, and drums. A friend of his told *People* magazine that Hinman had played Carnegie Hall, but unfortunately 'got in with the wrong crowd'. Gary Hinman was known to be kind, gentle, smart, and generous, and unfortunately that's what ended up resulting in his death and being the first Manson Family murder victim, killed by people he thought were his friends, people that he would allow to stay at his house. He was a Buddhist and wanted to go on a pilgrimage to Japan, but unfortunately he never went because he was killed before that was supposed to happen.

While in Topanga Canyon, he met Charles Manson, who he thought to be a genuinely talented singer-songwriter. However, within a year, things turned violent and Charles Manson ordered members of his cult to kill people for him. The first of these was Gary Hinman. He was killed because Manson believed him to be rich and wanted a piece of the pie and so he sent Bobby Beausoleil, Susan Atkins, and Mary Brunner to kill him. They demanded money from him, but he didn't have any so they called Charles Manson and asked what they should do and Manson told them to hold him captive while he was on his way. Charles Manson's right-hand man Bruce Davis drove him over there with Charles Manson armed with a sword that he cut Hinman with. The Manson Family tortured him for three days before killing him. As part of Manson's Helter Skelter race war ideology, Manson said to stage the scene of the crime as if Black Panthers had killed him. Bobby Beausoleil stabbed Hinman and he along with Mary Brunner and Susan Atkins took turns suffocating Hinman with a pillow while Hinman held his prayer beads and chanted a prayer. Like in the other Manson Family murders, they took the victim's blood and wrote a message with it, in this case 'Political piggy' with a bloody pawprint to make it look like the Black Panthers were responsible. Gary Hinman was murdered on 27 July 1969 and Bobby Beausoleil was arrested on 6 August in the car he had stolen from Hinman.

Beausoleil was found guilty of first-degree murder and sentenced to death. Because the Supreme Court of California ruled the death penalty unconstitutional in 1972 (that was later overturned, but California Governor Gavin Newsom placed a moratorium on executions in 2019. California has not carried out an execution since 2006.), all prisoners in California on death row had their sentences commuted to life imprisonment with the possibility of parole (notably, RFK assassin Sirhan Sirhan also had his death sentence commuted to life with the possibility of parole as well). Like Patricia Krenwinkel, Tex Watson, and Bruce Davis, he is still in prison. Even though he was recommended for parole, the sitting governor always rejected the recommendation.

ARTHUR LEE & BOBBY BEAUSOLEIL

When Bobby Beausoleil was only seventeen, he was in the band that ultimately became Love, but at the time they were called The Grass Roots (not to be confused with the '60s band put together by Lou Adler, P.F. Sloan, and Steve Barri). In an interview with *It's Psychedelic Baby Magazine*, he said he saw The Grass Roots perform at a local venue and he liked their sound and energy and that they were a band with a racially integrated line-up and he invited himself into the band. He was fired from the band after a short time in it.

FRANK ZAPPA & BOBBY BEAUSOLEIL

Bobby Beausoleil sang backup vocals on The Mothers of Invention album, *Freak Out!*. Of Frank Zappa, he said that as a teenager he followed him around and would hang out with him and listen to his music. He looked up to Zappa and found him funny, knowledgeable about music, and he wanted to join his band, but he was rejected because he didn't know how to read music.

KENNETH ANGER & BOBBY BEAUSOLEIL

While Kenneth Anger wasn't a musician, he had a lot of connections to classic rock and this is Bobby Beausoleil's strongest celebrity connection. If you look through Bobby Beausoleil's Instagram (run by his friends and family), you'll often see posts about Kenneth Anger on there.

After Beausoleil left LA because he found it to be too superficial, he went to San Francisco, but he never gave up on music. He found himself in the Haight-Ashbury district before it became the trendy hippie counterculture place. He was in a few bands, one called The Outfit, one eclectic one that he started called Orkustra, who played gigs with fellow Bay Area bands like The Grateful Dead, Country Joe & The Fish, Quicksilver Messenger Service, Jefferson Airplane, and more! The other band he formed were The Magic Powerhouse of Oz. While in Orkustra, he met filmmaker Kenneth Anger who was looking for someone to play Lucifer in his sequel of sorts, or rather an antithesis of *Scorpio Rising*, *Lucifer Rising* and as soon as he saw Beausoleil, he knew he was the one to play Lucifer. Beausoleil knew of Kenneth Anger and *Scorpio Rising* but had never seen any of his films. While at Anger's flat, Beausoleil read a lot about Thelema and the occult.

In the end, Beausoleil never appeared in *Lucifer Rising*, but rather those shots of him playing Lucifer were used in *Invocation of My Demon Brother*. However, Beausoleil still had significant involvement in *Lucifer Rising*. That film took a lot of time to complete because a lot of things fell apart and Kenneth Anger wanted to make an Aleister Crowley biopic, but it was never made. Mick Jagger distanced himself from Anger and didn't want to be in *Lucifer Rising*, but instead, his brother Chris appeared in the film, but Anger argued with him on set and fired him.

Kenneth Anger met Jimmy Page at an auction in London, where they were bidding on Crowley memorabilia. Jimmy happened to own a home in Scotland where Crowley used to live and invited Anger to stay over there with him. Anger wanted Jimmy Page to compose the soundtrack of *Lucifer Rising*, but it wasn't long until they had a falling out, with him calling Jimmy Page 'dried up as a musician'. Bobby Beausoleil found out about the falling out between Page and Anger and wrote to Anger from prison, offering to compose a soundtrack for *Lucifer Rising*. Compose a soundtrack from prison? Sounds like an impossible task! But he was able to do it thanks to a teacher in the prison who got Beausoleil access to musical instruments and recording equipment and so he formed a band in prison called The Freedom Orchestra. As well as his music being the soundtrack for the film, it was released on vinyl and sold mainly at screenings in the early '80s.

If you want to hear Jimmy Page's soundtrack for *Lucifer Rising*, it can be found on YouTube. Bobby Beausoleil recently made all his music and artwork available for free on the internet and information can be found on his official website, bobbybeausoleil.com.

CHAPTER 9

X Offender: Debbie Harry and Ted Bundy (1972)

Debbie Harry is best known as the frontwoman of new wave band Blondie. Years before she got famous, she allegedly came into contact with a famous serial killer before he became a household name. Thankfully, she survived.

DEBBIE HARRY

Debbie Harry was born Angela Trimble on 1 July 1945 in Miami, Florida. At just three months old, she was adopted by Richard and Cathy Harry from Paterson, New Jersey. She found out she was adopted at four years old and she said in an interview with the *Irish Independent* that her parents explained it to her 'in a really nice way' that made her 'feel quite special somehow.' She never knew her birth parents and doesn't even know what they looked like. The Harrys renamed their daughter Deborah Ann. She claims that her first memory was the day her parents adopted her, when they took her to the petting zoo.

She grew up in Hawthorne, New Jersey, a quiet middle-to-lower-middle-class commuter town. Growing up, she loved fairy tales and playing in the woods near her childhood home. She was an imaginative child and had psychic experiences at a young age, such as hearing a voice from the fireplace speaking to her. Her upbringing was a typical American one, attending church with her parents and being in the Girl Scouts. She loved the woods and all the mystery there, but she also loved New York City: the shopping, the entertainment, and how vibrant the city was with its sights, sounds, and smells. Growing up, her parents liked listening to opera, jazz, and big band music. Early on, she had dreams of being a star and people around her recognised her as beautiful. She sang in the church choir and acted in school plays. By the time she was in secondary school, she knew she wanted to be an artist or a bohemian, but her parents didn't agree with that – they wanted her to be more academic. She wanted to be like Marilyn Monroe and when she was fourteen, she started dying her hair that signature platinum blonde, just like her idol. She was also fascinated with the folk and beatnik scene in Greenwich Village.

She wanted to get out of that small town and be somewhere more exotic and cosmopolitan and so she made it happen. After graduating from Centenary College in Hackettstown, New Jersey, which she described as a 'reform school for debutantes', she got a job in New York City and moved into a rent-controlled apartment on the Lower East Side. She worked various odd jobs before getting famous including being a shop assistant at a housewares market, a secretary for the BBC's office in New York, a shop assistant at a head shop, a waitress at Max's Kansas City, a Playboy Bunny, and a go-go dancer.

In the late '60s, she was a backup singer in a folk band called The Wind in the Willows, named after Kenneth Grahame's famous children's book. The band's founder, Paul Klein, was the then-husband of Debbie Harry's high school friend Wendy Weiner. Paul and Wendy were Freedom Riders who travelled to the South to help register black people to vote. In the '60s, record labels would sign all sorts of bands and take chances on them, paying them some money and paying for studio time. In the summer of 1968, they released their self-titled debut album. Artie Kornfeld, one of the founders of Woodstock, produced the album and played bongos on it. Debbie Harry only sang lead vocals on one song on the album, 'Djini Judy'. The album went nowhere on the charts, only reaching number 195 on the Billboard Albums Charts. The Wind in the Willows were supposed to record a second album, but it was never released. Debbie Harry left the band shortly after the first album was released because of creative and personal differences with her bandmates; she felt like she was outgrowing the band, and she was tired of being a 'decorative asset'. She's more than just a pretty face and she wanted to write songs and have more creative input.

A few years after leaving The Wind in the Willows, she was in a girl group called The Stillettos with Elda Gentile and Rosie Ross. Chris Stein joined the band as a backup musician. He and Debbie Harry left and formed a new band. They were originally called Angel and the Snake, but they changed their name to Blondie after Debbie Harry told Chris Stein that truckers kept shouting 'Hey, Blondie!' at her all the time. Keep in mind though that Blondie is not Debbie Harry, hence why the band had buttons that had 'BLONDIE IS A GROUP' on them. Blondie went on to be a successful band with their breakthrough album *Parallel Lines* coming out in 1978. Hit singles 'Hanging On The Telephone', 'Heart of Glass', and 'One Way or Another' were on that album. Some other famous songs by them include 'Dreaming', 'Call Me', 'The Tide Is High', and 'Rapture'. The band broke up in 1982. The following year, Chris Stein was diagnosed with pemphigus, a stress-related autoimmune skin disease that often results in death. Debbie Harry took a hiatus from music and took care of her then-partner, which she described as not seeming 'like a sacrifice at all'. The couple broke up in 1987 but have remained friends and have worked together since then.

TED BUNDY

Ted Bundy was born Theodore Robert Cowell in Burlington, Vermont on 24 November 1946 to a single mother, Eleanor Louise Cowell. The identity of his biological father is unknown, but there are theories that the father was a sailor, in the Air Force, or the Army. There was even a theory that Ted Bundy's grandfather was his biological father, but a DNA test debunked that. Because his mother was so young, his grandparents took him to Philadelphia and raised him in early childhood as if he was their son, even telling him that his mother was his older sister. When he was about three years old, he and his biological mother moved to Tacoma, Washington since they had family living there. Eleanor married an Army hospital cook named Johnnie Bundy and he adopted her son and so he took his last name. He never felt close to him and actually resented his stepfather for not having much formal education or money. He wanted to be rich, so it's no wonder he made attempts at studying law and working in politics when he was a young adult.

Growing up, he was a socially awkward child who had an early interest in violence and gore. When he was three, he placed knives all around his aunt when she was sleeping. He allegedly told forensic psychiatrist Dr Dorothy Otnow Lewis that he assaulted his sister at a young age. He also was abusive to animals in childhood, a common early warning sign of a serial killer. When he was a child, he hanged a cat with rope and set the cat on fire and found it funny. While it wasn't proven he did it, an eight-year-old girl named Ann Marie Burr who lived in his neighbourhood went missing in 1961, when he was just fourteen. She was sleeping and someone broke into her family's house and kidnapped her. Ted Bundy lived a few blocks away from the Burr family, had a paper route in the area, and would visit his uncle, who was their neighbour. He confessed to Dr Ronald Holmes that as a teenager he 'stalked, strangled, and sexually mauled' Ann Marie and hid her body in a muddy pit. However, when evidence was analysed decades later, it was shown not to contain enough measurable DNA to link Ted Bundy to the case. The kidnapping of Ann Marie Burr is still a cold case even over sixty years later. One of Ted Bundy's childhood hobbies was reading detective magazines that had illustrations of women in danger, fearing for their lives. In his last ever interview, the day before he was executed, he said that he would look at porn when he was as young as twelve or thirteen. He confessed in that interview that he had a porn addiction. He also was a peeping tom in his teenage years.

In school, he did well, maintaining a B+ average. He was intelligent, but not brilliant or a genius in any way. After graduating from secondary school, he attended the University of Puget Sound and University of Washington and even took an intensive Chinese course at Stanford and took some classes at Temple University in Philadelphia. While in university, he worked various odd jobs to pay the bills. From 1967 to 1968, he dated Diane Edwards (also known as Stephanie Brooks), a woman from a wealthy California family. The relationship ended when Edwards moved back to California and Ted Bundy didn't get into law school. She broke up with him because she didn't find him strong or masculine enough and she didn't find him to be ambitious enough. The breakup left him devastated and there's a theory that when he started killing women, his victims often looked vaguely like Diane. Academically, he had some achievements. He changed his major to psychology, eventually graduating with a bachelor's degree in psychology from the University of Washington. He graduated with honours, earning mostly A's with a few B's here and there. He was accepted into the University of Utah law school, but never graduated.

In 1968, he started getting into politics, working for the Republican Party. He attended the 1968 Republican National Convention in Miami as a delegate for presidential candidate Nelson Rockefeller, who lost to Richard Nixon. He was also a driver and bodyguard for Washington state lieutenant governor candidate Arthur Fletcher.

In 1969, he travelled to the East Coast to trace his roots and find out the truth about his real father, after his cousin made fun of him for being an illegitimate child. His birth certificate read that he was an illegitimate child and a Penn State graduate and Air Force veteran Lloyd Marshall was listed as his father, but he didn't know him. He was devastated, but some happiness came into his life when he fell in love with Elizabeth Kloepfer, a single mother from Ogden, Utah. The pair met at a tavern in the University District. Elizabeth said she wouldn't normally pick up a man at a bar and take him home, but there was something about Ted that she really liked and she really wanted to marry him, while he wanted to wait until he graduated from law school. She even wanted to have a baby with him and he even got her pregnant, but the two couldn't afford to have a baby so she had an abortion.

Ted and Elizabeth dated until 1976, when he was convicted for kidnapping in Utah. By the end of her relationship, she got in contact with the police, giving them information about Ted. She started to connect the dots about why Ted was acting suspiciously and not answering the phone at times when she called him, but was still in disbelief. The two corresponded while Ted was in jail in Utah, against her psychiatrist's advice and she attended his kidnapping trial in Utah and sat with his parents and spent time with him when he was out on bail even when police were following Ted. After his conviction, she struggled with alcoholism, had difficulty coming to terms with what had happened, and at times regretted speaking to the police. Meanwhile, Ted started dating Carole Ann Boone, the woman he famously proposed to while on trial for murder in Florida and would go on to be the father of their daughter, Rose.

In the early '70s, he was kidnapping, raping, and murdering women in the University District (the neighbourhood they were living in) and Lake Sammamish State Park and of course these crimes made the news. The suspect was described as a man named Ted with a transatlantic accent who drove a Volkswagen and so happened to look like Elizabeth's then-boyfriend, but there were some discrepancies with the description, such as his height, the colour of his car, and the way he wore his watch. She didn't want to believe it at first and thought it was a weird coincidence because she was in love with him and even her friends were telling her it was a coincidence and he looked normal. However, he started acting suspiciously and had some unusual things in his apartment like plaster of Paris, crutches, and a meat cleaver that wasn't used for cutting meat. One day when Ted and Elizabeth were rafting, he violently pushed her off the edge of a raft and into the river and his eyes had this dangerous look she had never seen before. Another time, he closed the fireplace damper in Elizabeth's home and put towels under the door cracks so smoke would stay in the house. She had trouble breathing and was constantly coughing. The reason she survived was she stuck her head out of a window. He would later confess to her that he tried to kill her. After her co-workers said that the suspect named Ted looked an awful lot like her boyfriend, she called the police. But the police in Seattle didn't do anything because he didn't seem like a murderer because of how 'clean cut' and 'handsome' he was.

Ted moved to Salt Lake City after being accepted again at the University of Utah law school. Elizabeth decided to stay in Seattle, but she stayed in contact with him, often talking to him on the phone. Instead of attending class, he spent a lot of time kidnapping, murdering, and raping women and sure enough, the disappearances and murders ended up making the news. Elizabeth's friend Angie broke the news that similar crimes were happening in Utah and Elizabeth felt like her world was falling apart; just too many coincidences to be a coincidence. Elizabeth decided to call the Seattle police again to tell them she was afraid that 'a friend' of hers was involved and pointed out the similarities but kept saying that she felt like she was wrong and always had this fear when talking to them. She urged them to talk to the police in Salt Lake City since similar crimes were happening there. She later met with a police officer and brought photos of Ted and talked about her relationship with him, but the cop straight up told her that, even though he was on the list of suspects, he didn't look like a suspect because he didn't seem to fit the psychological profile but still, Elizabeth gave him some photos to show the witnesses to see if they identify Ted as the kidnapper. The most reliable witness said that Ted looked too old and put the photo back in the pile of suspect photos.

Still, Elizabeth visited Ted when he was in law school in Utah. It wasn't until a routine traffic stop on 16 August 1975 that Ted Bundy was arrested. The police officer noticed the gutted Volkswagen, questioned him, and searched the car – finding a bunch of tools used to commit murders and found he fitted the description of the suspect of a kidnapping that had happened months earlier. The kidnapping victim picked Ted out in a police line-up and said he was the culprit. Even after he was convicted of kidnapping in Utah (note: he was not tried for the murders in 1976), his co-workers felt like he had been railroaded and that he had to be innocent. Some people back in Seattle even donated to his defence fund for the kidnapping trial in Utah. A headline in the Seattle *Post-Intelligencer* about his arrest read *Ex-Evans Campaign Aide Held in Kidnap* with a photo of him with a caption that read: 'Is Utah "Ted" the Seattle "Ted"?'. He was sentenced to fifteen years in prison for kidnapping. He didn't just escape from prison once, he escaped twice!

While Ted was in law school in Utah, he also kidnapped and murdered women in Colorado; after detectives examined the Volkswagen Beetle he sold to a teenager and found some hair samples matching the missing and murdered women, he was extradited to Colorado to be tried there for murder. This time, Ted represented himself and so he was granted use of the law library and the privilege to appear in court unshackled, the perfect recipe for an escape. It was a warm June day when Ted made his first escape from the law library on the second storey of the courthouse, simply jumping out the window in his street clothes and running into the woods and eventually back into Aspen to steal a car and escape further afield. After six days on the run, he was caught. Ted requested a change of venue to a different county because his case was too high-profile in Aspen, so right before Christmas the judge granted the request and approved a transfer of venue to Colorado Springs, where the jailers are stricter and there's a higher rate of death sentences. With a transfer to a higher security jail on the horizon, Ted was not going to give up on escaping from jail. Escape was always on his mind and he would hint at it in letters he wrote to Elizabeth. While incarcerated at the Garfield County Jail, he studied his surroundings and noticed an opening in his cell where the lightbulb was and had a feeling he could escape through that if he lost a bit of weight and obtained a hacksaw. He starved himself and lost about twenty to thirty pounds so he could fit through the opening in the ceiling. Because of the Christmas break, most of the jailers were on holiday leave so there was only a skeleton crew guarding the jail. It would take some time before guards would realise he was gone. He arranged books under the covers to look like he was still sleeping and then he took off through the crawl space and ended up in the jailer's apartment, where he stole some street clothes and fled the scene. He hopped on a Greyhound bus to Chicago and from there made his way to the college town of Ann Arbor, Michigan. Word got out about him escaping from prison, but because of his chameleon-like appearance, no one recognised him. He knew if he wanted to be under the radar, he'd have to go further afield and so he stole a car and went to Atlanta before travelling to the college town of Tallahassee by bus. He continued shoplifting and stealing cash and credit cards from purses to survive even though he knew that if he was caught shoplifting, he'd end up being sent back to jail in Colorado. It wasn't long until he was killing again. He murdered two women from the Chi Omega sorority and a twelve-year-old girl from Lake City.

While trying to escape Florida, Bundy was apprehended. The police discovered that they had found someone on the FBI's Most Wanted list. He was indicted for the three murders on 27 July 1978. When Sheriff Ken Katsaris held a press conference, he dragged Bundy in front of the cameras. Bundy made some quips and famously ripped his copy of the indictment on camera. Bundy got the notoriety he wanted. His face was all over the newspapers and his trial made history, being the first one to be nationally televised. A trial of the century. In the end, he was given the death penalty. He was executed by electrocution on 24 January 1990, with crowds appearing at Florida State Prison celebrating his demise.

The story of Ted Bundy goes to show you that murderers and rapists don't always look like monsters that you can spot a mile away. They can look like ordinary people in your community and that's the scariest thing. It is also a case that is a product of its time, which demonstrates how primitive things were then compared to today, with DNA evidence and more interconnectedness between faraway places because of the internet.

DEBBIE HARRY & TED BUNDY

Debbie's encounter with Ted Bundy was not her first run-in with a creep. Growing up, she dealt with a lot of encounters with creeps. She wrote in her autobiography, *Face It*, that when she was a baby, her doctor told her parents that she had 'bedroom eyes'. She also said that when she was around eight years old her mum was babysitting her friend's daughter Nancy and her mum told her to take Nancy to the nearby swimming pool, which was two blocks away from their house. Debbie walked with Nancy to the swimming pool and on the way there, a creepy, dishevelled-looking old man in a parked car asked the young Debbie for directions with a map or newspaper covering his erection and him masturbating. The paper fell over and he exposed himself. She was terrified and she and Nancy fled to the pool. As soon as she got to the pool, she was in such a panic over what happened that she told her teacher, who was checking pool passes at the entrance, that she needed to go home and asked if she could look after Nancy. Debbie ran home and told her mother about the perverted old man who exposed himself to her and without hesitation she called the police. There were other incidents, such as a flasher in a trench coat stalking Debbie's family in the Central Park Zoo, and at the age of eleven or twelve while on holiday in Cape Cod with her cousins, they were hit on and stalked by these men in their late thirties – one of them turned out to be famous jazz drummer Buddy Rich. She said that these incidents were so frequent that it started to feel 'almost normal'. In the early '70s, she was stalked by an ex-boyfriend she names in her autobiography as 'Mr C.'. He followed her to her grandmother's house, to her job at a hair salon, and even broke into her apartment waving a revolver at her. She moved out of that apartment right after the break-in, but the stalking didn't end there. He stole her mail and threatened her bandmates. She went to the police, but they were no help.

Debbie Harry had a lot of close calls and talks about a bunch of them in her autobiography. She describes her close call with Ted Bundy as the 'nastiest' one. The first time she told this story was in an interview with a newspaper in 1989 and her retellings of the story have been consistent ever since, so there's reason to trust her story.

In the early '70s, glam rock was very popular and she was a big fan of punk rock pioneers and androgynous glam rockers The New York Dolls and she made it a point to go to as many of their shows as possible. One hot summer night, Debbie Harry was staying in Alphabet City with some friends and she found out about a party for The New York Dolls that was happening at an after-hours club in the West Village, all the way across the city, a little under a two-mile walk. Her friends didn't want to come along, so she walked alone. Doesn't sound that bad, but imagine that in platform shoes – the chic footwear of the day! On top of that, it was two in the morning; you know how New York is the city that never sleeps, always something going on. In those days, Alphabet City was seedy and taxis wouldn't go there and there was certainly no Uber, so Debbie Harry had no choice but to make the trek along Houston Street in her super tall Granny Takes a Trip platform shoes. She was understandably tired of walking and she tried walking barefoot, but it was dangerous because the footpaths were covered in broken glass shards. A man in a small white car circled her as she was walking and he eventually pulled up next to her and asked her if she needed a ride. She turned down the offer, but the man kept circling around and persisting. She turned him down a couple more times, but eventually she was exhausted and took a chance, even though getting into a car with a stranger was not something she'd do even when she was a hippie and everyone hitchhiked.

She got into the car with the strange man and noticed that he 'was not bad looking'. True to the description of Ted Bundy, the man had short, dark hair with a slightly wavy/curly texture. He was quiet and so stinky to the point where she desperately wanted to open the window a little more for some fresh air, but there was something very suspicious about the car. There was no crank to open the window and the whole car was completely stripped down with a bare-bones metal-framed dashboard with no radio or glovebox. She was terrified and went into a flight-or-flight response and went with her gut feeling – she was going to try to escape. The window was just cracked open enough to get her arm through and she managed to open the car door. He noticed and swung a fast left turn onto Thompson Street, which opened the car door and flung her out on her butt in the middle of the road. She was only a couple of blocks away from the New York Dolls' party. The bad news was, by the time she got there, the party was over. The good news (if you can even call it that) though was that she wasn't hurt and he drove off and didn't come back for her.

She put the incident out of her mind and didn't think about it for fifteen years or so. Sometime around 1989, she was flying to LA and read a story about Ted Bundy in either *Time* or *Newsweek*. The story talked about his modus operandi and how he found his victims and she found a lot of parallels between the stories of his victims and her close call that one hot summer night in 1972. He had just been executed by electric chair in Florida. When she read the article, the hairs on the back of her neck stood up just like when she was in that car, the only two times in her life she had that sensation. Eerie!

Some people have questions about Debbie Harry's story and doubt that it was Ted Bundy because there wasn't any evidence that he was in New York City at that time. However, there isn't evidence either that he wasn't there at that time. He had relatives on the East Coast and had travelled around the country quite a bit, so it's possible that he could have visited New York City at some point. In Ann Rule's book *The Stranger Beside Me*, a woman named Siobhan from Linden, New Jersey (which is right next to Staten Island) wrote to her saying that when she was a teenager in 1974 or 1975, she saw Ted Bundy in a gold VW and her story had a lot of similarities to Debbie Harry's. It was a rainy day, she was sopping wet, her umbrella was broken and she was desperate for a lift and so when Ted Bundy offered her a lift, she accepted even though it wasn't something she'd normally do. He drove her to a sketchy part of town instead of where she needed to go, and she had a bad feeling in her gut. As soon as the car stopped and she had an opportunity to get out, she poked him with his umbrella, shouted 'Fuck you!' at him, and exited the car. Ann Rule said of Siobhan's story that those were busy years for Ted but she couldn't track down his whereabouts on the East Coast. She concluded, 'I'm inclined to guess that Siobhan met someone other than Ted, but I wouldn't bet on it.' In both of these cases, he picked up young women/girls who were in desperate situations.

While the car Debbie Harry was riding in was similar on the inside to his 1968 Volkswagen Beetle, she said on RuPaul and Michelle Visage's podcast *What's The Tee?* that the car wasn't a VW bug because the dashboard was squarer and she felt confident of that since she has some knowledge of cars. She also acknowledged the questions about her story in *Face It*, but felt confident in her memory and wrote, 'it was him'.

One thing that sceptics point out is that Ted Bundy is not known to have committed murders until 1974. Most of his murder victims were in Washington state, Oregon, Utah, Colorado, and Idaho in 1974 and 1975, as well as an unidentified victim in California and three victims in Florida in 1978. However, some people believe that Ted Bundy may have killed women prior to 1974, but these are speculations.

CHAPTER 10

Jimmy Page and Lynette 'Squeaky' Fromme (1975)

While this legendary British rock guitarist didn't come into contact with a member of the Manson Family, it was still startling, as this near-encounter happened not long before the attempted assassination of President Ford.

JIMMY PAGE

Considered one of the best guitarists of all time, there isn't really an introduction needed for Jimmy Page. You know him as Led Zeppelin's guitarist, but before all that, he was an established session guitarist in London and was a member of The Yardbirds, the band that launched three of Britain's most legendary guitarists' careers: those of Eric Clapton, Jimmy Page, and Jeff Beck.

Jimmy Page was born James Patrick Page just outside of London, in a suburb called Heston on 9 January 1944, but he also lived in Feltham, not far from Heathrow Airport, and Epsom, Surrey. He was named after his parents: his father was also named James and his mother's name was Patricia. He was an intelligent kid who taught himself a lot of things and he was introverted, making it hard to relate to others. When he was twelve, he found an abandoned Spanish guitar in the house his family were living in in Surrey and there was a lot of mystery behind the item. Whose guitar was it? Why did they leave it behind?

Jimmy Page didn't think much of it until he started hearing rock and roll records and found his calling and so with just a couple of lessons to get him started, he mostly taught himself how to play guitar. He practised and practised and became a master of his craft. Like most British kids in the '50s, he got into rock and roll and skiffle. Skiffle was Britain's take on American country music, popularised by Lonnie Donegan, whose version of 'Rock Island Line' shaped a generation of aspiring rock stars. If you go on YouTube, you can find a video of a thirteen-year-old Jimmy Page playing a skiffle-style cover of the traditional song 'Mama Don't Allow No Music' and Lead Belly's 'Cottonfields' on a TV show called *All Your Own*, hosted by Huw Wheldon. In a brief interview between the songs, Page said he also liked to play Spanish guitar and that he had hopes of studying biological research at university to cure cancer; the latter comment has been memed by many Led Zeppelin fans.

He remained active in the local rock and roll scene, joining multiple rock bands in and around Epsom and playing in local clubs for their rock and roll nights. He loved playing acoustic folk guitar like Bert Jansch, and Chuck Berry and Bo Diddley songs. Over time, he saved up money to upgrade his guitars, going from a Spanish guitar to a Hofner President to a Futurama Grazioso to a Fender Telecaster, and a bunch of other more professional guitars.

As you can surmise from chapter 8, Jimmy Page has an interest in the occult and also astrology. Interestingly enough, his interest in the occult started when he was fifteen, he said in an interview with Chris Salewicz in 1977. He loved to read Aleister Crowley's *Magick in Theory and Practice*. He left school with four O-Levels because he had one goal in mind: to be a pop star; although he did spend some time in art school studying painting after collapsing at a gig due to fatigue. But that didn't last long because he was inspired by the British R&B boom to pick up his guitar and play full-time again. And so he went to London to do session work with lots of popular artists like The Who, The Kinks, Marianne Faithfull, Cliff Richard, Billy Fury, The Rolling Stones, Them, Donovan, Johnny Hallyday, Joe Cocker, Shirley Bassey, Lulu, Petula Clark, Sonny Boy Williamson, Chris Farlowe, Nico, and he played guitar on some of the incidental music from The Beatles' film *A Hard Day's Night*. He got a lot of work because there weren't a lot of session electric guitarists as skilled as him besides Big Jim Sullivan, who started his career backing OG British rock star Marty Wilde. He was making such good money as a session musician that he initially turned down joining The Yardbirds after Eric Clapton left the band. But he joined later when bassist Paul Samwell-Smith left the band, and with a shift in who played what, Chris Dreja moved to bass and Jimmy Page and Jeff Beck were on twin lead guitar. Page and Beck, along with John Paul Jones, Keith Moon, and Nicky Hopkins, did a one-off supergroup recording of 'Beck's Bolero', piquing Jimmy Page's interest in forming a supergroup together, but because of contractual obligations and no lead singer, the plan fell through. But something good came out of it when, according to legend, John Entwistle said the idea would go down like a lead balloon and somewhere along the line it turned into lead zeppelin, for more effect. According to an interview Jimmy Page did for *Trouser Press* in 1977, it was Keith Moon who came up with the band's name. Jimmy kept those two words in mind for a future project, dropping the 'a' in lead because he didn't want people to accidentally say the band name the wrong way; isn't English a crazy language with all its heteronyms and homonyms?

The Yardbirds went their separate ways in 1968 and Jimmy was the only one left and still had to complete some tour dates in Scandinavia as promised. What could he do? Form a new band and call them The New Yardbirds, so he hired an incredible line-up: Robert Plant, John Paul Jones, and John Bonham. When they came back from that tour, they adopted the name Led Zeppelin, so those who saw The New Yardbirds on the 1968 Scandinavian Tour were the first to see Led Zeppelin and they didn't realise it at the time. From there, Led Zeppelin released a string of masterpiece albums, were a popular live act, and stayed together until the death of John Bonham in 1980.

LYNETTE 'SQUEAKY' FROMME

Lynette Fromme may not have been involved in the Tate–LaBianca murders, but she was a devoted follower of Charles Manson and got into his cult early on in 1967, just as he got out of prison. She was in love with him and worshipped him, believing him to be psychic when he spotted her crying on a bench after being kicked out of her parents' house at only nineteen years old.

Lynette 'Squeaky' Fromme was born in Santa Monica on 22 October 1948. Her father, William, was originally from Brooklyn and was briefly in the Army but was discharged after six months due to poor performance in training so he went to California to build planes, a growing industry there at the time. He was educated with degrees from NYU and USC. Squeaky's mother, Helen, was originally from rural Minnesota and grew up in a large family. The family settled down in Westchester, then a conservative suburb of LA near LAX airport, which grew post-WWII thanks to families moving in and the growing aerospace industry.

Growing up, the red-haired Lynette, nicknamed Lynny, loved animals and nature and was known in the neighbourhood as very charming and a chatterbox. But behind that happy face and seemingly idyllic suburban upbringing was turbulence at home. The patriarch became a bitter, mean cheapskate and took it out on his wife and kids and Lynny wasn't the same whenever he was around. He was abusive and had anger problems. For Lynny, her escape and talent was dancing, with her joining and being the youngest member of the Westchester Lariats dance troupe. With her distinct red hair, she became a star; all eyes would be on her as she danced, but not everyone liked that. She faced a lot of jealousy and bitterness from her peers. Sadly, though, her parents weren't the most supportive of her dreams of being a performer. The Lariats were so successful that they performed at some of LA's most famous venues, at Laurence Welk's show, at Disneyland, and they toured all over the country and even visited the White House. When she wasn't dancing, she would run away to friend's houses and feel more at home there than at her parents' house. In secondary school, she was friends with future SNL actor Phil Hartman and hung out with peers who had more alternative, artistic interests. She also had an interest in the occult, conducting séances and using a Ouija board. While still in secondary school, Lynette's family left Westchester for Redondo Beach, a similar suburb with conservative politics and a lot of people working in aerospace. She got involved in her school's theatre programme and wrote poetry in her free time. She worked odd jobs because her family wouldn't give her very much money. She enrolled in college and after dropping out, she was kicked out of the house and subsequently joined the Manson Family. During the Manson Family's time at Spahn Ranch, the owner, George Spahn, gave Lynette her nickname of Squeaky because she would make a squeak noise whenever he touched her. While members of the Manson Family were in court, she would demonstrate in support of them and made clothes that the Manson Girls wore at their trial. She even went to jail for trying to serve a burger laced with LSD to a witness to the Tate murder, Barbara Hoyt. She was the glue that kept the Manson Family together, keeping the members on the inside and outside in touch.

Even though Charles Manson, Bobby Beausoleil, Clem Grogan, Bruce Davis and the Manson Girls were behind bars, the Manson Family didn't die out completely. By the mid '70s, girls like Gypsy Share, Ruth Ann Moorehouse, and Mary Brunner left the cult and Charlie Manson wasn't happy about that, sending empty threats to them. But he still had Squeaky Fromme on his side and she still sent correspondence to Susan, Patricia, and Leslie. And so the cult evolved into the Order of Rainbow. Charles Manson gave the girls new nicknames, each of them being assigned a different colour: Squeaky – Red, Sandra Good – Blue, Susan Atkins – Queen of Violet, Patricia Krenwinkel – Queen of Yellow, and Leslie Van Houten – Queen of Green. However, Atkins, Krenwinkel, and Van Houten rejected this 'queen' title when they'd stopped corresponding with Charles Manson and no longer wanted anything to do with him. Charles Manson started talking more about the environment and protecting the earth and so Squeaky and Sandy, who were on the outside, spread the message, but sporting new looks. Gone were the risqué swinging '60s miniskirts. Now, they were wearing modest robes that covered their bodies from shoulder to ankle. Sandra Good even said that she and Squeaky were 'nuns' 'waiting for [their] lord'.

In 1975, Squeaky attempted to assassinate President Gerald Ford in Sacramento, the capital of California. Even to this day, environmentalism is a very important issue to her and Charles Manson talked about the environment with his ecological belief system called ATWA – which stands for Air, Trees, Water, Animals – what he called a name for all life on Earth and a 'human quest to live in balance with our planet's life-support systems'. Lynette Fromme, Sandra Good, and Charles Manson were all outspoken when it came to ATWA. In the '80s, Charles Manson wrote a letter to President Reagan speaking out against the War on Drugs and urging him to do something about climate change. Fromme and Good, dubbed Red and Blue respectively by Manson, ended up in jail too and what landed them in there was taking ATWA to an extreme. As with any cult, the message first starts off as something reasonable, easy to agree with, benign, but then as you become more indoctrinated, it becomes more extreme.

In the '70s, carbon dioxide and greenhouse gas emissions were a problem, but instead of forecasting global warming, scientists had a theory that these aerosol pollutants would reflect sunlight away from the Earth, therefore resulting in global cooling. While there was a brief somewhat cooler period during the mid-20th century, the planet got hotter and hotter as the years went by with record-breaking scorchers almost every year.

In the '70s in California, smog was a huge problem, not just in the cities but also in the rural areas, as an Environmental Protection Agency study showed. Weeks before the report came out, President Ford asked Congress to relax provisions of the Clean Air Act, a move that environmentalists were not happy with and this led to multiple threats on his life. Weeks before the President was to appear in Sacramento, a man named Thomas Elbert called the Secret Service, threatening to kill the President. Lynette Fromme, also known as Red, was concerned about the redwood trees (part of the reason for her nickname) and she believed the smog from cars would cause them to fall and cause devastation to the environment. When she found out President Ford was coming to Sacramento and that the hotel where he was staying was near her flat, she hatched a plan: kill the President because he was killing the environment, to scare the government into doing something about pollution.

On 5 September 1975, President Ford spoke at the forty-ninth annual Host Breakfast. Because it wasn't certain that Governor Jerry Brown would speak at the event (he did appear in the end), the wealthy businesspeople organising it invited President Ford to speak. With California being the most populous state in the country, it was crucial for the President to go there to win over voters if he wanted to win the 1976 election. After he spoke at the Host Breakfast, he returned to the Senator Hotel, which was next to the California State Capitol, just separated by a bit of the Capitol Park. In Capitol Park, the president shook hands with the people who came to see him on his way to the Capitol to speak to Governor Brown. Squeaky Fromme was there too and she stood out in her long, bright red dress, but she wasn't there to shake hands and say hello. She pointed a Colt M1911 .45 pistol at him, he saw the large gun, there was an audible click, she shouted, 'It wouldn't go off!', and the Secret Service tackled her to the ground, taking her pistol. The ammo was in a detachable magazine in the grip, but no bullets were in the chamber. Thanks to her not knowing how to use the gun, President Ford lived. She didn't know that, in order to put the bullets in the chamber, she needed to pull back the gun slide.

The trial was historic with Gerald Ford being the first US President to testify at a criminal trial and Squeaky Fromme being the first woman to attempt to assassinate a US President. His testimony was via videotape from the White House (they didn't have Zoom then!). In the end, Squeaky Fromme was sentenced to fifteen years to life in prison for attempted assassination of a US President. At her sentencing hearing, she acted out and threw an apple at United States Attorney Dwayne Keyes because he said her punishment should be severe because she has shown herself to be full of 'hate and violence'. She escaped from a federal prison in West Virginia for two days around Christmas 1987 because she found out that Charles Manson might have testicular cancer and she wanted to see him. She didn't get very far and was found just two miles away from the prison fence. The following year, she was sentenced to an additional fifteen months for the escape and was sent to a more secure facility in Kentucky. She was paroled in 2009. She now lives in rural New York, with her boyfriend, an ex-con who also has a fascination with Charles Manson.

Squeaky Fromme wasn't the only one to try to kill President Ford; only seventeen days later and also in California, Sara Jane Moore tried to kill him, but in her case, she fired one shot at him, which missed. She fired one more shot as former Marine Oliver Sipple grabbed her arm, moving it away from the President. Instead, it ricocheted and hit a taxi driver. She was also sentenced to life in prison and paroled on 31 December 2007.

Even in recent interviews, Squeaky Fromme has said things

sympathetic to Manson, telling ABC News that she was still in love with him and that you don't exactly fall out of love with someone.

JIMMY PAGE & SQUEAKY FROMME

In a 2019 interview with The Church of Rock, Squeaky Fromme denied stalking Jimmy Page and even claimed that she didn't know who Jimmy Page was as a person, and that all she knew about Led Zeppelin was basically 'Stairway to Heaven' from the radio. She claims that someone connected to former Manson Family member Dianne Lake's book propagated that rumour that she stalked Led Zeppelin, saying that it could have been someone in the Manson Family who tried contacting Jimmy Page.

While the two never met, she allegedly knocked on the hotel room door of Swan Song (Led Zeppelin's record label) VP Danny Goldberg, while Led Zeppelin were in California, soon to play a show in Long Beach. She was described as nervous and requested to meet Jimmy Page to warn him of something evil that would happen at the concert. Since she wasn't allowed to see Jimmy, she wrote a letter, which was subsequently burnt, and was escorted away. The following week, she was all over national television because she had tried to assassinate the President. Danny Goldberg instantly recognised her. Not surprising because that red hair along with that strange behaviour stands out.

CHAPTER 11

Trampled Under... Fists?: Led Zeppelin and John 'Biffo' Bindon (1977)

It's important for rock stars to have security guards. Fans can be crazy and you can't play shows if you're hurt or dead. You need someone tough who can defend you. Sometimes though security guards can have some sketchy pasts and run-ins with the law and that's exactly what happened to Led Zeppelin's security guard for their 1977 US tour, John Bindon.

LED ZEPPELIN

In the previous chapter, we talked about Jimmy Page. In this section, we'll talk about the rest of the band: bassist John Paul Jones, drummer John Bonham, and lead singer Robert Plant. No intro is necessary for Led Zeppelin. If you've listened to classic rock radio, you're bound to know at least a handful of their songs like 'Communication Breakdown', 'Whole Lotta Love', 'Black Dog', 'Immigrant Song', 'Stairway to Heaven', and 'Kashmir'. They're easily one of the best-known classic rock bands around.

Just like Jimmy Page, John Paul Jones was an established session musician and arranger before founding Led Zeppelin. He was born John Baldwin in Sidcup, Kent (which is now part of South East London) on 3 January 1946. His parents were both musicians. His father, Joe Baldwin, played piano at silent film screenings and played piano and arranged for big bands in the '40s and '50s. His mother was a vaudeville singer and dancer. With show business running in the family, he learnt to play piano when he was six and also learnt the bass guitar and he performed with his father at various events as a piano/bass duo. Joe wasn't thrilled with the idea and thought that the bass guitar would be a fleeting fad, but little did he know his son would become one of the best rock bassists. With the US having military bases all over the UK, that meant a lot of opportunities for fledgling rock bands to play gigs to entertain soldiers and that's what John Paul Jones did with his teenage rock bands. At the age of sixteen, he left school and decided to go pro as a session musician, first playing bass on ex-Shadows rhythm section Jet Harris and Tony Meehan's song 'Diamonds', a song Jimmy Page played guitar on. Just like Jimmy Page, he became very well established in the session musician scene at a young age. He arranged the string parts on The Rolling Stones' 'She's a Rainbow' and he and Jimmy Page played on Donovan's hit 'Sunshine Superman'.

Jimmy Page and John Paul Jones's paths crossed a lot in the session scene. Jimmy Page tried to start a supergroup with Jeff Beck but couldn't find a lead singer because the best singers were all taken. Jimmy Page had some discussions with Peter Grant (whom he'd met through his work as a session musician playing on Mickie Most's productions) about the New Yardbirds, and then through Terry Reid he found Robert Plant, a blonde-haired singer from Birmingham who was in Hobbstweedle and Band of Joy. They still needed a rhythm section and Robert Plant knew the perfect guy: John Bonham. And perfect he was! The final member to join the band was John Paul Jones, whose wife found out that Jimmy Page was looking for a bassist for a new band he was forming because Chris Dreja didn't want to join the band.

Robert Plant was born on 20 August 1948 in West Bromwich, a town near Birmingham, in the West Midlands. His father, also named Robert, was an engineer, and his mother, Annie, was of Romani descent and had thick, curly black hair. Much like fellow curly blonde-haired lead singer Roger Daltrey, Robert Plant showed a lot of promise as a child in school, that was until rock and roll came into the picture and he heard Elvis Presley's music and found his calling. Before he adopted the boho look that he was well known for in Led Zeppelin, he styled himself in the en vogue mod fashions of the mid '60s and listened to Delta Blues music, a huge influence on his singing and Led Zeppelin's music. His parents were not supportive of him abandoning his studies to become a rock star. Instead of becoming an accountant like they hoped, he left school and his family home as a teenager and joined various blues bands in Birmingham and set a goal for himself: if he didn't find his career going anywhere by the age of twenty, he would give up. While in the Crawling King Snakes, he met John Bonham and the two became great friends. In 1967, with rock music becoming more psychedelic and fashions veering towards hippie, he found some new inspiration and got into the music coming out of California like Jefferson Airplane and Love. Finally, in 1968, he met Jimmy Page, quickly bonded over blues and folk music, and the rest is history.

John Bonham was born to John and Joan Bonham on 31 May 1948 in Redditch, fifteen miles south of Birmingham. His father was a carpenter and naturally there was a lot of hammering at home and like father like son, John started hammering and hitting things and this evolved to him making makeshift drum sets out of tins. His inspirations were Max Roach, Gene Krupa, Buddy Rich, Sandy Nelson, and later Ginger Baker and Keith Moon. When he was ten, he got a snare drum as a gift from his mother and finally at fifteen, his father bought him a used drum kit. It was a bit old and in poor condition but, like a lot of other classic rockers, there were many other places he'd rather be than school and so he left school as a teenager and pursued his dream of being in a rock band, earning a reputation for playing drums well and loudly. Bands in and around Birmingham wanted him. On a summer night in Oxford in 1968, Robert Plant bumped into John Bonham after three months of not seeing each other and he told him that he had to join this band called the New Yardbirds. At first, he wasn't sure because The Yardbirds were on the way out, but he decided to give it a shot since he had nothing to lose and because he knew that Page and Plant were great musicians, so it would be a pleasure for him to be in the band even if it went nowhere. But with a line-up that great, it was an inevitability that they would soar to the top.

It was magic at first rehearsal; everything clicked together so well, as if the stars had all aligned. From there, they hit the ground running, touring Europe under The New Yardbirds name until former Yardbirds bassist Chris Dreja sent Jimmy Page a cease-and-desist letter saying he could only use that band name for the Scandinavian tour dates due to a prior contractual obligation (the tour was planned before the Yardbirds broke up). Led Zeppelin it was then! And so, in October 1968, they recorded the nine tracks from their self-titled debut album in just thirty hours of studio time. The goal was to showcase the songs they'd play at their live shows, but unlike their predecessors, The Yardbirds, their debut wasn't a live album. It was a very ahead of its time album and one that helped create a genre: heavy metal.

Their manager, Peter Grant, thought that Led Zeppelin's music would be a smash hit in America and he wasted no time getting them to America and building a following there since FM radio stations were more receptive to playing longer, heavier rock songs while in Britain the BBC weren't as open to it and played 'safer' pop songs instead. America is only the biggest music market in the world, after all. If you've made it in America, you've truly made it. Just before Christmas 1968, Led Zeppelin flew to America to kick off their first US tour, their first date being in Denver on Boxing Day (the day after Christmas) opening for Vanilla Fudge and Spirit. While on tour in the US, *Led Zeppelin I* came out and they won over audiences in key markets like LA, San Francisco, and Boston with their incredible live shows.

Meanwhile, in their native England, it was taking a bit of time for their popularity to catch on because their music wasn't being played on the radio and their album was released later there than in the US, and so they went back into the studio to start recording their classic album *Led Zeppelin II*.

Within months they were back in America for their second tour, starting in spring 1969 and this time as co-headliners with Vanilla Fudge. During that tour, *Rolling Stone* slated Led Zeppelin's debut album, but Peter Grant told the band to ignore the rock press and focus on connecting with fans through the music and their live shows, while he would berate music journalists who criticised Led Zeppelin. The band gave very few interviews at that time. Who cares about some pretentious rock critic's opinion? The opinions of the fans matter most. While in the US they also booked some studio time to record their commercially successful sophomore album. The end of the '60s was a very busy time for Zeppelin between touring and recording sessions. It was a 'work hard, play hard' time for the band because when off stage and not in the studio, they partied like rock stars, all the cliches you can think of: sex, drugs, and rock and roll.

By 1970, the band members were buying nice houses and reaping the rewards of success. With Jimmy and Robert having kids, the band took a well-deserved break for a couple of months. Jimmy and Robert went to Bron-Yr-Aur in the Welsh countryside to relax and get away from it all. Robert Plant chose this location because his family would go there when he was growing up and he loved how Tolkienesque it was. This setting inspired the acoustic, Celtic-inspired sound of *Led Zeppelin III*, a departure from their earlier heavier releases. Folk guitarists like Davey Graham, Bert Jansch, and John Fahey were musical inspirations for the album. However, the Scandinavian-inspired opening track 'Immigrant Song' had a heavy sound and a war cry. The band toured extensively from January to April and then from late June to September, concluding with their first Madison Square Garden show before taking a break from touring to work on *Led Zeppelin IV,* with Jimmy and Robert returning to Bron-Yr-Aur for some inspiration and a distraction-free environment – a writing retreat if you will. 'Stairway to Heaven' was born during this trip and that would become the band's signature song and from there, it brought even more success to the band – cementing them as superstars. They toured Japan for the first time in 1971 and once again in 1972, and Australia in 1972 (their only ever tour there). No more travelling like plebeians, they were flying from city to city in a private jet and they started their own record label in 1974, Swan Song Records – who signed artists like The Pretty Things, Bad Company, Maggie Bell, and Dave Edmunds. Their 1973 Madison Square Garden concerts were filmed for the 1976 concert film *The Song Remains The Same. Houses of the Holy* and *Physical Graffiti* were major successes for the band and the audiences kept growing. The band set a record with their 1973 concert in Tampa with 56,800 fans in the audience, which broke The Beatles' 1965 Shea Stadium record.

In 1975, the band took a break from touring because Robert Plant and his wife, Maureen, got into a car accident while on holiday in Rhodes. During this time, Robert had the support of John Bonham and Jimmy Page and together they worked on the songs that would be on their 1976 album *Presence.*

In 1977, Led Zeppelin were touring once again and they went on their very last North American tour, which is where their connection with bodyguard/actor John Bindon comes in.

JOHN 'BIFFO' BINDON

John Bindon was born on 4 October 1943 to a working-class family in Fulham, London. His father was a cab driver and his mother was from Ireland; he was the oldest of three children. Early on in life, he had a reputation for being a thug and a troublemaker. He stole bicycles as a child and even was the leader of his own gang. As a teenager, he was nicknamed 'Biffo' for getting into fights. At the age of thirteen, he beat up a coal deliveryman and at fourteen, he had a reputation for being a heavy drinker. Eventually, the law caught up with him and he was sent to borstal, which is basically the British version of juvie, for possessing live ammunition. He would go in and out of prison a good bit in the early '60s. After getting out of borstal, the Kray twins allegedly hired the 6'2" tall Bindon as muscle to help them 'sort out problems' and he allegedly ran protection rackets of his own in the West End of London making as much as £10k a year from that, but the details of this are not known. Not only did he have connections to the Krays, but he also had connections to their rivals, the Richardson gang.

He got his start in acting in 1966 when he was discovered by director Ken Loach in a pub – just a matter of being in the right place at the right time – and he offered him a role as a violent, abusive husband in his gritty kitchen sink drama film *Poor Cow* – an escape from a life of crime, a hand up. He had no training as an actor, just a lot of confidence. Actor Billy Murray said in the ITV documentary *Real Crime: John Bindon* that he had no nerves at all, he wasn't scared of the media, cameras, directors, or producers. From that point onwards, he was typecast as a mobster, gangster, or thug and he played those types of characters in other movies. He was in the 1970 crime drama *Performance*, starring Mick Jagger, and that was a breakthrough role for him. He was also in the 1971 crime film *Get Carter* starring Michael Caine, the 1975 Stanley Kubrick film *Barry Lyndon*, and the 1979 film adaptation of The Who's concept album *Quadrophenia*. He also had acting roles in TV series like *Department S*, *Z-Cars*, *Softly, Softly: Taskforce*, and *Hazell*. For the most part, his roles were small, but as Konstantin Stanislavski said, there are no small parts, only small actors. Because of his stardom, he was hobnobbing with socialites like the daughter of baronet Sir John Hodge, Vicki Hodge (who was his long-time girlfriend) and even royalty like Princess Margaret. Apparently, pop star and friend of David Bowie's Dana Gillespie introduced John Bindon to Princess Margaret while on the private island of Mustique. She later snuck him into Kensington Palace to visit her. There's a photograph of him with Princess Margaret where he is wearing a shirt belonging to Dana Gillespie that says 'Enjoy Cocaine' in the Coca-Cola font, even though Princess Margaret denied having anything to do with him. During a party on Mustique, he would do his favourite party trick, hanging five half-pint beer glasses on his large, erect penis, earning him the nickname Big John. He also befriended actors Richard Harris and George Sewell. He partied with David Bowie and went to his Christmas Eve party in 1973, where he walked around with a big red dildo strapped to his forehead, according to Bowie's ex-wife Angie, and sang carols with the A-list attendees.

Even though he was doing quite well for himself as an actor, making as much as £20k a year, he wanted a change of pace so he worked as a security guard for David Bowie and Led Zeppelin, a big mistake for a guy who could not control his temper. His ex-girlfriend Vicki Hodge described him in *Real Crime: John Bindon* as 'fists for hire'. He did not want to give up on that gangster life. In 1968, he received the Queen's Award for Bravery for rescuing a drowning man in the Thames, but allegedly he pushed the man in and only dived in and 'saved' him when a cop passed by.

Not long after Led Zeppelin's 1977 North America tour (which he was fired from), he found himself in legal trouble, this time even more serious than his previous run-ins: he was charged with murder. In November 1978, he got into a fight over owing money for cocaine with a dangerous gangster named John Darke at the Ranelagh Yacht Club under Putney Bridge and stabbed him nine times in the back, chest, and throat. The club was crowded and a fight broke out. Darke had a reputation for carrying guns and knives with him wherever he went. Bindon himself was injured and was on the run, hiding his knife wounds. Soon after Darke was stabbed, Bindon called his girlfriend, Vicki Hodge, telling her he was seriously hurt and thought he was dying and he needed money and some essentials put in a bag and a lift to Heathrow Airport so he could fly to Ireland, where he had IRA contacts who could hide him and he could be far away from the cops in London who were looking for him. En route to the airport, Bindon and his friends allegedly destroyed evidence, according to an interview Vicki Hodge did with the ITV show *Real Crime*. He tried to hide the stab wounds from airport staff, but blood was flowing through the scarves and bandages he was wearing. The cover-up story for the airport staff was that he was badly injured playing rugby. Meanwhile, in London, Bindon's associates cleaned up blood and fingerprints at the Yacht Club and got rid of evidence and they were so effective that the police couldn't find much evidence that a bloody fight had occurred there. Vicki and John's sister, Geraldine, cleaned up any clothes or rugs with blood on them and burnt his snakeskin boots. Still, the cops were looking for Bindon, not knowing if he was still alive, and they knocked on Vicki's door. When Bindon landed in Dublin, his lung had collapsed and he was taken straight to hospital where doctors found his heart was nicked too. He willingly turned himself into the police, claiming that Darke had stabbed him and he was acting in self-defence, and he returned to London, where he was tried at the Old Bailey in October 1979, the same place that the Kray twins were tried for murder. While he was in custody at Brixton Prison, Vicki visited him regularly and smuggled in Mandrax (also known as Quaaludes) via a kiss. A prisoner told the police that Bindon bragged about being paid £10k to murder Johnny Darke, which contradicted his self-defence story. Still, he was acquitted. The jury believed his self-defence story and his claim that he'd been framed by detectives calling it a contract killing. Actor Bob Hoskins' appearance as a character witness helped influence their opinion.

Still, even after Bindon was found not guilty of all charges, the case irreparably damaged his reputation as an actor and he never appeared in a movie or TV show again. He broke up with Vicki Hodge in 1981 and former friends of his distanced themselves from him. He still didn't give up his gangster ways after avoiding a life sentence in prison. He was in and out of jail multiple times in the '80s, convicted of threatening a law student with a piece of pavement and holding a carving knife in the face of a detective constable, among other crimes. He became increasingly reclusive and died in poverty in 1993 in his small Belgravia flat, aged fifty.

LED ZEPPELIN AND JOHN 'BIFFO' BINDON

Peter Grant, also known as G, hired John Bindon to be Led Zeppelin's security coordinator on the recommendation of tour manager Richard Cole. The band's last North American tour was supposed to begin in March 1977, but because Robert Plant got tonsillitis and there was no way he could perform a three-hour long concert with no voice, the tour was delayed for a month, beginning on 1 April in Dallas. During this tour, there were heaps of bodyguards, with each band member having their own minder, and a lot of strict rules for the music press who got access to the band – basically the dynamic was the press were extras and Led Zeppelin were the stars: extras don't talk to the stars unless the stars talk to them first and if you fuck around, you'll find out.

While there were was a record-setting crowd at their 30 April Pontiac Silverdome show in Michigan with 76,229 people in attendance, there were a lot of difficulties and setbacks during this tour. For starters, the band were worried about their first few concerts because they had no instruments and no ability to practise before the tour. By this point, Jimmy Page was underweight and deep into a heroin addiction and even got sick with food poisoning while on tour, leaving one hour into a show in Chicago with severe stomach cramps. Bonzo was drinking heavily and was using heroin too, negatively affecting his stamina. On the whole, the band weren't performing at their peak. There were rioters and gate crashers at some of their concerts.

On top of that, towards the end of the tour, at the Oakland Coliseum, violence erupted between John Bonham, Peter Grant, John Bindon, and Jim Matzorkis, one of concert promoter Bill Graham's employees, while Richard Cole kept an eye on the door. What started the fight? Depends on who you ask. John Bonham's story was that right before the show ended, Peter Grant's eleven-year-old son, Warren, wanted to take one of the hand-carved 'Led Zeppelin' signs from the band's dressing room trailer with him as a souvenir, and one of Bill Graham's security guards, Jim Matzorkis, saw him try to take it and hit the young boy. Bonzo saw it and he was understandably upset; he went over with a coke-fuelled G and Bindon to beat up that security guard. John Bonham kicked the security guard in the crotch and the guard tried to hide in another dressing room trailer while G searched for him. Bill Graham tried to diffuse the situation and keep the peace, but couldn't calm G down and when he tried to get G and Matzorkis to make up, Matzorkis held out his hand hoping for a friendly handshake and G sucker-punched him. A coked-up Bindon joined in and put him in a full nelson while G punched him in the face, knocking out a tooth and Richard Cole stood outside keeping guard, armed with a metal pipe. Richard Cole's account slightly differed, saying that the security guard shoved Warren. The band's publicist, Janine Safer, said that Warren wasn't slapped and even told Bindon not to beat up the security guard because no one touched Warren. Bindon also, without provocation, knocked out a stagehand, Jim Downey, because he misinterpreted something he said as being about G's weight.

When they got back to their hotel and had a panicked meeting in G's suite, Bonham, G, Bindon, and Cole were arrested and the police surrounded the premises so they couldn't escape. Because of the incident, Led Zeppelin threatened to cancel the following night's show, which would result in a lot of angry, disappointed

Zepheads, and they used their star power to coerce Graham to sign a letter of indemnification, absolving them of responsibility (this waiver wouldn't hold up in court because it was clearly signed under duress) and he signed it just to get the band off his back, but the second show was full of tension and awkwardness. On Monday morning, the day after the concert, Peter Grant, John Bindon, John Bonham, and Richard Cole were arrested at the Miyako Hotel and paraded through the lobby in handcuffs, with disgraced body language: their heads down, no eye contact. In the end, all four pleaded no contest and received suspended prison sentences and fines.

Graham didn't want Led Zeppelin to play another show at one of his venues again and he got what he wanted – the 24 July concert was Led Zeppelin's last ever show played in the United States, but not for happy reasons. The tour ended early when Robert Plant's five-year-old son, Karac, died from a stomach virus, and the band cancelled their remaining tour dates so he could mourn and get the support of his family and loved ones. Robert Plant flew back to England with Bonzo, who attended Karac's funeral – Jimmy Page and John Paul Jones did not attend. Led Zeppelin's sombre ballad 'All My Love' and two post-Zeppelin songs 'Blue Train' and 'I Believe' were written in memory of Karac. The band all went their separate ways after the Oakland concert; G and Bindon went to Long Island, John Paul Jones went on a road-trip, and everyone else went to New Orleans in preparation for what would have been the next show. In a way, the band broke up until 1978. Robert Plant was devastated and angry at himself for not spending enough time with his family, spending too much time on the road, and he needed a break. Rumours spread that Led Zeppelin were breaking up, but that didn't happen until the death of John Bonham in 1980.

Meanwhile, behind the scenes, John Bindon was fired and Peter Grant later admitted that hiring him as a bodyguard for the band was the biggest mistake of his career as Led Zeppelin's manager.

CHAPTER 12

Oh No, It's DEVO: and John Hinckley, Jr. (1982)

Inspiration from song lyrics can come from anywhere, including from someone who tried to kill the President of the United States. The classic rock era was full of edginess and DEVO surely shocked people when they turned something that John Hinckley, Jr. wrote into a song. Decades later the drama resurfaced when Hinckley wanted a slice of the pie.

DEVO

Once again, we have another sibling band here. We've talked about The Kinks, Spandau Ballet, and The Beach Boys. What's with classic rock bands made up of brothers and having connections with true crime figures? Weird coincidence. This time, there are two sets of brothers: Mark and Bob Mothersbaugh (AKA Bob 1) and Gerald and Bob Casale (AKA Bob 2), plus Alan Myers as the drummer in their classic line-up, replacing Jim Mothersbaugh. Yes, there are two Bobs in the band. Millennials may recognise the Mothersbaugh name because of the popular, classic 1990s Nickelodeon cartoon *Rugrats*, which was Nickelodeon's biggest cartoon before SpongeBob. And we millennials have never lived in a world without 'Whip It', so we all know that song. And you might have heard 'Uncontrollable Urge' in *The Wolf of Wall Street* and MTV's *Ridiculousness*.

Anyway, DEVO are a very unique band and given the name, which comes from Gerald Casale's concept of de-evolution, the idea that the human race was no longer advancing, you can guess that they're a nerdy band, and you'd be right. Their music and stage presence are very science-fiction inspired, kitschy, and with a unique sense of humour. Musically, they can be described as alternative and new wave.

There's another true crime connection with the group, and it starts at their formation and even has something to do with their name. The band are Akron, Ohio natives and some of the band members – Gerald Casale, Bob Lewis, and Mark Mothersbaugh – went to Kent State. Yes, that Kent State, where there was a shooting on 4 May 1970, as told in the Crosby, Stills, Nash, and Young song 'Ohio'. DEVO weren't the only rock stars who were there. Two other Kent State alumni who were caught up in the massacre were The Pretenders frontwoman and fellow Akron native Chrissie Hynde (who was in a band with Mark Mothersbaugh at one point) and Chris Butler of '80s new wave band The Waitresses. Gerald Casale's friends Jeffrey Miller and Allison Krause were two of the four students killed when the Ohio National Guard fired sixty-seven rounds on students peacefully protesting the Vietnam War. Casale conceived the 'Theory of Devolution' after surviving the shooting. Of the Kent State Massacre and forming DEVO, Casale said in a *Washington Post* interview, 'I don't think I would have started DEVO had that not happened.' They made their first performance as DEVO (Sextet Devo) at the 1973 Kent State Performing Arts Festival.

Before releasing their first album in 1978, they made music videos, and yes this was before MTV. Early famous fans of the band, David Bowie and Iggy Pop, helped get them signed to

Warner Brothers Records. Bowie's friends Brian Eno and Robert Fripp were also early fans and Bowie said in 1977 that DEVO were 'the band of the future'. Bowie originally had plans to produce them, but that fell through. Instead, glam/art rocker turned ambient musician Brian Eno produced their debut, which was mostly recorded at famous Krautrock producer Conny Plank's (he notably worked with NEU! and Kraftwerk) studio in Cologne. It was well loved by critics, but DEVO's big breakthrough came in 1980 with their album, *Freedom of Choice*, the album with their best-known song 'Whip It'. This more electronic/synth-sounding album was a radical change from the previous album, which had a more punk sound, and this sound would become even more prominent in their next albums like *New Traditionalists* and *Oh No! It's DEVO*.

The band gained a loyal following because they weren't just an ordinary band and they didn't just have an image, they also stood for something and weren't afraid to take a stand on things, but also put a little humour into it, such as their involvement with the parody religion, Church of the Subgenius, and opening for themselves as a parody Christian soft rock band called Dove (an anagram of their band name).

Their 1982 album *Oh No! It's DEVO* is where you find the other true crime connection. Before we get to the true crime connection, here's some context. The album was produced by Roy Thomas Baker, who previously worked with Free, Nazareth, Queen, Hawkwind, Foreigner, The Cars, and others. The album gets its title from some people's reaction to DEVO releasing another album. Critics too sometimes didn't have nice things to say about them, such as calling them fascists or comparing them to Nazis and clowns. And in true punk/rock and roll fashion, this album was a response to that with Gerald Casale saying that this album answers the question: what would an album made by fascist clowns sound like? Don't apologise, just own the criticism and reclaim it! That's rock and roll!

A certain song on it though has some controversy surrounding it because of the lyrics and who wrote them. And let's just put it this way, to criticise President Reagan in the '80s was social suicide because America is one of those places that is super patriotic on the surface and a lot of people have a 'love it or leave it' attitude towards critics. While Reagan's approval rating during his presidency was so-so, he still won in a landslide in 1980 and 1984, winning 43.9 million votes and 489 electoral votes in 1980, and winning 54.45 million votes and 525 electoral votes (only losing Minnesota) in 1984, a historic election because no other presidential candidate matched Reagan's electoral vote count in America's history. Still to this day Republicans love Reagan and many will proudly call their party the Party of Reagan. Though I don't think that's a presidency to be proud of because of him fumbling the AIDS crisis and declaring a War on Drugs (complete disaster and incredibly racist), among many other horrible things.

JOHN HINCKLEY, JR.

John Hinckley, Jr. was born in Ardmore, Oklahoma on 29 May 1955 to a rich family and seemed to have a picture-perfect upbringing, which makes you wonder why he turned out the way he did. He was raised in the Dallas area. His father was Chairman and President of the Vanderbilt Energy Corporation. His mother didn't need to work and instead took care of her children. He was shy and not as academically inclined as his siblings. Growing up, he liked to play sports, especially basketball and football, and he was pretty well liked. However, he became more withdrawn when he entered secondary school, getting really into The Beatles and spending a lot of time in his room playing guitar. After graduating from secondary school, he travelled a lot around the country, going between Colorado, Texas, California, and the Northeast of the US. He intermittently attended Texas Tech dropping in and out of classes, but never graduated. He was a loner and didn't have any friends. In 1979, he bought his first gun and started going to shooting ranges, and from there amassed more guns. Hinckley originally wanted to shoot President Carter and was stalking him, following him from campaign stop to campaign stop. While travelling, he was arrested at the airport for having firearms in his luggage. The guns were taken away and he was only fined $62.50. That didn't stop him from buying more guns.

His parents were concerned with his mental health and sent him to a psychologist, who suggested that they cut him off financially so he would be forced to mature and be self-sufficient.

Like Squeaky Fromme, John Hinckley, Jr. tried to kill the President, although there are differences between their cases; however, both were eventually freed and both had infatuations and obsessions with people they wanted to impress, with Squeaky clearly wanting to impress Charles Manson (whom she actually knew).

John Hinckley, Jr was obsessed and infatuated with actress Jodie Foster, who later on came out at the 2013 Golden Globes. At the age of twelve, she was in the 1976 Martin Scorsese film *Taxi Driver*, playing a child prostitute named Iris, a casting that was very controversial at the time and years later she would say that everyone on set was uncomfortable about her character and that nobody knew how to direct her. However, that movie changed her life and was the launchpad for her career. The movie is about a taxi driver named Travis Bickle who plots to assassinate a presidential candidate and after that failed, he shoots Iris's pimp and he's called a hero. It's based on Arthur Bremer's real assassination attempt on segregationist George Wallace.

Ever since watching that movie at least fifteen times as a young man in his early twenties, Hinckley was obsessed with Jodie Foster and stalked her. At the time, he was estranged from his family and had recently been kicked out of a neo-Nazi group for being too extremist and he related to the loner main character, Travis Bickle. He started imitating his mannerisms from the way he dressed to his love of guns and even kept a diary.

He went as far as sending letters and poems to Foster, calling her, visiting her home to drop things off for her, and even moving near her when she started attending Yale. Foster just wasn't interested and the more she ignored him, the more he pursued her and became more extreme in his pursuit to win her attention.

Before trying to kill Reagan, he travelled from LA to Washington DC and wrote Jodie Foster one more letter saying that he was going to do something historic and that he wouldn't have done it had he won her heart and married her, but he never sent it so no one knew he was going to try to assassinate President Reagan, so he couldn't be stopped. Besides his obsession with Jodie Foster, he lamented the murder of John Lennon in his New Year's Eve monologue and said that the world was over and expressed that he didn't want to live in 1981. Weirdly enough, like John Lennon's killer Mark David Chapman, Hinckley had J.D. Salinger's *The Catcher in the Rye* in his possession, but at his hotel room.

On 30 March 1981, President Reagan was at the Hilton in Washington DC giving a speech and Hinckley was waiting nearby with his Röhm RG 14 .22 LR revolver. As Reagan walked to the limo waving to the crowd, Hinckley fired six shots. One of those bullets ricocheted off the president's limousine and hit President Reagan, who was being pushed into the limo by Secret Service agent Jerry Parr, who reacted just in time to prevent Reagan from being shot in the head, saving his life. Once the car doors closed, the limo sped off. At first, it was believed that the assassination attempt could have been a Soviet plot, but the truth was, Hinckley acted alone. As for Jodie Foster's reaction? She told *Esquire* in a 1982 interview, 'I am sorry for people who confuse love with obsession and hurt by those who have inflicted their confusion on me. Obsession is pain and a longing for something that does not exist. John Hinckley's greatest crime was the confusion of love and obsession. The trivialisation of love is something I will never forgive him. His ignorance only prods me to say that he's missing a great deal. Love is blissful. Obsession is pitiful, self-indulgent. This is a lesson I've learnt. I'll always be wary of people who proclaim their love for me.' Since then, she has only made a few statements about the incident and has cancelled interviews because producers wanted to talk about Hinckley.

Being so close to the President and having a lot of responsibility for their protection and their life, Secret Service agents have special training and part of that means that they have to do anything to save the President's life, including taking a bullet for them. For years, it was kept a secret that President Reagan nearly died. He was spitting up blood, losing 40–50% of his blood supply, and was taken to the emergency room with a team of dedicated trauma doctors instead of the White House because of a split-second decision, and that saved his life. When he woke up, he famously made this joke to the medical staff, 'I hope you're all Republicans.' It really was a close call for him.

At the time, no one died, but Hinckley injured four people: President Reagan, Secret Service agent Tim McCarthy, White House Press Secretary James Brady, and Washington DC police officer Thomas Delahanty. Thirty-three years later, in 2014, James Brady died of complications related to his injury so the medical examiner ruled that his death was a homicide. However, Hinckley had been found not guilty by reason of insanity of all charges against him. Charging him with homicide would be double jeopardy and because of the year and a day law, a common law standard that death cannot be legally attributed to acts or omissions that occur more than a year and a day before the death, in effect in Washington DC at that time, he could not be tried for homicide.

Two years later, on 10 September 2016, Hinckley was released from St Elizabeths Hospital and was deemed to no longer be a threat to himself or others, but there were many conditions on his release: no alcohol, firearms, weapons, violent media, Jodie Foster memorabilia, porn, or erotica. His internet access was to be monitored, he wasn't allowed to speak to the press, and he was forbidden from contacting Reagan's family, Brady's family, Jodie

Foster or anyone related to or working with her and he had to stay with his mother. Little by little, restrictions were lifted and John Hinckley moved closer to being a free man.

A court-ordered risk assessment was supposed to be conducted in 2018, but none was conducted. That same year, a judge ruled that he could move out of his mother's house and into his own home. In 2020, a judge ruled that Hinckley could publicly display and promote his art and music online. In September 2021, a federal judge ruled that Hinckley would be unconditionally released in June 2022 provided he complied with the conditions of his current release order and was of sound mind.

His release was controversial, with President Reagan's daughter, Patti Davis, calling his release 'terribly sad and wrong'. In a 2016 blog post discussing her feelings on Hinckley's release, she expressed doubts that Hinckley's mental health had improved and said that he only got released because his family were wealthy and could afford a good, patient lawyer who would fight for him. She closed that blog post with this: 'I will forever be haunted by a drizzly March afternoon when my father almost died, when Jim Brady lay in a pool of blood and two other men – Thomas Delahanty and Timothy McCarthy – were gravely wounded. If John Hinckley is haunted by anything, I think it's that he didn't succeed in his mission to assassinate the President.' Five years later, she continued to speak out against Hinckley's release, but her brother, Michael, supported Hinckley's release, stating that his father forgave him and would have approved of his release.

DEVO & JOHN HINCKLEY, JR.

At the time *Oh No, It's DEVO!* was released, Hinckley had just been found not guilty by reason of insanity. One song on the album, 'I Desire', adapted some lines from a poem Hinckley wrote and turned it into a love song. DEVO described the poem as 'poetic sociopathy' and were blown away by it. The band got permission from Hinckley to use verses from his poem after reading it in a tabloid, and even got permission from Jodie Foster before recording it, making sure she was aware that it wasn't an endorsement of Hinckley or his actions.

As you can expect, it was DEVO's most controversial song and it led to the FBI calling the band and threatening them, as Mark Mothersbaugh, one of the songwriters later said. The band's record label, Warner Brothers Records, were not thrilled with the idea of having to pay royalties to the guy who nearly assassinated President Reagan. This is different from The Beach Boys singing a Charles Manson song because Charles Manson sold the rights to 'Cease to Exist' before The Beach Boys recorded it. Hinckley never sold any rights so he would have been entitled to royalties, even if he was institutionalised.

What was Hinckley's reaction at the time of the song's release? He liked the notoriety and he loved that he was part of a new wave song. He expressed his love of the genre, requested that 'I Desire' be played fifty-eight times a day, and said he listened to David Bowie's 'Heroes' when he stalked Presidents Carter and Reagan in a letter to the Morning Zoo crew of Dallas album-oriented rock station KZEW, The Zoo. The station shut down in 1989 and has been replaced by an adult contemporary station and later a hip-hop station.

In October 2021, Hinckley opened a Twitter account as a way to promote his music, which he had just been allowed to start streaming on Spotify and YouTube. Talk about an '80s reboot! He describes himself as a singer-songwriter and outsider artist and said in a tweet that he believes in 'peace, love, and understanding' and that's what he writes about. His Twitter is mainly about his art and his music and sometimes he shares what he's been listening to, much of it classic rock like Leonard Cohen, Bob Dylan, The Velvet Underground, The Clash, Elvis Costello, The Kinks, The Byrds, Neil Young, The Pretenders, and The Ramones, but there's some newer music he likes too, like Ty

Segall, Foo Fighters, The Black Keys, Rhiannon Giddens, and Car Seat Headrest.

He tweeted on 24 October that he co-wrote DEVO's 'I Desire' and that he hadn't seen royalties from *Oh No, It's DEVO!* in thirty-five years. The tweet made the news and Gerald Casale of DEVO responded saying that it's possible that Hinckley's telling the truth about not receiving royalties, but that DEVO don't control payment of royalties, that would be the record label's job. He added that he wouldn't get a lot of money because the song wasn't a hit and it was just one song on the album that he co-wrote lyrics for.

As for recording an album that sounded like something fascist clowns would make, you can say this was mission accomplished. Taking creepy lyrics from someone who nearly murdered the President and setting it to a disco beat is pretty clownish and fascistic sounding.

Musicians Who Killed

You thought that classic rock was all peace, love, and flower power? You thought murderers were just creepy monsters? Think again. Murderers don't all look the same. They don't all have the same life experiences. And they certainly don't all have the same jobs. Yes, even the rich and famous who seemingly have it all have killed people. I find that these are some of the most interesting true crime stories and these stories remind me why I am fascinated with true crime in the first place: how is it that someone can have it all and yet take another person's life? What leads them to do something so heinous? How does someone go from living like a prince to dying like a pauper?

In this section, you'll be reading the stories of a country musician who killed his wife, an R&B singer who stabbed someone at a party, a revolutionary music producer who killed his landlady, a conga player who missed out on Woodstock because he killed someone, a funk singer who got hooked on drugs and murdered two drug dealers, a punk rocker who was accused of killing his girlfriend and was charged for it but killed himself before he could be tried, a rock drummer who killed his mother and who played with some of the best guitarists ever, a legendary producer behind a revolutionary sound and production style who killed an actress he had only met hours before, and two rock legends who accidentally killed people.

In each chapter, there will be a section on the background on the musician themselves, all about their personal and professional life, and a section about the crime, including information about the trial and the musician's time in jail – if available/applicable.

To say that prisoners are seen as an afterthought is an understatement. No one thinks about them or sees them as a priority, they're forgotten people. But what happens when a famous person lands behind bars, even if it's not for murder? Then people start to think about jail. Katy St. Clair said it well in this *East Bay Express* article published in 2002: 'When musicians get sent up the river, it tends to humanise a population that still remains in the throwaway pile for most of America: prisoners. Don't think that James Brown was the first black man to get a stiff sentence for trying to outrun a cop. He just reminded us that stuff like that goes on, and for a moment we actually remembered there were other people like Brown in jail.'

CHAPTER 13

Spade Cooley (1961)

ABOUT SPADE COOLEY

Not classic rock, but country music has some links to rock music and is part of the popular music landscape and I think it's important to talk about Western Swing musician Spade Cooley and the murder of his wife.

Fiddle player and band leader Spade Cooley was born Donnell Clyde Cooley in Oklahoma on 17 December 1910. His family were fiddle players and were of partial Cherokee ancestry. As a child, he was forcefully taken away from his family and taken to a residential school for Native Americans in Oregon.

During the 19th and 20th centuries in the US, hundreds of thousands of Native American children were separated from their families and forced into boarding schools that would erase their culture and force them to conform to white American culture. They weren't allowed to have long hair, use their Indigenous names, wear clothes from their culture, speak their native language, or practise indigenous faith. Children at these schools were often sexually, mentally, and physically abused and many children died, with dead bodies thrown in unmarked mass graves. Even in the 2000s there were still thousands of children in these residential schools. These racist institutions have taken many lives and have had lasting damage on Native American communities, with intergenerational trauma. These schools are still under investigation in the US and Canada with many horrifying things being uncovered as the years go by.

The dust bowl hit the Great Plains in the '30s, resulting in a mass exodus of people from the area, economic impact, and damage to the ecology of the area. It was a significant historic event referenced in John Steinbeck's *The Grapes of Wrath* and the music of Okie folk singer Woody Guthrie. Like many other families, Spade Cooley's family moved to California. He didn't want to be a sharecropper like his family. Instead, he had his eyes on Hollywood, with big dreams, and he showed up one day to a studio with just a fiddle and six cents in his pocket. His stage name, Spade, came from him winning three straight flush hands in poker with all spades.

He played western swing music, which is a type of country music that originated in the southern and western US in the 1920s and '30s and was popular until the '40s, and he became known as 'The King of Western Swing' and got multiple top-ten hits in the 1940s. When he got to Hollywood, he became a big success with TV shows, appearances on radio and in films, and was a celebrity, making six figures a week in today's money. He was friends with Roy Rogers and Ronald Reagan.

He lived like a rock star, spending money on lavish clothes and, of course, he had lots of lovers. He ended up developing an alcohol and drug problem, and he had a temper and jealousy problem, taking it out on his wife. His marriage with Ella Mae Cooley (née Evans) was turbulent and they both cheated on each other. After his fame was fading, his show was cancelled, and he fired his orchestra, he went on his own and moved to the desert, where he bought a nice, isolated home on a ranch where he could keep a close eye on and control and abuse his wife and he started working on plans to start an amusement park called Water Wonderland. Disneyland was a new park at the time and he wanted to start something that would rival that, but it was never realised because he murdered his wife.

THE MURDER

Spade and his wife Ella Mae met because she was a backup singer in his band starting in 1943. They got married in 1945. It was his second marriage. They had three children together: Melody, Donnell Jr, and John. When Ella Mae confessed to cheating on him, the violence escalated and he treated her like a prisoner. She told her doctor she was afraid of her husband and told her attorney that he was physically abusing her and feared for her life, saying that if she left him, he would kill her and the kids. Because their marriage had so many problems, including a history of violence, Ella Mae filed for divorce and started sending money to two men, Bud Davenport and Luther Jackson, so they could invest it and she could have something to live off after the divorce. Davenport and Jackson were also aware that she feared for her life and was being beaten. Spade Cooley and two business associates visited them and threatened them. He then got a confession from his wife that she was cheating. On the evening of 3 April 1961, weeks after she filed for divorce, he killed her. He first beat her in the living room, knocking her to the floor, then beat her in the bedroom, choking her, pulling her hair, stomped on her, and raped her with a broom handle. His teenage daughter, Melody, walked in and wondered what was going on, and Spade took his wife's body to the bathroom, killed her, and called her a slut right in front of his daughter. To ensure she was dead, he put out a cigarette on her nipples. He then molested Melody, kissing her and groping her breast. The crime scene was bloody and Ella Mae had injuries all over her face and body. She was only thirty-six years old.

Hours after the murder, a nurse named Dorothy Davis arrived at the house to check on Ella Mae. Spade Cooley claimed that it was an accident and Ella Mae slipped and fell in the shower, and that's what he told the police at first – but that defence fell apart when medical experts were consulted and when they heard Melody's eyewitness testimony. At this point, Ella Mae had been moved and her body lay diagonally across the bed. Davis checked her pulse and heard no heartbeat and said she had to be dead. She called the hospital and the sheriff's department to get an ambulance.

The following day, Spade Cooley made a voluntary statement to the sheriff's deputies and, as usual, this was something used at trial. After his first claim of his wife dying because of an accident fell apart, he claimed that he did not intend to kill his wife and that it was a crime of passion where he 'blacked out' and lost consciousness of his actions because he found out about his wife having an affair. He alleged that his wife told him that she was part of a 'free love' sex cult and that's what drove him crazy. However, this claim fell apart because he had known about his wife's infidelity for a while and had hired a PI to expose his wife's lover and they were undergoing divorce proceedings.

The murder case went to trial and psychiatrists found him to be legally sane to stand trial, but he still went with the insanity defence. And before the trial he had a heart attack, and he got another heart attack during the trial. The six-week trial started in July 1961 and it was a trial of the century of sorts in Kern County (a mountainous, arid county in the Central Valley of California, bordering Los Angeles County) because of its length and because it involved a celebrity. People would gather at Bakersfield Superior Court before the trial to vie for one of the limited seats in the courtroom. Finally, on 19 August, a jury found him guilty of first-degree murder.

When you have money, the criminal justice system is more lenient on you and Spade Cooley was no exception. Typically, if you were a convicted murderer, you were sent to one of two notorious prisons: San Quentin or Folsom. And the death penalty was a big possibility. Not only was Spade Cooley rich, but he also had heart problems so he was imprisoned in the California Medical Facility in Vacaville, where he lived like a prince in comparison to regular prisoners: a private room all to himself rather than a prison cell he'd have to share, and he kept busy in prison carving violins and teaching music. He kept a vegetarian diet behind bars, a bit odd for a convicted murderer. His friend Ronald Reagan was the governor of California from 1967–1975 and he wanted to pardon Spade Cooley – but he died before the pardon was finalised, and in 1968, the California State Adult Authority granted him parole and even let him out of hospital to perform a benefit concert for the Deputy Sheriffs Association of Alameda County, where he was treated like a star – full house, standing ovation, autographs and all. Funnily enough, he didn't know where he was going when he was granted furlough; all he knew was he was going to perform somewhere. You might say it was one last hurrah for him, because he died of a heart attack during the intermission. He would have been released on 22 February 1970 had he not died. The lesson from all of this is, when you're rich and well connected and commit a crime, you're babied and given special treatment.

CHAPTER 14

Little Willie John (1964)

ABOUT LITTLE WILLIE JOHN

Much of what's known about Little Willie John is that he was an R&B star turned prisoner who died young – at the age of thirty, but there was more to him than that. Stevie Wonder said of The Prince of the Blues in the foreword to *Fever: Little Willie John's Fast Life, Mysterious Death, and the Birth of Soul: The Authorised Biography* that Little Willie John was a big influence on him and that all the aspiring soul and R&B singers who grew up in the '50s would listen to him and Jackie Wilson for the riffs. Dion DiMucci also said, 'Little Willie John did not know how to sing wrong'. Bob Dylan also was fascinated with Detroit's R&B scene and he loved Little Willie John's 'Fever'.

R&B singer-songwriter Little Willie John was born William Edward John in Cullendale, Arkansas on 15 November 1937. When he was four, his family moved to Detroit, Michigan, where he was raised. There was a lot of black migration from the South to the North, where it was more industrialised and there were better economic opportunities. His family were poor and they lived in housing projects in Detroit. This being during the Jim Crow era, the growing Midwestern city was segregated, like many other cities across America. Which meant that black families couldn't live where they wanted because of redlining and restrictive housing covenants. Little Willie John's childhood was difficult with his father beating him for sneaking out of the house and for speaking in a sassy, smart way. This led to him running away from home.

He had nine siblings and he formed a gospel group called The United Five with some of his siblings. The United Five sang with the Dixie Hummingbirds, Mighty Clouds of Joy, and Soul Stirrers (Sam Cooke led that group). Like many black families, the John family went to church. Black churches are known for their gospel music and that's where many black singers in America started their careers. Besides gospel music, the blues, especially B.B. King, were a big influence on Little Willie John.

Friends at church saw a lot of potential in The United Five and said that they could make it and so they tried to get the word out about them so they could get more performances and attention. The standout, Little Willie John, was an energetic performer with an emotional voice and got the attention of Greek-American R&B bandleader, talent scout, producer, TV show host, and DJ Johnny Otis and influential black music executive Henry Glover. At the age of sixteen, he made his first recordings and there were stories about him in the newspaper saying that he was really smart and Duke Ellington and Stan Kenton wanted him to tour with them. This motivated him and he didn't want to keep going to school, he wanted to tour and record and that's what he was doing by the age of eighteen, which would earn him the title The Smallest Man with the Biggest Sound.

In 1955, Glover got Little Willie John a record deal with King Records, the label he worked for. He was called Little Willie John because he was short. His peak years as a musician were the mid to late 1950s, when he got multiple R&B chart hits like 'All Around the World', 'Need Your Love So Bad', 'Fever' (also a crossover pop hit), 'Talk to Me, Talk to Me' (also a top-twenty crossover pop hit), among others. This was during a time when rock and roll was insurgent, rising up the charts and beginning its chart music takeover. The music world after this would never be the same again. He even performed at the Cavalcade of Jazz concert in LA in 1958 with famous musicians like Sam Cooke and Ray Charles. He also performed on TV multiple times; he notably performed on *American Bandstand* three times. Sadly, though, no footage of these TV performances survived. The only film of him that survived was him playing claves in a TV show. At nineteen, he got married to his wife, Darlynn. They had two sons: William Kevin and Darryl Keith. He loved spoiling his family with gifts and he was very protective of them and helped his family out a lot financially.

As well, he was outspoken and unapologetic about being black. He was upset about the whitewashing of rock and roll and said black people had been making music like that for a long time before white rock musicians came on the scene. It took white people time to get hip to it and black musicians were the trendsetters, not the followers. He took a strong stance in favour of the Civil Rights movement and urged musicians to get involved. Social justice was very near and dear to him.

If you look at popular music history, you'll see that fame doesn't last forever. Very few famous musicians can stay relevant for decades on end. Eventually, there's a lull in a musician's career because the music scene changes a lot – in this case from R&B to styles that incorporated some rock and roll, like soul, and thank goodness the music scene evolves, grows, and changes with new advances and fresh faces. However, that means that famous musicians of yesteryear, especially ones who weren't A-listers or got a bad deal, often end up financially unstable. Remember that being a musician or any sort of creative doesn't come with health insurance, pension, and other benefits that many nine-to-five workers come to appreciate (even then, companies are chipping away at this; thanks a lot, capitalism!). On top of that, the show business crowd don't always have the best influences and the job is tough, so many musicians turn to vices like drugs and alcohol to cope and they get addicted and turn the person into someone completely different, maybe someone they never imagined themselves becoming. The early '60s was tragedy after tragedy for Little Willie John with friends and idols dying or getting seriously injured one after the other: Jesse Belvin joined the '27 Club' (an informal list of musicians who died at the age of 27) when he died in a car accident in 1960; Jackie Wilson was shot in 1961; Dinah Washington died in 1963; Ray Charles was arrested for possession of drugs in 1964; and that same year, Sam Cooke was shot and killed. Around this time, Little Willie John's behaviour was growing erratic, with him getting into fights and missing gigs. He lost his backing band and it was a downward spiral.

Like Ian Curtis of Joy Division, Little Willie John had epilepsy and would get seizures. They weren't that much of a problem in his childhood, but as a touring musician, things got worse with the bright lights and the constantly on-the-go lifestyle. It also didn't help that it's hard to eat on tour and that he would drink too much or take too many drugs. His seizures got worse as he drank more and more heavily. He also liked to play with guns, but for show and to play pranks, not to threaten anyone. He was just a silly, mischievous young man. Back in the '50s, it was very easy to get a gun provided you had an ID and so some fellow musicians like Jimmy Scott, Billy Davis, and Johnny Ace had guns.

He got in a little trouble a few times with the law, being charged with making calls on a bogus credit card, but he was released if he promised to pay the long-distance phone call charges. He was also arrested for possession of marijuana, but his family believe he was set up because it was common for police to raid musicians' hotel rooms and dressing rooms.

Hearing that The Beatles covered his song 'Leave My Kitten Alone' must have raised his spirits because it's an honour to have the biggest rock band in the world covering your song, but things took a quick turn south not too long after that.

THE CRIME

While on bail, Willie left Miami (where he was living) for the West Coast for tour dates. Not too risky then as it would be now, as police departments weren't as interconnected and communicating with each other as much and there was no social media then so the authorities in Florida wouldn't know his exact whereabouts. Little did he know, he would play his last ever concert as a free man on that trip, at the Magic Inn in downtown Seattle. He was to play six shows there over the weekend of 16–17 October 1964. It was not the nicest venue, but a job is a job and he needed money because he wasn't getting chart hits like he used to. Not only did the British Invasion have an impact on pre-British Invasion rock acts from America, it also had an effect on R&B acts, with new names becoming dominant in R&B. Once upon a time, James Brown wasn't sure if he could beat Little Willie John, but post 1964, James Brown became a much bigger star. Willie wasn't taking that well at all; it was a real hit to his ego. At 1.30am, after the show, he went to the jazz club, Birdland, and sang a couple of songs after he had a couple of drinks. Then he went to another club and met up with singer/guitarist Little Bill Engelhart. He was a white man who loved black musicians and was a big fan of Little Willie John, even giving him his new record and seeing him every time he came to Seattle. He noticed that Willie wasn't like he used to be: he was drunk and acting silly, grabbing his cane and walking around with it. Willie invited Bill to go to a party with him, but Bill rejected the invite.

Willie and some friends partied at this illegal after-hours party house popular among the black community with some white patrons on 23rd Avenue run by Theodore Roosevelt Richardson. At the party, there were a lot of troublemakers and bad influences, but there were some upstanding citizens who were there, such as attorney Jim McIver. One of the men who came along to the party house was a man named Kendall Roundtree. He had quite the rap sheet with a lot of arrests for offences ranging from assault to armed robbery. He was a big guy at 6'2" and over 200 pounds, so Willie was diminutive in comparison at only 5'4" and at most 130 pounds. Roundtree was loud and looking to pick a fight. One of Willie's friends left her seat to go to the washroom and Roundtree took a seat where she had been sitting and said some threatening and sexist things and shouted obscenities. Willie said he was talking crazy and was trying to mind his own business, but Roundtree punched Willie in the face and he ended up on the floor with a bloody mouth. The party house owner tried to break up the fight and calm down tensions, but Roundtree kept attacking Willie. Next thing we know, Willie was holding a steak knife and Roundtree was wounded, but no one saw him stab anyone. Black people often don't trust the police and in this case partygoers didn't want to call for help because they also would be incriminating themselves because they're at an illegal venue. Willie called for an ambulance and both an ambulance and the police showed up. Most people fled, and those who were questioned told conflicting stories.

Willie's story was that he took phenobarbital and then drank seven to eight cognacs and had a seizure when he arrived at the party house and he had no recollection of anything. His business manager, Eddie Moore, said that he didn't have a seizure and wasn't even drunk. He said he was tired and he claimed he saw Willie stab Roundtree. Others corroborated this story. He was arrested and charged with second-degree murder. He posted $10,000 bond and pleaded not guilty, fleeing Seattle, even though he wasn't supposed to leave the state. While out on bail, he went to San Francisco and LA to sing at clubs. He was brought back to Seattle and eventually got permission to see his family. Around Christmas, he went back to his hometown of Detroit to see his family and that's where he found out Sam Cooke had been murdered. He was devastated, crying on the floor while listening to his records.

The trial began on 12 January 1965 and lasted three days. Because he was a high-profile musician, his trial was a memorable one, especially for the prosecutor, Art Swanson, who said in *Fever: Little Willie John's Fast Life, Mysterious Death, and the Birth of Soul* that he remembered more details from the Little Willie John trial than any other trial he did in his over forty years as a prosecutor. Attorney Bill Lanning represented Little Willie John and he was popular among musicians, but he wasn't at his best at this point in his career and failed to make a case that there was reasonable doubt that Little Willie John stabbed Kendall Roundtree. Swanson felt like Little Willie John's counsel wasn't competent. It didn't help that the jury was not a jury of Little Willie John's peers, with it being lily white and middle class and racial biases such as anti-blackness being ingrained in many white people, especially in the Pacific Northwest, a part of the US where few black people live due to a racist history. When Little Willie John took the stand, he was overconfident and bragged about his many accomplishments as a musician, even embellishing it and acting a bit like a smart-arse. He was found guilty of manslaughter with a weapon.

The verdict was big news and Willie's friends and fans were shocked and felt it was an injustice because they believed he was trying to defend himself against a big, threatening man. It was a very unfortunate situation of Willie being in the wrong place at the wrong time.

While awaiting sentencing, Willie was out on bail and played some tour dates, but he was in even more legal trouble because he was charged with cheque fraud, with him being accused of paying for a charter flight with a bad cheque from a bank that didn't exist. He was brought back to Seattle in August 1965 and was taken into custody. Even then, his spirits were still not completely down; he was determined to continue recording music and he had Capitol Records behind him. Capitol were interested in Little Willie John and other black musicians after they had a lot of success with Lou Rawls, an R&B singer from Chicago. Having a big record label behind him meant that he could get out of jail for a bit to record an album. This new music was supposed to be a big deal, with the Wrecking Crew as backing musicians, but the album wasn't released for over forty years, and even now, it's hard to find.

Willie started serving time in Walla Walla State Penitentiary on 6 July 1966. While there, he took classes to work towards a high school diploma and even performed for the inmates. His epilepsy was still a problem in prison and he was punished unfairly because of his seizures. Trying to look on the bright side and make the best of a bad situation, he felt like prison was a wake-up call for him and said in a letter to his family that he would have ended up like Dinah Washington, Sam Cooke, or Otis Redding if he had been free. On the outside, he had support from Joe Tex, who called Little Willie John Soul Brother No. 1 in response to his rival James Brown calling himself that. James Brown visited Willie John in prison and had previously loaned him money for bail. Still, Willie was yearning for parole the entire time he was in prison, asking friends and family to write letters to the parole board in support of him.

His death is a mystery and no one really knows what exactly caused it. Was it pneumonia? A heart attack? Neglect after he was beaten? On one visit, James Brown saw Willie in a wheelchair looking unwell, coughing and sniffling. At this point, Willie was fatalistic; he felt the only way he was getting out of prison was in a body bag. On 26 May 1968, his family got the bad news that he had died in the prison hospital. He was only thirty.

CHAPTER 15

Joe Meek (1967)

ABOUT JOE MEEK

In the 1960s, there were a lot of gay men behind the scenes in rock and pop music producing and managing rock bands: Larry Parnes, Brian Epstein, Kit Lambert, Simon Napier-Bell, Robert Stigwood, Tony Stratton-Smith, and of course Joe Meek. There's more to gay culture than show tunes and disco; rock and roll has a gayer history than you think. The arts scene has always been a more accepting place for LGBT people, with more progressive attitudes and like-minded people, art being an excellent outlet to express yourself, and individuality being encouraged. But it wasn't always a complete safe haven and gay men in the music industry were still discriminated against, teased, and gossiped about.

Joe Meek was an innovative record producer and sound engineer from England who worked with a lot of the big British stars of the early '60s, pre-British Invasion era. His biggest accomplishments as a music innovator were pioneering space-age music, years before Pink Floyd, Gong, and Hawkwind put that genre on the map and defined it. Joe Meek used techniques like overdubbing, sampling, and reverberation as early as the late '50s, pre-dating psychedelic rock. You could maybe say he was Britain's Phil Spector – both innovative, eccentric producers with a chequered history. Later in this book, we'll be looking at Phil Spector and the 2003 murder of actress Lana Clarkson, which happened on exactly the same day Joe Meek killed his landlady, Violet Shenton, and then himself – 3 February, just 36 years later.

Joe Meek was born Robert George Meek to parents George and Biddy Meek in a market town near the Welsh border called Newent, in Gloucestershire, in South West England on 5 April 1929. From a young age, he had an interest in electronics, building circuits, radios, and maybe even the first TV in the region, all in his grandmother's shed. As part of the Silent Generation, he was required to do national service (this was in place until 1960, so baby boomers were not required to do this). While serving in the Royal Air Force (RAF), he worked as a radar technician, piquing his interest in outer space; even better that the space race was just around the corner! Just before he worked in the music industry, he worked for the Midlands Electricity Board, where he polished his music production techniques using company resources. This explains how he grew to become one of Britain's most innovative producers.

In the mid 1950s, he moved to London, switched industries and worked as an audio engineer, making his foray into the music industry. He made history in 1956, producing Humphrey Lyttelton's jazz instrumental 'Bad Penny Blues', the first British jazz record to get into the top twenty. Paul McCartney based the piano riff from 'Lady Madonna' on Johnny Parker's boogie piano riff in this song.

Joe Meek had a great work ethic and really had a one-track mind when it came to what he did. Everything in his life was about music and electronics and he fully dedicated himself to it, eschewing a social life. His approach to music production was marching to the beat of his own drum and keeping an open mind, breaking the conventions and giving things a go even if the old guard said it wasn't possible. He also dealt with a lot of homophobia at work.

After leaving IBC Studios and being fired from Denis Preston's Lansdowne Recording Studios, he went out on his own and set up his own production company called Meeksville and a record label called Triumph, the name of the production company being a reference to Motown's Hitsville USA. But there were some hiccups with finding investors and business partners to start an independent record label. Despite three singles that Meek had worked on being in the top ten all at once in 1959 – 'What Do You Want to Make Those Eyes at Me For?' by Emile Ford and The Checkmates, 'Sea of Love' by Marty Wilde, and 'Mr Blue' by Mike Preston – he had a reputation for being unstable, difficult to work with, and having a temper fuelled by drugs, so even if his work was good, many didn't see him being worth the headache to work with. Eventually, though, he found business partners.

Meeksville was run out of his flat on 304 Holloway Road in Islington. This is where the big hits were recorded. Because it was a music studio, it would get noisy and not everyone was thrilled with that, especially the landlords, who would knock on the ceiling with a broomstick. Meek would passive-aggressively respond by cranking up the volume.

He produced hits like the teen tragedy song 'Johnny Remember Me' for actor and singer John Leyton, 'Telstar' for The Tornados (the first British rock band to get a number one in the US), 'Just Like Eddie' (a tribute to Eddie Cochran) for German-born singer Heinz Burt, and 'Have I The Right?' for The Honeycombs.

While he was better known for his behind-the-scenes work, he also made music of his own and was a visionary, releasing a space-themed electronic concept album about humans living on the moon called *I Hear a New World* in 1960, way before concept albums took off in the late '60s and early '70s. It was an ambitious project inspired by his love of space, fascination with the space race, and belief in aliens. It wasn't a commercial success and an original pressing is incredibly rare, with fewer than a hundred copies being pressed. He wasn't the first to make a concept album, though; concept albums were out as early as 1940 with Woody Guthrie's *Dust Bowl Ballads* and in the following decade, Frank Sinatra took that another step further with albums like *In The Wee Small Hours* and *Frank Sinatra Sings for Only the Lonely*, making popular music a true art form. Nat King Cole released his concept album *Wild Is Love* the same year as Joe Meek's space-themed concept album.

Meek may have been a great producer, but he wasn't perfect and he made some poor judgement calls such as saying that The Beatles weren't worth signing to a record label after hearing their demo tape, signing a band on the condition that they fire their singer – a teenage Rod Stewart, and rejecting The Kon-Rads – a band with a young David Bowie on saxophone.

He notably struggled with mental illness, mood swings, paranoia, psychotic delusions, possibly an eating disorder (he used diet pills), and acted more and more erratically as time went on, accusing Phil Spector of stealing his ideas when he answered a phone call from him, thinking that Decca Records had wiretapped his house to steal his ideas, going out covered up in the fear of the Kray twins stealing his acts and blackmailing him about his homosexuality, and thinking his landlady was spying on him. Simply put, he wasn't a trusting person and he looked at everyone with suspicion. To put it in modern terms, if he was playing *Among Us*, he'd call everyone 'sus' and an imposter.

He was fascinated with the idea of communicating with the dead. This could come from his hometown of Newent being a superstitious place, with it being near the Forest of Dean, a woodland known for witches' covens and ghost stories. He grew up with these legends and stories and they were a source of inspiration for him. He would go to graveyards with his recording equipment to try to communicate with the dead.

He was obsessed with Buddy Holly and believed that he spoke to him in dreams after he died. And that obsession with him began in January 1958 when he and a friend were doing a tarot card reading and his friend predicted that Buddy Holly would die on 3 February. Joe Meek screamed and feared for Buddy Holly's life. 3 February 1958 came and went and nothing happened, but Joe Meek still felt the need to stalk him and meet him at a concert venue in London, where he delivered a message warning him of impending doom. The twenty-one-year-old Texan rock star handled the situation like a pro and thanked Meek for his concerns and accepted the note. It just so turned out that the prediction happened to be right, and he, the Big Bopper, and Ritchie Valens died in a plane crash in the early hours of 3 February 1959. It was a cold winter and Buddy Holly was tired of being on that crowded, freezing tour bus and wanted to travel in relative comfort and warmth. After that, Meek held séances trying to contact Buddy Holly. Interestingly enough, there's a little coincidence with Buddy Holly on the day of the murder-suicide. Life is full of coincidences, isn't it?

THE MURDER

Growing up gay in the 1930s and '40s was very difficult, no matter where you were in the world. Joe Meek was different from his brothers, who had more stereotypically masculine interests like sport. Besides electronics, he loved theatre and crossdressing. In the same shed where he would tinker with electronics, he put on plays with friends. He was very much a mama's boy and was bullied and called a sissy for his androgyny and crossdressing.

London in the '60s was still a homophobic place and it wouldn't be until 1967 when homosexuality would be legalised in England and Wales. Joe Meek was much freer to be himself and hook up with men in London than in his hometown, where his mother would watch him like a hawk. Joe Meek's first run-in with the law was in November 1963 when he pleaded guilty and was fined £15 (which would be about £321 in 2020) for cruising in public toilets at Madras Place in London. He called the charges a 'pack of lies' and believed he had been set up. He was a famous man at the time and this would be all over the newspapers and no doubt his family would find out what happened. He couldn't imagine how hurt his family would feel if they heard the news. As well, how would this affect his professional life? He had to deal with blackmail threats from then until the day he died.

Around the time of his death, he was also sued for plagiarising the melody of 'Telstar' from 'La Marche d'Austerlitz' from the 1960 French film *Austerlitz*, a movie he'd never seen because it hadn't even been shown in Britain at the time that he wrote 'Telstar'. He never made money from 'Telstar' in his lifetime, as the lawsuit was settled in his favour weeks after his death.

The year 1964 was a year of big changes and the year many people think of as the year the '60s truly culturally began. In the previous years, the music trends changed from pure rock and roll to pop ballads to guitar group instrumentals and there was a big change coming and it was a threat to Joe Meek, who was hoping it would be a flash in the pan. That big change was Merseybeat, with groups like The Beatles, Gerry and the Pacemakers, The Searchers, The Merseybeats, The Swinging Blue Jeans, and Billy J. Kramer and the Dakotas changing the scene. The '60s would never be the same again thanks to beat music. Other cities in the UK followed Liverpool's lead and had their own beat scenes: London had the Tottenham Sound and Birmingham had Brumbeat.

Much to Joe Meek's dismay, The Beatles were everywhere and here to stay. He didn't understand the big deal because The Tornados had got a number-one in the US before them, but The Beatles got more chart toppers in the US. It was definitely a hit to Meek's ego and a reminder that the entertainment industry is fickle and everyone's time in the spotlight comes to an end. It didn't help that he recorded a young Tom Jones (then known as Tommy Scott) with Welsh beat group The Senators, but Decca Records screwed him over and didn't release their single. According to Tom Jones' former Senators bandmate Vernon Hopkins, Meek fired a gun at The Senators when they were recording at his small studio in London. When Meek wasn't happy with the band's performance, he yelled at them, telling them that they were playing the music wrong before aiming a pistol at them and firing it. Thankfully for The Senators, it turned out to be a starting pistol filled with blanks. Still though, that's scary! On another occasion, Meek allegedly groped and tried to kiss Tom Jones.

Good news though came in the form of The Honeycombs' 'Have I The Right?' topping the charts in August 1964 with its prominent stomping sound. However, because Tottenham beat group The Dave Clark Five's 'Bits and Pieces' came out months before and had that signature percussive stomp, producer Joe Meek was accused of ripping off that Dave Clark Five sound even though he was a sound engineer on Anne Shelton's 1956 hit 'Lay Down Your Arms', which had that same stomping sound. After that little bit of success, Meek's productions faced rejection after rejection and his bank balance was dwindling. His temper and attitude made him his own saboteur.

Just weeks before the murder-suicide, a Suffolk tractor driver named Fred Burggy found two suitcases with the dismembered body of seventeen-year-old Muswell Hill warehouse worker Bernard Oliver inside. His hair was freshly cut and his nails were manicured, and he had been sexually assaulted and strangled. The police couldn't identify the body straight away, so they released a photo of the boy's head to the media and Oliver's family recognised him straight away. Policed questioned his family and had intentions to question every gay man in London (since at that time gay men were considered sex offenders since homosexuality wasn't legalised). That included Joe Meek, who had been convicted of cottaging, and in the weeks leading to the murder-suicide, he was always on the lookout to see if police were spying on him, and his assistant, Patrick Pink, believed Meek was being spied on too. Joe Meek's mental health was already unstable at this point, and these allegations sent him into an even worse tailspin, even though things were looking up with a possible job offer at EMI. To this day, the murder of Bernard Oliver is an unsolved mystery.

On the eighth anniversary of Buddy Holly's death (the day the music died), 3 February 1967, Joe Meek killed his landlady before killing himself. He had a feeling ever since Buddy Holly died that he would die a violent death at a young age, before the age of forty, since he identified a lot with him. Meek's anger problems were getting worse and his relationship with his neighbours and landlord was growing more and more strained with them being upset with him over late-night sessions and not paying the rent on time due to financial difficulties (even though you'd never know it looking at him because he placed a lot of importance on looking stylish and living luxuriously). He felt lonely and unloved because he hadn't found his soulmate. His roommate and crush (who did not return feelings because he was straight), Heinz Burt, had a shotgun. In his spare time, Heinz liked to hunt and when he wasn't hunting, he left the shotgun in the 304 Holloway Road flat, and Joe Meek had access to it.

Joe Meek never really got along that well with his landlady, a woman in her fifties named Violet Shenton – it was a love–hate relationship, and that's how many of Joe's relationships were. When he was in a good mood, he was great to work with, but that could all change like the flip of a switch. Violet would do favours for Joe and was a good listening ear, but Joe hated her because she would ask for peace and quiet on behalf of her husband; he took it personally and would yell at the couple. Musicians don't make the best roommates for those who value tranquillity. Meek also believed that she could be spying on him and stealing his ideas. And Violet most of all was frustrated with Joe Meek not paying his rent on time, but she was always calm and gentle when asking for rent money.

According to a radio interview Patrick Pink did speaking about Joe Meek's last hours, Joe was acting like his paranoid self as usual, feeling like he was being spied on and asking Patrick to mime to the music and write things down so they couldn't be heard if the flat was bugged. Patrick prepared breakfast for Joe, and Joe only ate a slice of toast and drank a lot of coffee and communicated through writing that he was still being spied on. He took the note writing another step further at this point, by burning his notes and any 'evidence' that could be used against him by police or blackmailers. Patrick, being concerned, offered to call a doctor and Joe angrily shouted that he didn't need a doctor. He went back to work in the studio to work on Patrick's tape and told Patrick to get his landlady, Violet Shenton, to come and see him and so he brought her upstairs. Joe and Violet had an argument over the rent book and just as she turned around to head down the stairs, Joe shot her in the back and she tumbled down the stairs. Patrick ran out to see what was going on and saw Mrs Shenton dying, catching her and hearing her last breaths. Patrick ran up the stairs and as he was halfway up the flight of stairs, Joe shot and killed himself. Unfortunately for Patrick, people initially thought he had killed both Meek and Shenton, with a crowd of people in front shouting 'murderer' and 'hang him' at him. After five hours of questioning at the police station, he was released. Pop star Heinz, the owner of the gun, was questioned too. The coroner's investigation showed that Joe Meek killed his landlady and then himself. Nevertheless, there are many mysteries and questions around this murder-suicide.

Sadly, the outer-space loving Joe Meek didn't live to see man make it to the moon or a Britain where homosexuality was legal.

CHAPTER 16

Marcus Malone (1969)

ABOUT MARCUS MALONE

Marcus Malone was an original member of Carlos Santana's band and was one of those 'I was almost famous' stories. The Memphis-born percussionist's nickname was 'The Magnificent' and he was a major influence on the band's early improvisational sound, even though he never played Woodstock, the festival that would launch the band into stardom. He joined what was then known as the Santana Blues Band in 1967, when a friend of Carlos Santana's spotted him in North Beach, playing congas and standing out in a group of conga players. Carlos Santana said in his autobiography *The Universal Tone: Bringing My Story to Light* that Marcus was self-taught and had no knowledge of Cuban or Puerto Rican music, but he was willing to learn. Of Marcus's personality and appearance, Santana said that he was sharp-dressed, with a love of wearing burgundy, he drove a brand-new Eldorado, he was tough and didn't show a lot of emotion, and that he was a player and a street hustler. His lifestyle was different from everyone else in the band; while they were hippies who liked tripping on acid and smoking pot, he was focused on women. In the early days, the band would rehearse in Marcus's mother's garage.

Just as Santana were going places and becoming a popular live act at the Fillmore, he was arrested for killing someone and the band knew he was in big trouble. Santana needed another conga player and he was replaced with the man he had replaced, Michael Carabello.

Marcus did, however, have a songwriting credit on fan favourite and Santana concert staple 'Soul Sacrifice' and Santana credited him with making their cover of Babatunde Olatunji's 'Jingo' something special with that improvised approach.

Little else is known of his life because he was a private person who didn't speak in much detail about his past. However, he was proud of his brief time playing with Carlos Santana.

THE CRIME

Very little information is available about his case, but on 5 January 1969, he stabbed a San Francisco man named Edward Amido, who succumbed to his injuries a few weeks later. Marcus was allegedly caught in bed with Amido's partner. He was free for much of the year on bail and maintained that he stabbed Amido in self-defence. It's also alleged that Malone was on probation for narcotics offences. A *San Francisco Examiner* article from 26 November 1969 only describes Malone as a twenty-five-year-old musician, not mentioning his former affiliation with Carlos Santana, who would have been famous at the time the article was published. It appears that it took around a year for the case to go to trial. In the end, he was convicted of manslaughter. Afterwards, he was imprisoned in the notorious San Quentin State Prison. Coincidentally, Carlos Santana played a concert in San Quentin in 1988, fifteen years after Marcus Malone was released from prison.

AFTER PRISON

Unlike a lot of the other stories in this section, Marcus was released from prison, but it's a sad story and a sad example of how America treats ex-cons. If someone has done their time and paid back their debt to society, you can't keep punishing them forever. Generally speaking, people deserve another chance. People shouldn't be dumped out of prison with no hope, no support, and no chance of redeeming themselves. Whether or not you think Marcus defended himself and whether or not you think he should have been released, no one deserves to be homeless.

Marcus Malone was released from prison around 1973 and for forty years it was like he had dropped off the face of the earth. No one knew where he was or what he was doing. Carlos Santana speculated that he may have worked in clothing design in North Beach for a time, but it can't be confirmed for sure. Marcus's family moved to Oakland in 1978 and it seemed like he followed them there because that's where he spent most of his years. It's unknown how many years he was homeless.

Suddenly, in December 2013, a reporter named Stanley Roberts from local TV station KRON-TV came across Marcus by chance when he was covering a story on illegal dumping. In the story, Marcus said he worked as a landscaper and composer. He was shown to be living in a trailer. Marcus told the reporter that he used to be in Carlos Santana's band.

One might be sceptical of a homeless person saying that they used to work with a famous musician, but it turns out that, after fact-checking, he was telling the truth. For decades, Carlos Santana had tried looking for Marcus, but couldn't find him, so his manager contacted Stanley Roberts at KRON after the segment aired and Roberts reunited the two. Carlos Santana's first words to him in forty-five years were 'Marcus "The Magnificent" Malone' before greeting him with a hug. Santana told him that it was an honour to be in his presence and that he had always cherished him. Marcus had been homeless for many years and he described homelessness as 'a constant day-to-day struggle on trying to keep food in your body, keep your health up, and struggling period trying to find work [in] different places, anything that you can do for anybody you can do it for'. Some nights he was sleeping rough, outside in the cold. A lonely and painful life. Even while homeless, he wrote songs and made music.

The story made international news and Stanley Roberts and Carlos Santana were interviewed on CNN about the reunion with Marcus Malone after so many years of no contact. In an interview with CNN Santana expressed how he had been looking for him for years because he wanted to send him royalty payments for his songwriting credit on 'Soul Sacrifice'. Those payments went to his family on his behalf. Santana publicly stated that he wanted to give Marcus an apartment of his own and some congas and offered him a chance to play on his upcoming album, *Santana IV*, reunited with some of the original band members.

What happened since that CNN story? Marcus did indeed rehearse with Carlos Santana, but in the end he didn't play on the album because, as Santana told *Rolling Stone*, 'I could tell he hadn't played in years. He didn't have the strength or stamina.' In a *Las Vegas Sun* article from 22 January 2014, he said that he gave Marcus a new set of congas and got him an apartment, but he's 'not invested in the final outcome of his life' because he doesn't believe in telling people 'who to be, what to do, or how to do it' because that would be an imposition.

According to a 15 July 2014 Facebook post on a page run by Marcus's family, he said he hadn't heard from Carlos Santana in seven months and he's still living on the streets of Oakland and he's still hoping that Carlos Santana stands by his word. He said, 'I'm still on hard times. But the upside is that I've reconnected with so many old friends and made new friends after the story aired. I've had people actually come and find me to offer me food, a ride, or just a kind word so no matter what comes from this, the love that people have shown me that don't even know me has been overwhelming and for that I'm eternally grateful. Always remember in the rhythm of life that no matter what happens, "the beat goes on".'

Things took a tragic turn on 18 June 2016 when Marcus was involved in a freak accident that landed him in hospital and on life support. A tyre flew off a moving car and hit him. He made progress as far as recovering, but five years later, on 12 October 2021, he died after things took a turn for the worse health wise. He was seventy-seven.

CHAPTER 17

Rick Stevens (1976)

ABOUT RICK STEVENS

Rick Stevens was the lead singer of Oakland soul/funk horn group Tower of Power in the early '70s. The band describe their brass-heavy sound as 'East Bay Grease', the title of their debut album. Like Janis Joplin, Rick Stevens (born Donald Charles Stevenson) was born in Port Arthur, Texas, but unlike Janis he wasn't raised there. When Rick was a few years old, his family moved to Reno, Nevada and raised him there until they all moved to Oakland when he was a teenager. When he was just four years old, he started singing in church. He was the nephew of R&B singer-songwriter Ivory Joe Hunter, known as the Baron of the Boogie and the Happiest Man Alive. The prolific Ivory Joe Hunter was a big influence on him and would visit Rick Stevens and his family on breaks when he wasn't touring. Like a lot of black teenagers who got into music, he got into doo-wop in the '50s and joined a group. Before he moved to Oakland, he performed in Reno nightclubs, where he earned the nickname 'Mr Twister'. He got his stage name from when he performed in nightclubs and was told that he didn't look like a Donald Stevenson and that Rick would be a more fitting name for him.

When he moved to Oakland, he continued playing in local bands like The Idolistics, Rick and the Ravens, Four of a Kind, and Stuff. In 1969, he and his Stuff bandmate Willie James Fulton joined Tower of Power. Like many other bands starting out, Tower of Power played covers and they often played songs by artists like James Brown, Otis Redding, and Wilson Pickett. As Tower of Power became more popular, they played shows with groups like Santana and CCR. Tower of Power had some famous fans too like Aretha Franklin, who said she wanted to them to tour with her, and Queen bassist John Deacon who listed them as one of his favourite groups.

Rick's signature songs were 'Sparkling in the Sand' from *East Bay Grease* and 'You're Still a Young Man' from *Bump City*, with the latter being one of Tower of Power's biggest hits, reaching number twenty-nine on the Billboard charts. He wouldn't stay for long, with him leaving during the recording their 1973 self-titled album, which doesn't credit him for his background vocals. Lenny Williams replaced him as lead vocalist. Rick Stevens befriended him, and they kept in contact even while Rick Stevens was behind bars.

Rick's drug use was one of the reasons he left the band in 1972, with him earning the nickname, 'The Junkie'. By that point, he had been using cocaine, heroin, and methamphetamines for years and his drug problems worsened over time because he was surrounded by other musicians doing drugs. He later described his drug use in an interview with Story Connection TV as 'snorting and shooting up like a jackass in a jumpsuit'.

Stevens' departure from Tower of Power was a sad one and bandmate Emilio Castillo praised his vocals in an *East Bay Express* interview, calling him 'one of the greatest singers that ever lived. Unbelievable,' adding that had he not been addicted to drugs, he would have been a huge star.

Stevens joined Brass Horizon in the mid '70s, but by this point his drug use was becoming a major problem, putting himself and his family in harm's way, and this meant that his new band couldn't take off.

THE MURDER

Like a lot of musicians, Rick Stevens had drug problems and drugs are expensive; they can get you into debt and because you're buying them on the black market, there's a lot of sketchy and dangerous people dealing drugs and you don't know what you're getting. Rick Stevens owed money to brothers Harry and Andrew Austin and he shot and killed them on 18 February 1976 in a cabin in the Santa Cruz Mountains. He described that situation as a life-or-death situation; someone was going to die and it was either him or them. The Austin brothers, who were drug dealers, were sending him and his family death threats and so he met with the dealers in a cabin in the mountains, bringing a gun with him for self-protection and told them to leave him and his family alone. Things took a nasty turn when one of the drug dealers tried to grab his gun and turn it towards Rick, and then the gun went off while they were fighting over control of it.

They weren't the only people he killed, though. The following day, he killed Elliott Wickliffe in San Jose and was arrested at Edenvale Elementary School not long after. He was thirty-five when he was arrested. Even though it had been a few years since Rick left the band, his Tower of Power bandmates were shocked to see that he was arrested for first-degree murder and manslaughter. Founder and band leader of Tower of Power Emilio Castillo said that the whole band were in total shock and that they were all 'hanging out with some pretty heavy hitters in the drug scene, so stuff like that could happen at any time.'

While on trial, Rick Stevens was incredibly gracious and was prepared for whatever the court was going to throw at him. He was fully prepared for a death sentence for the first-degree murder charge when the jury found him guilty. He told the jury in a very classy way, 'I know this was not an easy decision for a lot of you who felt I deserved it. I have no ill will toward you. God bless you all. Thank you.' Initially, he was sentenced to death for the murders, but in a stroke of luck, the California Supreme Court found the death penalty unconstitutional and he was back in court with a new sentence, this time seven years to life, but it would be decades before he got paroled. The judge, John S. McInerney, told him during his resentencing, 'I'm happy that I don't have to sentence you to San Quentin's gas chamber again, but I'm going to sentence you to new life.'

He later said the trial and charges were completely fair, and therefore he never appealed. He was a class act in prison and his record was spotless, never landing in trouble.

Life is full of learning experiences and even the worst experiences are still a learning lesson. In Rick Stevens' case prison was a wake-up call and might have even saved his life. Maybe if he hadn't gone to prison, he could have spiralled into addiction even further and ended up dying young because of it. He told NBC Bay Area in an interview, 'I had to go to prison in order to grow up'. While in jail awaiting trial, he quit drugs cold turkey, and that was just the start of him turning his life around and redeeming himself in the public eye.

He made the most of his time in prison and three things helped him out. His first lifesaver was music, with him describing music as his 'guardian angel'. When he went to prison, there were a lot of Tower of Power fans who respected him and took care of him, giving him gifts and in return he treated them as equals, with respect. He told NBC Bay Area, 'I don't care if they were Chicanos, Black, Asian, or Caucasian. Everybody just gave me the respect.' And in an interview with *SF Gate*, he said he continued performing in prison because he 'refused to be institutionalised'.

He would organise gospel shows in the prison chapel with fellow inmates.

Because of his good behaviour, he was allowed furlough on some occasions so he could perform in public, such as at the State Capitol to sing for politicians. There are some perks to being famous and talented, that's for sure.

The second thing that helped him in prison was religion. He was said to have found God and he did a lot of reading, soul searching, and praying. He didn't just read Christian books, he read Jewish and Muslim texts too and paid a lot of attention to the news. Besides that, he kept busy working as a warden's assistant and as a 'quasi counsellor' for his fellow inmates. A pastor described Rick Stevens' changes in prison as regeneration and transformation rather than rehabilitation because rehabilitation means returning back to how they were before. He also described him as 'a student of the Bible'. Judge McInerney said that Rick Stevens 'really did find God in prison'.

Last but not least of the things that kept his spirits up in prison was his supportive family. At that time, there were conjugal visits for prisoners and while locked up, he conceived two children, one in Folsom and the other in Vacaville. His family would visit him every week. Visits are one of the few special things that prisoners have to look forward to and not everyone gets them because it requires a lot of time, patience, and commitment.

Even though he kept a positive attitude in prison, he was frank about the ugly side of prison, telling the *Mercury News*, 'I've had my back up against the wall. In prison, you might find yourself in a cell with a guy who is a complete a-hole. You don't sleep until you ask the guards if it's cool. Sometimes you have to ask for a "cell swap". A lot of times, that happened.' He said the famous 1994 prison drama *The Shawshank Redemption* is quite accurate to how prison really is with lots of stupid things happening both in jail and on the outside.

Rick Stevens was paroled on 20 July 2012 at the age of seventy-two after serving thirty-six years behind bars, which would end up being just under half his lifetime. Coincidentally, Jerry Brown was the governor of California when Rick Stevens entered prison and he signed off, approving his parole, thirty-six years later, which Stevens noted in that interview with *Story Connection*.

He served time in San Quentin, Vacaville, Folsom, the California Men's Colony in San Luis Obispo, and Mule Creek State Prison. Thanks to his 'pit bull', dynamite attorney, Peter J. Boldin, he got out of prison after seventeen parole hearings where he was turned down for political reasons, even though his behaviour in prison was exemplary and he was always remorseful of his crimes. Boldin knew the law very well and said that the parole board couldn't use the crime to find him unsuitable for parole, they had to have a legitimate reason outside of that and they couldn't find that, so they granted him parole. Even after he got out of prison, he gave back to inmates and played gigs and gave talks in prisons to give the prisoners hope and inspire them to turn their lives around.

Once released, he moved into his oldest son's house in Antioch, a suburb of Oakland in Contra Costa County. He was happy to eat real food with flavour like garlic chicken, potato salad, and macaroni salad; it's the little things that matter, right?

Months later, he reunited with his Tower of Power bandmates who were happy to see him back. The reunion was emotional, with Emilio Castillo saying that Rick was 'very apologetic' and that he was just glad to see that he was okay. Castillo was a big ally to Rick and tried to get him temporarily released on furlough to play on their fortieth reunion DVD, but the prison wouldn't allow it. But once he was back to singing and performing, he was happy to be on stage again, his true calling. Another famous supporter and friend of his is Michael Carabello of Santana, who played in a band called the Four of Us with him in the '60s before they were famous.

He died of liver cancer on 5 September 2017 at the age of seventy-seven. He had ten children from four marriages and they all loved him unconditionally.

CHAPTER 18

Jim Gordon (1983)

ABOUT JIM GORDON

Jim Gordon is a name that you may not know, but you've certainly heard a song that he's played on and you definitely know of musicians he's worked with and oh boy did he have an incredible CV! You might say it rivals that of British session drummer Clem Cattini! He worked with musicians such as Duane Allman, Joan Baez, The Beach Boys, The Byrds, The Carpenters, Cher, Dave Mason, Eric Clapton, Frank Zappa, George Harrison, Harry Nilsson, Joe Cocker, John Lennon, Mariya Takeuchi, Tom Petty, Steely Dan, and more! If we're talking songs, you've probably heard his drumming on 'Classical Gas', 'Wichita Lineman', and 'Layla'.

His story is one of the most baffling to me and is a great example of why true crime appeals to me and fascinates me. How does someone go from successful in life by anyone's standards to being a murderer and with many people not seeing it coming? Buckle your seatbelts and get ready for the story of Jim Gordon, and no, we're not talking about the character from *Batman*!

Jim Gordon was born on 14 July 1945 in LA. His parents were middle class and appeared to be your typical happy-go-lucky picture-perfect family in the San Fernando Valley: Gordon's father worked as an accountant and his mother was a nurse. However, from a young age he struggled with his mental health – he was anxious and heard voices in his head, which were an escape and friends of sorts for him. His other big escape though, and the more constructive one for sure, was music. He was a creative kid and at the age of eight he made his own drum set out of rubbish bins and played along with the radio. His parents saw a lot of potential and bought him a real drum kit and signed him up for lessons, which quickly built up his skills and got him compliments such as 'prodigy' and 'genius'. Drumming also built up his confidence, making him feel like he was somebody, and he became a lot more outgoing in secondary school and more liked by his peers; he was elected class president and had a girlfriend.

The world was his oyster when he was seventeen years old. UCLA offered him a music scholarship and his parents urged him to go for it, but Jim's heart wanted something else. University wasn't the place he wanted to be: he wanted to make music and tour. To be a superstar! He was so good at what he did that, before he turned eighteen, The Everly Brothers hired him to be in their touring band and so, in 1963, he flew to England with them with a fake ID. Not giving up further education entirely, he took classes at a community college and pounded the pavement, networking and doing anything to get an 'in' in the music industry, taking any jobs that were available, and that helped with word of mouth – everyone just had to hear this whizz kid. A big fan of his was Wrecking Crew session drummer Hal Blaine, who offered him gigs and jobs he couldn't take because of scheduling conflicts.

Another big break for him was playing drums for some Sonny & Cher recordings, but an even bigger break came in 1966 when Brian Wilson hired the then up-and-coming drummer to play on some tracks on their famous masterpiece of an album, *Pet Sounds* – a fan favourite and critically acclaimed.

However, there was a dark side to fame. When you get into

the music industry, there's a lot of bad influences and vices around you and after some years of being in the industry, he was not only smoking pot, but trying harder drugs that had hallucinogenic effects and this can mix very poorly with mental illness, such as LSD making Syd Barrett's behaviour more and more erratic over the years. There's research showing that psychedelic drugs can treat depression and other mental illnesses by changing the structures of neurons, but with any treatment, it should be supervised by a medical professional. In Jim Gordon's case, sometimes the psychedelic drugs helped, but other times they didn't. While on tour with Joe Cocker in 1970, he punched his then-girlfriend Rita Coolidge in the face. She was left traumatised with a black eye for the rest of the tour and immediately broke up with him, completely cutting all ties. His peers saw it as something random and out of character for the usually pleasant drummer and many of them gave him the benefit of the doubt because he'd always been so kind and positive. It helped that his drumming skills were still top-notch.

Even with that hiccup, things were still going well for the Wrecking Crew drummer. He made connections with Eric Clapton through playing in Delaney & Bonnie and Friends and he played on George Harrison's incredible solo album, *All Things Must Pass*. He took a break from Wrecking Crew session work when he was invited to join the supergroup Derek & The Dominos and so he travelled to England and stayed with Eric Clapton, which meant opulence and an all-you-can eat buffet of drugs and alcohol. And his drug consumption was even greater than that of Eric Clapton and Bobby Whitlock. His bandmate, Bobby Whitlock, said that cocaine, heroin, and whisky 'will make you a crazy dude'. The supergroup was a mix of great musicians from both the US and UK: Bobby Whitlock, Carl Radle, Jim Gordon, Duane Allman, Eric Clapton, and Dave Mason. They only released one studio album in 1970, the double album *Layla and Other Assorted Love Songs*. Jim Gordon didn't just play drums on Eric Clapton's 'Layla', he came up with the ending of the song while goofing around on piano with chord changes and melodies, and so he won a co-writing credit on it. He even played that piano coda too!

Even though he was deep into drugs, the early '70s was a busy and successful time for him with him working with a who's who of rock and roll and spending a lot of time in England. By the mid '70s, he came back to LA and that's when things took a turn for the worse, mentally. Everyone saw there was something off about Jim Gordon. While tripping on acid in his friend and fellow session musician Gary Coleman's camper van driving down the Hollywood Freeway, he was acting arrogant and yelling at drivers about how they'd want his autograph if they knew who he was and that he was a star. The fame and drugs got to his head. Gary's wife, who was in the van at the time, told him that Jim was a bad influence and that he was 'going to kill someone someday'.

THE MURDER

Mrs Coleman's prediction sadly turned out to be right. In the late '70s, before the murder, it was a downward spiral for Jim Gordon with him becoming even more unreliable as a musician and his personal life was a mess with two divorces and constantly being admitted to psychiatric hospitals with no improvement in his mental state. Professionally, the mental decline culminated in him losing all his jobs. Finally, when Paul Anka hired him for a gig in Las Vegas in 1979, he walked off the stage after a few bars of the opening song.

The voices were getting louder and louder, telling him to give up drumming and how to live his life. In Jim's head, the voices were like those of his mother, who would become his murder victim. He saw her as the enemy and he claimed that it was her voice telling him to kill her.

On 3 June 1983, Jim's life would change forever when he decided to 'make the voices stop' once and for all. He took a hammer and an 8.25-inch-long freshly sharpened butcher's knife and drove his white Datsun 200SX from his home in Van Nuys to his mother's flat in North Hollywood, oddly enough making sure to follow the rules of the road, even though he was about to commit a murder. He rang the doorbell and his seventy-two-year-old mother answered the door and saw her son looking clearly unwell. Suddenly, before she could even defend herself or call for help, he attacked her, first with a hammer, bashing her skull four times. As she fell to the floor, she screamed. Once his mother was on the floor, he stabbed her in the chest with the butcher's knife three times to ensure she was dead. After that, he went back to his home, where the police found him lying down in his living room, where they notified him of his mother's death. At first, they didn't even consider him a suspect, but Jim straight away confessed to the murder and was then arrested, crying in the cop car saying how sorry he was, but saying she tormented him. And so he went from rock star to prisoner.

He was found guilty of second-degree murder in 1984 and was sentenced to sixteen years to life. The defence tried to argue that he was not guilty by reason of insanity, but California law makes it difficult to prove that someone is legally insane. However, his schizophrenia diagnosis was unanimously accepted, except by Jim Gordon himself, who saw himself as 'pretty normal' and insisted that he didn't 'feel that crazy' and continued to insist he was acting in self-defence. He had a mental illness, but he needed to face the consequences of his actions.

In the thirty years he was eligible for parole, he was turned down each time because he never attended a parole meeting, and he was still deemed to be a danger if he were freed. In 2018, his family and legal counsel asked the parole board not to grant him parole because they feared he'd hurt someone else once released, even though he had no record of violent behaviour since 2001. According to the California Department of Corrections and Rehabilitation, he last served time in the California Medical Facility in Vacaville, and before that, he served time in the California Men's Colony in San Luis Obispo and Atascadero State Hospital. On 14 November 2019, he waived his right to a parole suitability hearing for three years. He died of natural causes while incarcerated at the California Medical Facility in Vacaville, California on 13 March 2023. He was seventy-seven years old.

CHAPTER 19

Phil Spector (2003)

ABOUT PHIL SPECTOR

Love or hate Phil Spector, you can't deny how much of a genius and innovator he was as a music producer. He was easily one of the greatest music producers of all time. If you take his personal life out of the equation and just pay attention to his work as a producer, the stuff he was doing with his Wall of Sound technique was revolutionary and game changing. You've heard it on songs like 'He's a Rebel', 'Da Doo Ron Ron', 'Baby I Love You', 'You've Lost That Lovin' Feelin'', and 'River Deep – Mountain High' and you've heard his influence in artists like The Beach Boys and Bruce Springsteen. You may not know the terminology and how it works, but you can recognise that big sound that sounds big no matter how you listen to it: on a little portable radio, a fancy stereo, on your headphones, even on your phone speakers. Obviously for optimal enjoyment, stereo or headphones is the best way to immerse yourself in the Wall of Sound, but I'm not gonna tell you how to enjoy your music. It's time to talk about Phil Spector's life and how he went from the most successful music producer and tycoon of teen to convicted murderer.

Phil Spector was born Harvey Phillip Spector on 26 December 1939 in The Bronx to a Jewish family. His parents, Ben and Bertha, were Russian Jewish immigrants who slightly changed their last names from Spektor to Spector. Ben was born in what is now Ukraine and Bertha was born in Paris, where her family immigrated before going to the US. And yes, both his parents' last names were Spector, and Phil Spector told *Tearing Down the Wall of Sound* author Mick Brown that they were first cousins. When Phil Spector was young – about eight or nine years old, his father killed himself after suffering from depression and the pressure of supporting a family. On his gravestone, the epitaph read 'To know him was to love him', a line that would inspire an early Phil Spector song. A few years later, his mother moved the family across the country to LA because they had family there and she could find work. Bertha raised her kids by herself. Because his mum worked to support the family, Phil Spector was a latchkey kid.

He and his sister, Shirley, couldn't have been any more different. Shirley was a beautiful tall girl with blonde hair, who landed modelling jobs as a teenager and had dreams of being a movie star. Meanwhile, Phil was a short, skinny, awkward boy with a round face and wavy hair that would significantly thin in his early twenties. He was very self-conscious of his looks. What he lacked in looks, though, he made up for with his intelligence, being a good student, and musical talent. Much like Jim Gordon, music was his outlet to show that he was someone. As a teenager, he got into jazz and blues music (and like everyone else his age, rock and roll and R&B too), and he even learnt to play guitar. Seeing Ella Fitzgerald in concert on his birthday changed his life and he read all about jazz music, one of his favourite publications being the weekly jazz magazine *Down Beat*. He ended up writing a letter to the magazine about Barney Kessel being overlooked and it got published and his sister got in contact with Barney Kessel's record label and asked if her brother could meet him. Kessel recognised Phil Spector's name and agreed to meet him. This was another early life-changing moment for Phil Spector, meeting his idol, who advised him that jazz was on the way out and that he should go pop if he wanted to strike gold and make it big. And that's exactly what he did.

However, he had a mouthy side to him and his words would sometimes get him into trouble and fights. He also was a bit rebellious and would sneak out of his mother's home even when his mother told him not to. He hated being doted on by his mother and older sister. His mother suspected that he had a mental illness, and lo and behold, he was later diagnosed with bipolar and was prescribed medicine for that and schizophrenia. In the music industry and in his personal life, he had a reputation for being a control freak and Napoleon-like figure. He was also very mysterious, disappearing from the public eye for long periods of time and rarely giving interviews. But he had a goofy/prankster side to him, such as the time he was staying at a hotel in New York with The Teddy Bears and Fidel Castro got in the same lift as them with his entourage of bodyguards and Spector made faces at him behind his back. But underneath was a self-loathing man who was very insecure about his looks and concerned about what people thought.

While in his last year of secondary school, Phil Spector played 'Rock Island Line' at a talent show and won. After that, he and his friend Marshall Lieb appeared on KTLA's *Rocket to Stardom*, which was a talent show that showcased young amateur talent, and the pair won the prize, another big step up! *American Bandstand* was a popular show in those days and as Phil Spector watched it, he knew he needed to record his own music. And so he got out and worked for it, networking and speaking to people who worked at music studios, one of his favourites being Gold Star Sound Studios in Hollywood. There, he talked to fellow Fairfax High School graduate Stan Ross, who helped him get his big break. It was through that time at Gold Star in the '60s that

Spector came up with this Wall of Sound technique that involved layering, overdubbing, and using echo chambers to create this Wagnerian sound with excessive instrumentation. Like with Joe Meek, these ideas were very big and tested the abilities of the equipment and veteran producers weren't sure if it would work, but with persistence, he did it and created this revolutionary music production technique. He wasn't just a producer, he was a songwriter and auteur, not so different from Joe Meek, who you might say was his British counterpart.

He got his first big break in 1958, at only eighteen years old, when he wrote The Teddy Bears' 'To Know Him is to Love Him', which topped the charts thanks to it being played on Dick Clark's *American Bandstand*. It's debatable if he produced it or not, since Lew Bedell claims that he wasn't doing any production work, but rather only playing guitar and piano. The Teddy Bears were a group made up of Spector, Leib, Harvey Goldstein (who left early on), and Annette Kleinbard (later known as Carol Connors). Session drummer Sandy Nelson also played on their records and would later go on to have hits like 'Teen Beat' and 'Let There Be Drums'. The song was later covered by Peter and Gordon, Bobby Vinton, and Dolly Parton. Unfortunately for The Teddy Bears, 'To Know Him is to Love Him' was a one-hit wonder, but it wouldn't be the last success for the members as individuals.

A chart topper under Phil Spector's belt was enough to give him confidence and people around him noticed the difference in how he acted, but the dark side was that he became even more manipulative and controlling, even telling his girlfriend at the time, Donna Kass, that he wrote Ritchie Valens' hit 'Donna' and sold the rights to it. That was a lie and was exposed when she saw the real Donna, Donna Ludwig, Ritchie's high-school sweetheart, crying when she heard the news of his death.

Through promoter Lester Sill, he got a connection to work as an apprentice for Tin Pan Alley songwriting duo Jerry Leiber and Mike Stoller, who notably wrote hits for Elvis Presley, The

Coasters, and The Drifters. They were sceptical at first about taking Phil Spector on as a protégé and weren't impressed with 'To Know Him is to Love Him', which they described as 'white-bread trash', but they could see talent and potential in him as not only a producer, but a songwriter and musician.

This apprenticeship was great experience for him and his biggest hit at that time was co-writing Ben E. King's hit 'Spanish Harlem' with Leiber. He was making a name for himself. In the early '60s, he worked with R&B artists like Ruth Brown, LaVern Baker, and The Top Notes. He produced the original recording of 'Twist and Shout', performed by The Top Notes and later popularised by The Isley Brothers and The Beatles. He wrote two other Ben E. King songs with Doc Pomus, 'First Taste of Love' and 'Young Boy Blues'. While there, he befriended Atlantic Records founder Ahmet Ertegün. He idolised him and was fascinated with his stories of musicians he worked with, his style, and knowledge of music. Likewise, Ertegün liked Spector because he found him funny and unique. Both bonded over their love of black culture: jazz, slang, and soul food. Spector even worked as his personal assistant and as a staff producer for a time. Another person he worked with was music publisher Don Kirshner, who saw his potential as a music producer and a great interpreter of songs, but not so much as a songwriter. Kirshner thought of him as eccentric and charming, but manipulative and prone to using people.

In 1961, he and Lester Sill started a record label called Philles Records, an amalgamation of their two names. Previously, Sill worked with Lee Hazlewood, but Hazlewood didn't want to work with him anymore and went back to working with twanging guitarist Duane Eddy. Phil Spector made history with this career move, becoming the youngest record label owner. He loved the freedom that came with it and he could call the shots and do things on his own terms. That label released music from The Crystals, Bob B. Soxx & the Blue Jeans, Darlene Love, The Ronettes, The Righteous Brothers, and Ike and Tina Turner. And this is where Spector found a lot of success, producing multiple chart hits and shaping the '60s girl group sound. However, this label was short-lived, shutting its doors in 1969 – not even surviving a decade. Even with the label shutting its doors, the music will be remembered and loved forever.

In 1962, Phil Spector produced The Crystals' song 'He Hit Me (And It Felt Like a Kiss)'. The song was a Gerry Goffin-Carole King composition inspired by Little Eva's boyfriend beating her. It was controversial even then in the relatively conservative early '60s, with it getting little airplay and being widely protested. Phil Spector's production made the song all the more grim and it was an omen of his treatment of Ronnie Spector.

That same year, he created the Wall of Sound, born in LA at Gold Star Studios. And what better song to premiere this new production technique than 'He's a Rebel'? He wanted The Crystals to sing it, but they couldn't make it to LA, so instead The Blossoms recorded the song. The song reached number one in November. Another key part of the Wall of Sound was a group of seasoned session musicians called The Wrecking Crew. Gold Star may not have been the prettiest, state-of-the-art studio, but it was where Spector could be his best and most creative because he loved working with the people there because of that family sort of relationship. He'd never waste an opportunity and that control room was the perfect environment for listening to and mixing the songs to perfection because you'd be enveloped in the music. Everything he did had to be a masterpiece and so he paid careful attention to detail and tested each song on a small radio to see if it passed muster. The hard work paid off and, at just twenty-three, he was America's most successful record producer, a young visionary. But even that didn't eliminate his insecurities and he was regularly seeing a psychologist, Dr Kaplan.

Phil Spector married his first wife, Annette Merar, the lead vocalist of the Spectors Three in 1963. The marriage fell apart because he was busy, constantly travelling and working on music, becoming less and less available to his wife. While working with The Ronettes, he fell in love with Ronnie. It was doomed from the beginning because even when he said 'I do' to Annette, he was thinking of Ronnie Spector, a beautiful mixed-race singer with a beehive, heavy make-up, and tight-fitting dresses. In 1964, Annette moved out and Phil Spector begged her to come back, offering to drop The Ronettes if she did. He really didn't want to. He never admitted to cheating on Annette with Ronnie, but it was obvious.

The Ronettes had a great live following in New York City getting their start at the Peppermint Lounge and were signed to Colpix, but they didn't have any commercial success with anything released under that label. Ronnie's sister Estelle made the bold move to call Phil Spector and ask for an audition and he signed them and they became his top priority when it came to recording, but not when it came to paying their royalties. Their hits 'Be My Baby' and 'Baby I Love You' are some of the most perfect examples of Wall of Sound and gave them their meteoric rise to fame. In 1966, they opened for The Beatles on their last American tour and they broke up the following year. In 1968, Ronnie married Phil and went from being a superstar to essentially a prisoner who feared she would die if she made one wrong move.

Throughout the '60s, Phil Spector crafted this persona by making TV appearances, always making sure to dress well, have his hair styled perfectly, and turn on the charm. There was some mythologising going on with his backstory, such as a claim that he had goals of working as an interpreter at the UN when he went to New York in the early '60s, as told in Tom Wolfe's January 1965 profile of him published in the *New York Herald Tribune*. He also made cameo appearances in the sitcom *I Dream of Jeannie* and the road trip film *Easy Rider*. He had plans of making a documentary called *A Giant Stands 5 ft 7 in.*, but it was never made.

As the '60s progressed, Spector's girl group sound faded away (partially because of his insecurities, not wanting Ronnie to outshine him), with Berry Gordy's Motown becoming dominant with groups like The Supremes and Martha & The Vandellas. He saw Gordy as a rival, but the two were more alike than they thought. Controlling, determined to succeed, incredible production skills, and didn't treat their musicians well. The '60s was a decade of change and every couple of years, the music trends changed; a beautiful thing for music fans, but frustrating for people in the industry who didn't have their pulse on what the public wanted and who struggled to adapt and change with the times.

Still, Phil Spector continued to produce music in the '70s, notably producing The Beatles' *Let It Be*, John Lennon's iconic solo album *Imagine*, and George Harrison's iconic solo album *All Things Must Pass*, after a three-year break from producing. He was bored and eager to work again in his natural habitat, the studio. In the late '70s he produced albums for Dion DiMucci (*Born to Be with You*), Leonard Cohen (*Death of a Ladies' Man*), and The Ramones (*End of the Century*). However, he became more reclusive, but it wasn't the first time he had become more closed off to the media and public.

The first time that happened was after Tina Turner's 'River Deep – Mountain High' flopped on the American charts (it was a smash hit in the UK, however). And when you listen to it, you'll be surprised to find out it wasn't a success in the US. It's a masterpiece, an opera, Phil Spector's best production and yet it was slept on. Rodney Bingenheimer and Brian Wilson were left speechless when they sat in on the studio session for the song; they were blown away. You can easily tell how much blood, sweat, and tears went into it, and it was his biggest production. Some suspected that racism sabotaged it; others thought it was that Spector was getting pretentious, too big for his boots and people wanted to see him knocked from the pedestal. To cope with the song receiving only a B+ from *Cash Box* and *Billboard*, he called 'River Deep – Mountain High' his goodbye where he went crazy. Like going out with a bang. He admitted to *NME* in an interview in the '70s that he was indeed an egomaniac. In private, he was depressed, gutted and felt betrayed by the American record-buying public. Around the same time, his close friend, comedian Lenny Bruce, died and that made him even more depressed. Things come in threes and as The Ronettes were invited to tour with The Beatles on their final American tour, Spector was his usual controlling self and forbade Ronnie from going on tour under the guise of wanting her to stay in LA to record. He would get even more controlling as time went on and more and more people saw how dangerous he was. It was an open secret, but because of how respected Phil Spector was in the music industry and his persona that he had carefully crafted, who would believe them? The stories resurfaced when Phil Spector murdered Lana Clarkson on 3 February 2003. Oddly enough, a coincidence with Joe Meek, who murdered his landlady that same day thirty-six years earlier.

THE MURDER… AND ALL THE CLOSE CALLS BEFORE IT

If anyone saw this coming, it was Ronnie Spector, and a lot of other musicians Phil Spector worked with throughout his career. She said that Phil Spector threatened her with death, saying there's a glass coffin (not too different from *Snow White*) in the basement and her body would be in it if she ever left him so he could 'look at her forever'. For Phil Spector, it was like, 'If I can't have you, no one can,' that's how much he hated rejection. Luckily, she lived and escaped from that nightmare of a mansion.

Ronnie came from a conservative family and her mum, Beatrice, didn't like that she was seeing Phil Spector and she was desperate to bring her home to New York. As the taxi left for the airport, Spector threw a lot of money at Beatrice, begging to let Ronnie stay in California. She brought her back to New York for a short time, but Phil Spector tracked Ronnie down and brought her back to California, proposed to her, and married her. The wedding was his way: low-key and small, with the wedding party going to a Mahalia Jackson concert afterwards.

Their marriage had a rocky start with an argument as soon as the newlyweds arrived at Spector's mansion. Ronnie married Phil because she wanted to be a solo star and he could produce her music and Phil just wanted a trophy wife on his arm. From there, Ronnie's life became lonely and restricted with Phil watching her every move and forbidding her from leaving the house, with Phil claiming it was because he loved and cared about her and her safety. Not only were her movements controlled, but also her finances and who she could see. He separated her from her family and friends so he could have control over her. She was being abused on so many levels and it wasn't long until she first tried to file for divorce.

In the meantime, she developed a problem with alcohol and her mental health suffered. The mansion became even more prison-like after the Tate–LaBianca murders, when Phil Spector installed and implemented more security measures like fences, electric gates, barbed wire, and attack dogs, to turn the mansion into a fortress. On the rare occasions when Ronnie went out, she had to have a minder and inside the car was a blow-up mannequin of Phil Spector; his eyes were always on her in some way. He was controlling because he feared rejection and loneliness and he had an ego problem. Ronnie's drinking problems worsened to the point of her ending up in a car accident and suffering seizures. Spector sent her to rehab, and life at the mansion was so restrictive, that rehab was paradise in comparison and she'd deliberately binge-drink to go back to rehab.

In a desperate attempt to save their marriage, Phil Spector adopted five-year-old twin boys Gary and Louis without his wife's knowledge and gave them to her as a 'Christmas present'. Anyone who does something like that is unlikely to treat their kids well and it's no surprise that their brother Donte ended up homeless, HIV-positive, and addicted to drugs. The twins later said their father abused them. Donte alleged that his father would threaten him and the twins by putting his hand on his gun. He alleged that after Ronnie left, Spector would force the kids to watch him have sex with his girlfriends and even forced them to simulate sex with the girlfriend. Donte said this happened when he was ten years old, and Gary said that he had been a victim of the same thing too.

It was thanks to Alcoholics Anonymous meetings and the support of her mother that Ronnie was able to finally make her escape from Phil Spector. As the story goes, she escaped from him one summer day in 1972, running barefoot from the mansion to a car, where she and her mother got away. She was penniless and was living in a hotel afterwards; as you can expect, the divorce was nasty and a legal mess.

Ronnie Spector died on 12 January 2022 at the age of seventy-eight of cancer. She outlived Phil Spector by very close to a year.

Phil Spector once again disappeared from the public eye in 1974 when he got into a near-fatal car accident in Hollywood where he was thrown through the windshield of his car. The only thing keeping him from being declared dead at the scene was a faint pulse detected by a cop. He was taken to hospital, where he underwent hours of surgery and 700 stitches on his face and head.

Jazz guitarist Barney Kessel's sons remember meeting Phil Spector for the first time and him greeting them with his .38 calibre pistol in a shoulder holster, clearly visible. He even invited them to shoot old 45s that he thought were rubbish. Guns were just another way for Phil Spector to overcompensate for his insecurities. And insecure he was when he saw David Geffen go from awkward teenager hanging around Gold Star Studios to being a successful manager and even richer than him. One day, at a session with Cher, he punched David Geffen and called him a homophobic slur. And in 1973, while John Lennon was recording *Rock 'n' Roll*, Phil Spector pulled out his revolver and fired a shot in the studio, right near John Lennon. Lennon shouted back 'Phil, if you're going to kill me, kill me. But don't fuck with my ears. I need 'em.'

But why would people continue to work with him if they knew he was so crazy and dangerous? A former employee and lover of his, Devra Robitaille, said it was almost a thrill and part of it was you never knew which Phil Spector you'd see: the charming, charismatic Phil or the frightening, sinister Phil? He also would love-bomb her every time she tried to leave him, sending dozens of roses to her door to lure her back. He even threatened to kill her one night when she wanted to leave his mansion because the tensions were too much for her.

That's human nature, people like thrill, uncertainty, and risk-taking. The alcohol amplified both sides of Phil. A little alcohol made him even funnier and even more of a smart-ass, but too much and he became a monster. And insecure he was. Even though he influenced greats like The Beatles, Bruce Springsteen, and The Beach Boys and he was working with legends like Dion, Leonard Cohen, and The Ramones in the mid to late '70s, he wasn't selling records like he did in the early '60s.

Leonard Cohen needed to record another album and he got an offer in 1977 to record an album with Phil Spector producing it. Everyone around him was aware of Spector's reputation and told him not to go for it, but he did anyway. His close friend Joni Mitchell especially advised him not to do it because she knew how tempestuous the recording sessions with John Lennon got. Turns out, she was absolutely right and sadly, Leonard Cohen saw the dangerous side of Phil Spector first-hand. There were a lot of arguments between Cohen and Spector and it one day culminated in Spector walking up to him with a bottle of Manischewitz (an inexpensive, extremely sweet Jewish wine) and holding a pistol in his other hand and holding it up to his neck and saying, 'Leonard, I love you,' and Cohen replying back, 'I hope you do, Phil.' That album, *Death of a Ladies' Man*, was released in 1977 and because it was a radical departure from Cohen's previous work, it alienated fans and got negative, confused reviews. Cohen himself wasn't proud of the album and thought of it as a failed experiment. It was his worst-selling album.

The next group he worked with were The Ramones for their 1980 album *End of the Century* and you'd think that's a weird match, especially sound wise: punk is supposed to be raw and Phil Spector's sound was so polished. Why would punk rockers want to work with some dinosaur music producer from the early '60s? On the surface, The Ramones may look like punk rockers, but deep down inside, they had more pop leanings than you might realise and it's evident when you listen to their music. They weren't like The Clash, Sex Pistols, or Buzzcocks. Rather, they were more influenced by groups like The Who, MC5, Stooges, and New York Dolls. Joey Ramone especially loved '60s girl groups like The Crystals and The Ronettes. And who better to work with than Phil Spector when you love that music? The Kessel brothers, Dan and David, were huge fans of The Ramones and brought Phil Spector to their show at the Whiskey a Go Go where they played with Blondie and where The Ramones and Spector first met. Spector was interested in producing Debbie Harry as a solo artist (he even approached her while she was only in her bra and underwear in the dressing room), but Debbie Harry was savvy and knew about his reputation and understandably declined after he pulled out a gun, stuck it in her boot, and said 'bang'). It was through the Kessels that Phil Spector got that connection to The Ramones, but Dee Dee Ramone said it might have been the record company's idea for them to work together because they thought the collaboration could potentially be a hit.

Dee Dee Ramone said that his first impression of Phil Spector was that he looked like Count Dracula and he didn't recognise him when he first saw him in a cloak, beard, and dark aviator sunglasses, and only after the fact did he know that strange-looking man was none other than Phil Spector. Spector especially liked Joey and chatted with him about music and they got along well.

One night at Phil Spector's mansion, Spector and Joey Ramone went to another room to have a private meeting upstairs and the rest of the Ramones were downstairs in the piano room. They were bored and Dee Dee tried to go upstairs to see what was taking so long and next thing he knew, Phil was shouting and waving his pistol and clearly knew how to use it and he was quick. Dee Dee was bored and wanted to go back to the hotel and was angry that Spector was trying to steal Joey from the band and told Spector as much. And next thing he knew, Spector pointed a gun at his heart telling him, 'You're not going anywhere, Dee Dee,' and motioned for them all to get back into the piano room. For the rest of the night, he was playing 'Baby I Love You' on the piano. The Ramones recorded a cover of that song on Joey's insistence they do a Spector song for *End of the Century*. After a frustrating two weeks in the studio with Phil Spector, Dee Dee and Marky Ramone booked the next flight to JFK airport. Dee Dee said it was a miracle the album came together in the first place. Interestingly enough, it was their most successful album, charts wise, but there were no hit singles from it.

Johnny Ramone said that after he was frustrated with Phil Spector making him play the opening chord of 'Rock 'n' Roll High School' over and over again he got up to leave and Phil Spector told him, 'You're not going anywhere'. Johnny described him as a little man with lifts in his shoes, a wig on his head, and a man who carried four guns – one in each boot and one on each side of his chest. Two bodyguards accompanied Spector wherever he went. Johnny Ramone wrote in his posthumously released autobiography, *Commando*, 'After he shot that girl, I thought, "I'm surprised that he didn't shoot someone every year." But if he would have shot any one of us, it probably would have been Dee Dee. Somehow, he irritated him even more. Dee Dee drove him crazy and Dee Dee didn't like Phil either. He would complain that Dee Dee would show up stoned; meanwhile Phil would be drunk.'

If you don't want to take musicians' words for how dangerous

Phil Spector was, here's some more foreshadowing. Phil Spector had a criminal record and in 1972, was arrested and charged for pointing a gun at a woman at the Daisy Club in Beverly Hills. He was fined $200 and sentenced to a year's probation, where he wasn't allowed to have any deadly weapons.

A few years later, in 1975, he and an entertainment lawyer named Marty Machat (who was his connection to Leonard Cohen, as Cohen was one of his clients) argued with a woman at the Beverly Hills Hotel. The valet, Kevin Brown, wanted to know what all the ruckus was about and he ended up being pulled into it when Phil Spector allegedly pointed a revolver in his face and told him to back off before driving off in a silver Cadillac. Afterwards, he pleaded guilty to a misdemeanour firearms charge and was sentenced to two years' probation, once again where he wasn't supposed to possess dangerous weapons. A slap on the wrist once again. There are two different criminal justice systems in America: one for the commoner where they get long sentences and a different one for the rich where they can essentially get away with serious crimes.

Phil Spector retired for real from music in 1980, at the age of forty-one, quite a young age for retirement. That same year, John Lennon was shot just outside the Dakota Building, where he lived, and he was devastated once again, like he was when Lenny Bruce died, and Allen Klein said that dealing with loss was hard for Phil because he knew that at some point that he would die too. Yoko Ono gave him one of John Lennon's guitars as a gift. He became reclusive and very hard to reach, even to his close friends like Nino Tempo, who believed he was reclusive as a status symbol because he had multiple secretaries and of course a mansion with beefed-up security. In 1982, he and his girlfriend Janis Zavala had twins, Nicole and Phillip Jr. Even though the '90s weren't an eventful decade for him, he was starting to be recognised, honoured, and remembered because the '60s were now retro, and at some point, retro is cool again and if music sticks around in culture for so long, it becomes classic. Still, the '90s was a sad time with Phil Spector's son, Phillip Jr., dying of leukaemia, which is said to have killed whatever belief he had left in God, and his mother, Bertha, dying in 1995. On top of that, he was going through a few legal battles with musicians that he didn't pay royalties to, like Darlene Love and The Ronettes. Without the singers, there would be no record, so it was incredibly unfair to not pay these women who sold millions of records.

On Groundhog Day 2003, Phil Spector decided to go out and get drunk, so he hopped between different bars and clubs before eventually landing at The House of Blues and that's where he'd meet his victim, the tall, beautiful, blonde former actress Lana Clarkson, who was working at the club as a VIP lounge hostess because her acting gigs were drying up and she needed to pay the bills. In most murder cases, the victim knows their killer (especially when the victim is a woman), but with Phil Spector, a far from ordinary man, this wasn't an ordinary murder case and not an ordinary trial either. This was the first time Clarkson and Spector had met and it ended violently and tragically. Sadly, Clarkson is better known for her death than her accomplishments in her life, and that's tough for her family. It was a matter of being at the wrong place at the wrong time.

When Lana Clarkson first saw the diminutive, eccentrically dressed former music producer, she didn't know who he was, refused to let him into the VIP lounge, and thought he was some old woman who was lost and didn't belong there. Little did she know, it was Phil Spector and hours later, she'd be dead. At 2:30am on 3 February, she, Spector, and his driver, Adriano De Souza, left the nightclub and Spector invited Clarkson to his Pyrenees Castle in Alhambra. At first, Clarkson didn't want to go back there with him, but he insisted multiple times after giving her a lift to her car, and she decided to hop into the limo to go to the Pyrenees Castle. De Souza dropped the two off and went to the back and waited by the limo for Clarkson to be ready to go home.

Suddenly, at 5am, a gunshot was fired and a startled De Souza tried to see what was going on and then Phil Spector came out with a revolver, blood on his hand, and he said, 'I think I killed somebody'. De Souza first called Spector's assistant Michelle Blaine (daughter of Wrecking Crew session drummer Hal Blaine) before calling 911, when he told the operator, 'I think my boss killed somebody,' and told them that his boss was Phil Spector.

Five officers showed up to the home and in the meantime, Phil Spector tried to clean up the scene and changed his clothes. The cops saw him with his hands shoved in his pockets and asked him to take them out and put his hands above his head. He was uncooperative and then two cops shot him with a taser. As the police entered the home, they saw Lana Clarkson's dead body slumped in a chair with a bloody face and broken teeth. Phil Spector told the police that he didn't mean to shoot Lana Clarkson, it was an accident, and he could explain. The police arrested him straight away and took him to the Alhambra police station.

A drunken Spector shouted insults at the police and when he was being interviewed, he acted like a big shot, talking about how he worked with George Harrison and a bunch of other famous musicians. Coincidentally, the officer questioning him, Derek Gilliam, is the nephew of Monty Python's Flying Circus member, Terry Gilliam. Gilliam knew George Harrison, who was a close friend of Monty Python and helped finance their films.

After hours of questioning and Phil Spector telling tall tales about what happened such as claiming that Lana Clarkson forced herself into his castle and killed herself there. Acting like a megalomaniac, he was released on $1 million bail, thanks to his lawyer, Robert Shapiro (who you may remember as being part of O.J. Simpson's dream team). Since the police were gathering evidence and conducting an investigation at the Pyrenees Castle, he had to stay at a hotel for a few days. He avoided the paparazzi because the police and hotel were nice to him and let him

221

leave through a back entrance. Phil Spector being a rich music producer, you know he was going to spare no expense when it came to putting a legal team together. No way did he want to live the last years of his life in prison, a far cry from the luxuries and opulence he was used to. Yet, he was shooting himself in the foot with his statements to the media and bizarre videos claiming he was innocent. His lawyers tried to get him to stay quiet, but one does not simply tell an egomaniac to shut up. At one point, he arrogantly claimed that the police had no intention of pressing charges against him, and he'd be cleared as soon as his computer was returned to him. An exclusive interview with *Esquire* for their July 2003 issue was sympathetic, favourable, even fawning towards Spector and dismissive of the victim, Clarkson, just seeing her as a pretty blonde aspiring actress when she was more than that. The author, Scott Raab, even wrote that when he saw Phil Spector looking dishevelled and frail, 'I want to take him in my arms and hug him, and so I do. I kiss him on the cheek and, still holding his narrow shoulders, I say, "Phillip, how are you?"' and described him as a 'very nice man'. He also described some of the women who were at his mansion as 'more or less bimbos'. In the interview, Phil Spector said that it's the 'anatomy of a frame-up' and that Lana Clarkson 'kissed the gun'. It's an article to take with a grain of salt, for sure.

Of course, being rich, life on bail was still full of luxury, but even luxuries can't hide the fact that you could be charged with murder, you have a trial coming up, and you could very well find yourself a convicted murderer and sentenced to life in prison. And lo and behold, on 20 November 2003, Phil Spector was charged with murder and the use of a gun in the commission of a violent felony. Why bother with the second charge? Doesn't murder imply the use of a weapon in committing a violent felony? Isn't murder enough? Well, even with a murder conviction, there still may be a possibility of parole, so another charge ensures that they will spend more time behind bars – a sentence enhancement. Phil Spector could have had a speedy trial, but he wanted to bide his time and delay the inevitable.

The Phil Spector trial, or rather trials, was no doubt a trial of the century and the highest profile celebrity murder trial in California since the O.J. Simpson trial in 1995, which was called a trial of the century and the most publicised criminal trial in history. From the 1994 car chase in the Ford Bronco that interrupted coverage of the NBA Finals to Simpson being found not guilty thanks to the 'if it doesn't fit, you must acquit' argument, it was all over people's television sets and what everyone was talking about at the bar, the water cooler, school, wherever! Similarly, the Spector trial was all over people's TV sets; even though the 2007 trial was the only one televised, there was still a lot of news coverage about the 2009 retrial. Even if you're too young to remember it, that photo of Spector in court with the giant blond Afro wig is very memorable, to the point of it being a meme. His legal team managed to convince him that he can't be wearing outlandish wigs, so he kept it 'conservative' with a blond Karen-looking pageboy wig in the first trial and a brown mullet in the second trial.

Behind the scenes for Spector, it was a mess, with him dismissing his lawyers, including Robert Shapiro. Shapiro's replacement, the fiery Leslie Abramson, quit after Spector interrupted her multiple times during a press conference. Mob boss John Gotti's attorney, Bruce Cutler, replaced her. When Spector's legal team tried to have the grand jury testimony sealed, they said he was a public figure and deserved privacy, but the DA said that because Spector's career peak had been in the '60s, many people born after that had no idea who he was. As you can imagine, this was a blow to his ego and he went on a tirade after that, comparing the government to fascists and Hitler, possibly invoking identity politics. In a Trumpian move, he asked the Governor of California at the time, Arnold Schwarzenegger, to help out a 'fellow artist' and called the indictment a travesty of justice. The entitlement that money and fame give a celebrity! Phil Spector was used to getting anything he wanted for so long, but that would end soon. The first trial in 2007 ended in a hung jury and the State of California were certainly not going to let a dangerous long-time abuser be a free man so they re-tried him in 2008 and in 2009 he was convicted of second-degree murder and sentenced to nineteen years to life in prison. He was sixty-nine when he was convicted and there was only a slim chance that he'd live to ninety or even get parole. Of course, he tried to appeal, but each of his three appeals was a failure.

While being behind bars meant that Phil Spector wouldn't get to keep his wigs and fancy clothes, it still didn't stop him from being a weirdo and acting out. YouTuber California Convictions, a former inmate who served seventeen years in the California penal system, has told many crazy stories about Phil Spector from the perspective of an eyewitness. Allegedly, Phil Spector would often get visits from his wife, Rachelle, but he would be ungrateful and always yell at her every time she visited and at every visit Rachelle would spend as much money as she could on the vending machine to buy snacks for her then husband, who would hoard them, refuse to share, and flex in front of the other inmates. And he acted just as bratty as he would on the outside when he didn't get his way or things went wrong, like when he didn't have enough money on his books to purchase the things he wanted from commissary. He threw a tantrum, stomping, trying to shout even with a raspy voice, and would say the most unlikeable phrase, 'Don't you know who I am?', and generally displayed a lot of insecurity. While in prison, Phil Spector would allegedly buy morphine from inmates and even tried to hire bodyguards, whom he would pay $180 a month for twelve hours a day of work, a lowballing cheapskate. In California prisons, boots are a prized possession with the most expensive and coveted ones being $75, but medical shoes are allowed in medical wings of the prison and those are more expensive and coveted, being worth $300. They're not pretty, though. They're thick, plastic, white shoes custom-made to the prisoner's measurements with the prisoner's name and prisoner number written on the back. They were a status symbol. Phil Spector being old, he bought a pair of those shoes and a prisoner stole them from him. As you can expect, he threw a fit and yelled as loudly as he could.

One last story about Phil Spector's time in prison. As you know, aspiring musician/cult leader/convicted murderer Charles Manson was also locked up in California after the Tate–LaBianca murders and got a life sentence. When he found out Phil Spector was going to jail, he of course tried to reach out to him about making music together. Both served time in Corcoran, but at separate institutions, so this collaboration wouldn't have been possible. Spector's ex-wife, Rachelle, said that Manson's contacting of her husband was creepy and that he wasn't interested.

Phil Spector died on 16 January 2021 of COVID. He had tested positive for COVID the previous month, December 2020, and was taken to hospital on New Year's Eve and intubated sometime in January. He was eighty-one and would have been eligible for parole in 2024. Even at the end of his life, he maintained he was innocent, claiming that Lana Clarkson killed herself with his gun. Spector's daughter, Nicole, believes him and claims that he was 'easy prey' for prosecutors and that evidence shows that he didn't commit a murder at his home because there was no physical evidence that he pulled the trigger, according to Spector's defence lawyers. Allegedly, Nicole Spector is trying to get the Innocence Project to work to exonerate him, according to a Sky News interview with Sheena Joyce, director of a Sky Original documentary called *Spector: The Man, The Music, The Murder*.

CHAPTER 20

Sid Vicious (1978)

NB: The reason I decided to put the Sid Vicious chapter after Jim Gordon and Phil Spector's chapters is because while he was arrested and charged with the murder of his girlfriend, Nancy Spungen, he was never tried because he died only months after Nancy died – and usually murder trials take place many months or even years after the murder. Because the presumption of innocence (innocent until proven guilty) is a legal principle in America, we can't say that Sid Vicious murdered Nancy Spungen for sure. However, because this case is so famous, I think it has to be included somewhere in this book. There will be a lot of use of 'allegedly' because Sid Vicious was not tried or convicted. There were also no eyewitnesses, unlike the case of Joe Meek whose assistant, Patrick Pink, witnessed the murder-suicide, as discussed in chapter 15.

ABOUT SID VICIOUS

Music and style trends are responses to what came before them and punk was a response to a few previous subcultures and styles of music: hippies and psychedelic rock, glam/glitter rock, and progressive rock. Punk is a lot simpler and more back to basics than these genres. It rejected prog rock's pretentiousness and glam rock's excessiveness. While both hippies and punks were political, punk rock was bolder and louder about its anti-establishment message. Punks were also frustrated with the hippie culture and found it fake. Punk also took some retro influences from '50s rockabilly and rock and roll and the fashion of the time, although punk turned it on its head and took it leaps and bounds further, always pushing the envelope. Politically, the 'swinging party' of the '60s was over, or rather for the working class there never was a party. The Labour government were doing typical establishment things by making big promises to their working-class base, only later to betray them by not actually doing anything, and that opened the door for the Tories to take over by using the working class as pawns and also not caring about them, rinse and repeat, and you can see where we are now. In the mid 1970s, just before punk took off, there was a recession and inflation and whenever politics is a shitstorm, that means riots, strikes, and yes, protest songs too.

Punk rock started around the same time on both sides of the Atlantic with the major scenes being in London and New York. One of the best known of the British punk bands of the '70s were The Sex Pistols, a controversial band known for the diss track to the monarchy 'God Save The Queen' – said to be the 'most heavily censored record in British history'. What's more punk rock than your album being banned by the BBC and pretty much every radio station across the country? And that was far from their only controversy. They'd swear on TV appearances too. Most notably, they performed their anti-establishment songs on a boat on the Thames during Queen Elizabeth II's Silver Jubilee, as part of a publicity stunt organised by their manager, Malcolm McLaren, and Virgin Records owner Richard Branson. As they passed by the Houses of Parliament, they played 'Anarchy in the UK'. Ironically, as the police neared their boat, they were playing 'No Fun' and, just like that, the party was over and some of the Sex Pistols' entourage were arrested.

While The Sex Pistols were a short-lived band with a turbulent history, breaking up just after their disastrous US tour and only releasing one album, *Never Mind The Bollocks, Here's The Sex Pistols*, there's no doubt they had an impact on rock and roll history.

The Sex Pistols had working-class roots in founding members Steve Jones and Paul Cook and lead singer Johnny Rotten – who was from a working-class immigrant Irish family. Early on, the band members used stolen equipment and instruments because they couldn't afford them and they liked the rush of stealing things. Rotten and Vicious were classmates at Hackney Technical College in the early '70s and in those days Vicious was a big David Bowie fan who loved fashion.

Sid Vicious is obviously not his real name, pretty obvious stage name, but that's because Simon John Ritchie (although some media refer to him as John Simon Ritchie) is a kinda boring, not punk rock name, and in rock, it's all about the image and marketing and a name is important to that. His name came from bandmate Johnny Rotten, who took the name Sid from his hamster (named after Syd Barrett) and Vicious from the Lou Reed song.

Sid Vicious, then known as Simon, was born on 10 May 1957 in Lewisham, which is part of London. His mother, Anne Beverley, was in the Army and at one point moved to Ibiza with her baby. His biological father was a Grenadier Guard at Buckingham Palace, but he abandoned Anne and Simon. One thing that is important to note is that Anne also used drugs and was said to be a drug mule or even a dealer, and this was definitely a bad influence on her son and enabled his drug habits later on. According to Eileen Polk, who worked at punk clothing store Revenge and was a friend of Sid Vicious, when Sid was in jail in New York, his mother would sneak in heroin and she had this trick where she'd hide it in her metal-covered boots, which would set off the metal detector, and with a little sleight of hand, the drugs would be moved to the cuff of her trousers, then she'd walk through the metal detector and not be searched for drugs. It's even said that Anne's actions ultimately led to her son's demise. Photographer and close friend to Sid Vicious, Peter Gravelle, said that Sid's mother not only bought his last dose of heroin that ended up killing him, but she also administered it, the reasoning being to prevent him from going to prison.

Sid Vicious was always a rebel and didn't really like school, except for art class, but he left art school because he found it rigid. He also struggled with his mental health at school and when he talked about suicide, he was pulled out of class to go to counselling and he brought his friend, John Wardle (aka Jah Wobble), who joked that he 'might as well end it all' and in response, Sid nodded, startling his friend. At times, Sid was a squatter living in run-down Victorian dwellings with his friend, Johnny Rotten, who was kicked out of his parents' house for chopping his hair short and dying it green.

The two liked to hang out on Kings Road, especially around the thrift shop Acme Attractions and Vivienne Westwood and Malcolm McLaren's rocker/Teddy Boy clothing store Too Fast To Live, Too Young To Die, which was later renamed SEX and became a fetish fashion shop selling latex clothing and bondage gear. Malcolm McLaren and Vivienne Westwood had travelled to New York in the early '70s, where they saw the New York Dolls and they liked what they saw, and they saw the potential and appeal of punk and so they became affiliated with them, outfitting them in outrageous stage wear, and even managing them for a short period of time. Malcolm McLaren found music to be lucrative and he wanted to form a group that he could manage, and what better place to find band members than in his shop? Fashion is just one piece of the puzzle. If you want to sell a subculture, you gotta have both image and sound.

Around the same time, Chrissie Hynde worked there and even tried to convince Johnny Rotten and then Sid Vicious to marry her for a visa, but Rotten pulled out and when she and Sid Vicious went to the registry office, they saw it was closed and Sid Vicious couldn't go the next day because he got in trouble, something that would happen a lot in his twenty-one years living on this planet.

One day, while hanging out at Malcolm McLaren's shop, McLaren asked Johnny Rotten if he could sing and from there, he was recruited as The Sex Pistols' lead singer. Johnny Rotten invited Sid Vicious to join the band as a bassist after original bassist Glen Matlock was fired for liking The Beatles when everyone else in the band hated them. Before that, he had played with other bands, once playing drums at Siouxsie and the Banshees' first gig at the 100 Club Punk Festival in 1976 and he was a member of The Flowers of Romance. He nearly joined The Damned and could have been their lead singer, but he didn't go to the audition. This led to some violence because Vicious believed that he was sabotaged. When The Damned played their set at the 100 Club Punk Festival, Sid Vicious allegedly threw a glass towards their singer, Dave Vanian, but pieces of it hit a girl in the eye, injuring her. He was arrested and in custody at the Ashford Remand Centre, passing the time reading a book about Charles Manson that Vivienne Westwood had lent him.

John Lydon said of Sid Vicious's father and the band signing their record deal in Julien Temple's *The Filth and the Fury: The Voices of The Sex Pistols*, 'And you know the EMI signing, when we did it that day [in front of Buckingham Palace], Sid's old man could have been one of those guards inside. Heaven. Imagine that Sid's signing a very expensive contract while his old man's on guard inside the fence. It's genius.'

Sid Vicious wasn't known for his bass playing – in fact he didn't really play on the album at all, not only because of his lack of skills but because he was ill with hepatitis (from drug use), but he did make a pretty big contribution to punk by inventing the pogo dance, as a way to mock poseurs who came to Sex Pistols shows but who weren't part of the punk scene. The pogo dance is pretty self-explanatory: you jump up and down like a pogo stick with your arms held tightly to your sides. It's said to be a precursor to moshing, so Sid Vicious really did have some cultural impact.

Now that we have some background information on Sid Vicious and The Sex Pistols, let's talk about his relationship with Nancy Spungen and the murder of Nancy Spungen.

THE RELATIONSHIP AND THE MURDER

The sad thing with murder cases is that (barring situations where there are witnesses) there are only two people who really know what went down, and one of them is not alive to tell the story. And in the case of Sid and Nancy, neither can tell their story. All we can do here is talk about what we know happened and be as objective as possible.

In a lot of books about The Sex Pistols and news articles about her murder, Nancy Spungen is portrayed as a bimbo, slut, junkie, social climber, and someone who wanted to sleep with rock stars and no one around Sid Vicious seemed to like her. Kind of a Yoko Ono effect, all the blame goes to the wife or girlfriend, it's a misogynistic trope. The characterisation of Nancy in the media is a one-dimensional caricature and it doesn't do her justice and it's very hurtful to her family, who loved her very much, and people victim-blame them too for what happened to Nancy. She wasn't perfect; no one is. She deserved better though.

Nancy Spungen was born on 27 February 1958 in Philadelphia to middle-class Jewish parents Frank and Deborah Spungen, who worked as a travelling salesman and an owner of an organic food store respectively. She was raised in Philadelphia and a suburb called Huntingdon Valley. She nearly died of oxygen deprivation because she was choking on her own umbilical cord when she was born. Her skin was turning blue, but luckily doctors saved her life by giving baby Nancy a heart stimulant and blood transfusions and she appeared not to suffer brain damage. Doctors even said baby Nancy was a fighter, full of life, kicking and screaming during the procedure. She wanted to live and so eight days later, mother and baby were cleared to go home and were discharged from hospital.

However, she continued to have health problems and her mother described her birth as being 'neurologically traumatic'.

She was a firstborn and her mother was only twenty years old and finishing up her senior year at the University of Pennsylvania (she worked hard and ended up getting her degree too) when she gave birth to her. Deborah was the only pregnant student on campus, because in those days few women went to university and if you got pregnant, typically you dropped out to become a stay-at-home mother. The pregnancy was unplanned and Deborah's husband, Frank, was stationed in Fort Knox with the Army Reserves since she found out she was pregnant. The young couple had big dreams of getting good jobs in New York City. Her family were upset that she got pregnant so young because she had a lot of potential and a bright future ahead. Instead, life had different plans for the Spungens. And a year and a half after Nancy was born, Deborah gave birth to another daughter, Susan (Suzy), because why not have another kid? And two years after that, they had a son, David.

Deborah Spungen speculated that Nancy's traumatic birth led to her self-medicating with heroin and other drugs ever since her teenage years and she expected her daughter to die young, imagining it in her head for years and years. It wasn't a matter of if, but when. She was hoping that when her daughter died at a young age, it would at least be a dignified death, but that was far from the case. Instead, it was violent, she was victim-blamed, became a laughingstock on national television, and there was a whole media circus surrounding it with the Spungens constantly receiving phone calls, but we'll talk more about that later in this section.

Nancy was a bright girl who excelled in school. She was very articulate from a young age with an excellent vocabulary. Her motor skills weren't as strong though and it frustrated her, leading to her acting out. It was like a brain–body mismatch and it wasn't her fault. She was so strong academically that she could do schoolwork that was grade levels ahead of her, and she skipped third grade. Starting at the age of nine, she had an interest in rock and roll that started with her listening to recordings of the Broadway musical, *Hair*. From there, she got into The Beatles, The Doors, Cream, The Rolling Stones, The Who, Jimi Hendrix, Janis Joplin, Jefferson Airplane, and Led Zeppelin. She also loved reading books by authors like Sylvia Plath, Kurt Vonnegut, J.D. Salinger, Tennessee Williams, and F. Scott Fitzgerald. At just ten years old, she had an interest in social issues because she liked reading the news: anti-war and pro-environment. As a teenager, she got into photography and developing her own photographs. At fifteen, she got accepted to the University of Colorado and started attending when she was sixteen.

But she had many behavioural issues dating back to her early childhood. As a baby, she would cry constantly and at just three months old, her doctor prescribed her phenobarbital, which Deborah described as an 'easy solution', but one that 'covered up whatever the real problem was'. She threw tantrums frequently as a toddler. She had night terrors. She struggled to make friends. She'd bully her siblings, both verbally and physically. She despised her father and would cuss at and insult him frequently. She'd have hallucinations, seizures, and psychotic episodes which were dangerous to herself and others. She would self-harm. At age eleven, she started threatening suicide. Still, doctors insisted Nancy was normal and that whenever she'd get violent, she was just 'acting out'. It took a long time for her to receive a diagnosis of schizophrenia. Eventually, her parents put her in a special boarding school for children struggling with mental illnesses, but it was a struggle finding one that would accept her. For a few semesters, her parents sent her to a therapeutic boarding school three hours away in Connecticut. While Nancy was away, Deborah opened a health foods store, then sold it, and worked for Western Union in sales. At thirteen, while at a different boarding school for kids with mental illnesses, she started smoking marijuana and taking drugs.

At fourteen, she ran away to New York City. At sixteen, she stole her mum's car after failing her driving test three times.

Nancy's behavioural issues were so bad that her father would often leave the house and go to New York City for days at a time, leaving her mother stuck with the kids at home, and never really able to go out because the family couldn't afford a babysitter. It put a strain on their marriage, and at one point, they were discussing divorce. Both Frank and Deborah had affairs. And in those days, you couldn't just talk about your marriage problems, it was gauche to air out dirty laundry like that.

During her first semester in the summer of 1974, Nancy flourished at the University of Colorado. She was happy to be living in the real world independently, but when she returned home it wasn't long before she was back to being like her old self. When she returned for the autumn semester, she was partying and hanging out with what her parents described as 'street people', young people who weren't students, but rather people who hung around the university and sold drugs. It wasn't long before she was arrested with her new friends, who would steal ski equipment and store it in her dorm room, and for buying drugs from an undercover federal agent. She ended up expelled from the university because of it and had to leave the state in order to avoid prosecution, as a deal made with the juvenile officer, but she didn't know about the deal and her father only told her she was going home. She was furious and made her father out to be evil. Understandable, because it's a harsh punishment for a teenage girl and drug use shouldn't be considered a crime. At that point, she was done with university and in a conversation with her parents about her future she made a prediction about how her life would end up, saying that she would die in a blaze of glory before her twenty-first birthday, and it would end up a headline. Eerie for her parents to think about after she was killed. Getting a job? She tried but found it difficult and never managed to keep a job for long.

At seventeen, she determined that she wanted to be a rock and roll groupie because she loved the lifestyle and what rock and roll stood for: rebellion, anger, self-expression, individuality. She often went to rock concerts and would get to go backstage and meet bands. The most famous band she met were Queen; she got to go backstage and talk to them about music and party with them. She apparently partied (and claimed to have hooked up) with members of Bad Company, Aerosmith, The Who, The Allman Brothers Band, The J. Geils Band, and The Pretty Things. Her friends were sceptical of her stories.

Months before her eighteenth birthday, she had had enough of Philadelphia. If she wanted to work, it would have been in the music industry and there was plenty of work in that field in New York City. She moved there and her parents helped support her financially, but she spent the money on drugs and they refused to give her money because they didn't want to enable her drug habit. For the first couple of months, she would frequently call her parents while under the influence of drugs, but it wasn't long before she got immersed in the punk scene and would frequently be at the famous clubs Max's Kansas City and CBGB where she'd see bands like Blondie, The Ramones, and The New York Dolls perform. She started working as a go-go dancer near Times Square, making $200–300 a night, enough to fuel her heroin addiction. Even though her parents were ashamed, they still kept in contact with her and would visit, as Philadelphia wasn't too far from New York. They tried their best to get her to kick heroin for good, but she relapsed.

At the end of 1976, punk was becoming popular in London and Nancy really wanted to go there. All her friends had been there and she wanted to see it for herself. And so, in the spring of 1977, she was clean and on her way to London. Contrary to urban legend, she didn't pay for her ticket to London through sex work; her parents helped her out because they wanted to see her dream come true.

By that time, The New York Dolls, whom she had been following in New York, had broken up and its members had gone on to different bands. She travelled there to follow Johnny Thunders and Jerry Nolan of punk band The Heartbreakers, but she ended up falling in love with a musician in another band. She met The Sex Pistols at a party, as they were on their rise to stardom, England's latest sensation. Johnny Rotten said in his autobiography that he fobbed Nancy off on Sid because he thought they were perfect for each other, describing her as a 'filthy cunt'. Nancy often complained to her family about no one liking her, and her cries weren't unfounded; Johnny Rotten said that no one in the London scene liked her and everyone saw through her. She had a reputation for whinging all the time and that got on a lot of people's nerves. Chrissie Hynde of The Pretenders described her as an opportunist and a bad influence on Sid Vicious. Nancy's mother said that while Nancy claimed to have befriended a lot of musicians, none of them contacted the family to offer condolences, so either the friendships were unrequited, not as close as Nancy thought, or they were too embarrassed to say anything because of Nancy's notoriety.

Sid and Nancy were basically a punk rock Romeo & Juliet, star-crossed lovers, their lives ending in tragedy. Not a relationship to be romanticised. It's weird seeing young classic rock fans waxing poetic about their relationship, it wasn't pretty, it wasn't romantic. Not relationship goals. If you'd rather hear it from a source close to them, their friend, Eileen Polk, said in a 2011 interview with Dig Gallery that their romance would not have had a happy ending. In her words, 'Sid and Nancy were the most self-destructive people I ever met. I think that they actually believed that they were supposed to act the way they did; to play some kind of role as "punks". They thought that they were supposed to get totally inebriated and get into fights and smash things up. They played the roles of disintegrating rock star criminal and moll to perfection. I don't think under these conditions they were meant to live very long.'

She described their relationship as being like a 'nuclear reaction' and that both of them were suicidal and '[they] should have gotten more help from people who cared.'

Sid and Nancy quickly fell in love. According to Johnny Rotten, Nancy was Sid's first girlfriend and he was probably a virgin when he met her. After a period of couch-surfing with friends, the couple moved in with Sid's mother. What the two had in common was they were young, into drugs, constantly getting in trouble, and always begged for money. In total, Nancy's stay in London lasted eighteen months before she returned to New York with Sid, who cared more about having fun and enjoying the perks of being a rock star than actually making music or practising bass guitar. He allegedly beat Nancy, breaking her nose and tearing her ear off and once dangled her out the window of a hotel they were living in. She wasn't the only target of his violence. He beat up *NME* journalist Nick Kent with a bike chain in the 100 Club. While out on bail, Sid Vicious beat up Patti Smith's brother, Todd. Whether or not Sid murdered Nancy, we'll never know for sure, but Sid Vicious's history of violence didn't help him and if he had lived and it had gone to trial, it wouldn't have helped his case.

The Sex Pistols went to America for a tour in January 1978 but Malcolm McLaren banned Nancy from the tour, and like a lot of things in Sid Vicious's life, it was a disaster. You thought The Kinks' 1965 US tour was a fiasco, get ready for The Sex Pistols. The whole thing was weird and very disorganised with the tour all being organised at short notice.

They only played a few dates in the US, mostly in the South in places like Atlanta, Memphis, San Antonio, Baton Rouge, Dallas, and Tulsa but with one date in San Francisco. Not exactly cities known for punk scenes, just really weird choices, but there's a reason behind this. According to Jon Savage's book *England's Dreaming*, Malcolm McLaren wanted to make unorthodox choices because he hated how incestuous the music industry was in America with LA and New York as its centres. When he went to the US earlier in the decade, he felt excluded. He also thought that the Deep South was more real than America's largest cities and punk rock would shock the audiences more there. The Sex Pistols were supposed to play dates up north, but they had trouble getting visas because of the band members having criminal records: Steve Jones – theft and breaking and entering; Sid Vicious – assaults; and Johnny Rotten – possession of amphetamines. Luckily, the band had the might of a major record label, Warner Bros, behind them and their attorneys worked hard to get The Sex Pistols a visa for the US, but there were strings attached: it would only be valid for two weeks and the band's label had to post a surety of $1 million on the group's behaviour.

Musically, the gigs were awful: they had their British tour manager named Boogie doing the sound instead of a professional sound engineer; Johnny Rotten's voice was flat, the guitars weren't in tune, and rhythm section – what rhythm section? You don't go to a Sex Pistols gig for the music. Instead, you got violence and Sid Vicious shouting homophobic slurs (likely saying them to be edgy, I can't say for sure that his intentions were homophobic, but still not a good look) and spitting at the audience. Unprofessional behaviour. At the end of their last gig in San Francisco, Johnny Rotten appropriately left the audience with these last words, 'Ever get the feeling you've been cheated?'

Off stage, Sid Vicious was constantly looking for drugs and became very dependent on heroin. Johnny Rotten fell ill. Days after the tour concluded, the band broke up. Sid returned to London and later, he and Nancy went to Paris for a month before coming back to London. Sid Vicious's fifteen minutes of fame were pretty much over as the punk world had moved onto better bands. In August of 1978, Sid and Nancy travelled back to America and Sid met Nancy's family for the first time. Her family were shocked at their appearances: pale, gaunt, tired, and wearing loud punk clothes. Nancy was excited about coming back to New York with Sid and she became his manager and she seemed really happy.

When her parents dropped them off at the train station, that was the last time Deborah saw Nancy alive. Frank saw her briefly in New York, dropping off things for them.

After they left Philadelphia, they went to New York, where they moved into the famous Hotel Chelsea, which is linked to many classic rockers: Bob Dylan, Jim Morrison, Jimi Hendrix, Janis Joplin, Leonard Cohen, the list goes on. While in New York, Nancy tried to help find Sid gigs, but his music career was pretty much over and he only got a couple of opportunities to perform at Max's Kansas City. The audience came for the notoriety, but they didn't have anything to stay for, as Sid's not much of a musician. They were broke, sick, and taking lots of drugs. Mentally, Sid was not doing well and Nancy suffered beatings.

Just after Yom Kippur, Deborah got the call that she feared the most, from the NYPD. Nancy was dead and Sid Vicious had been arrested. Nancy died on 12 October 1978. What happened?

In the last twenty-four hours of Nancy's life, she and Sid were in their room at the Hotel Chelsea, just a normal day, visitors were coming in and out. Sid took Tuinal barbiturate tablets and he was pretty much out of it and fell asleep at 1am, with Nancy next to him. The two had an argument, but it's not known what it was about. On the morning of 12 October, Nancy was stabbed in her abdomen with a hunting knife and went to the bathroom, with blood dripping on the bed and on the bathroom floor. She was moaning, which neighbours heard. Hours later, Sid Vicious woke up, stumbled to the bathroom, saw Nancy bleeding, pulled out the knife and rinsed it, and called the front desk asking for help before shouting in the hallways, 'Something's happened to my girl'. Afterwards, he was acting bizarrely, wandering around the hallways and even initially confessing to the murder. He reportedly told police, 'I did it because I'm a dog. A dirty dog,' but he later retracted the confession, claiming he remembered nothing. He was arrested and indicted that day. Five days later, he was released on $50,000 bail, posted by his record label. One condition of his bail was that he couldn't leave the state and that meant he couldn't go to Nancy's funeral, which was held in Philadelphia. He was sad that he couldn't go and the only place he wanted to be was with Nancy. In an interview after he was released from jail, when asked where he wanted to be he said, 'Under the ground,' and nodded when asked if he was serious. He was even hospitalised for a suicide attempt after butting himself with a smashed light bulb. He tried to jump out of a window at Bellevue Hospital, screaming something like, 'I want to be with my Nancy!'

Sid definitely had the support of a lot of people. Mick Jagger paid Sid's lawyers, according to Johnny Rotten, and he never made a spectacle of it. Malcolm McLaren said that Sid was capable of anything, but that he 'didn't think that he could kill someone, especially his girlfriend, unless it was a botched double suicide.' Chrissie Hynde, on the other hand, said that 'no one was particularly surprised' to hear that Sid was arrested for allegedly stabbing Nancy.

In December 1978, Sid Vicious was back in jail. This time, for smashing Todd Smith, Patti Smith's brother, across the face with a beer bottle at a Skafish gig at Hurrah's. According to a blog post that Jim Skafish wrote, Todd was just working at the Skafish gig, watching the stage to make sure that no equipment malfunctioned and that the gig went well; his usual job was working as his sister's road manager. Sid was flirting with Todd's girlfriend, Tara (a drum roadie for Skafish), and Todd politely told him to stop flirting until after the show and so he attacked him. It was an unprovoked attack and Todd was taken to hospital, where he received multiple stitches. Skafish's road manager, Jimy Sohns (former singer of '60s group The Shadows of Knight), punched Sid in the face and kicked him out. This was Sid's last public appearance, as Sid was arrested again and sent to Rikers Island for fifty-five days. During that time, he was forced into a detox programme and he suffered from withdrawal symptoms. Rikers Island is notorious for being basically hell, and allegedly Sid was attacked and raped in jail.

He got out of jail on 1 February and the next day he died of a heroin overdose in a Greenwich Village apartment, as earlier stated, likely given to him by his mother, who was an enabler for his heroin addiction. At the apartment, he and friends celebrated him getting out of jail. Sid had been clean for such a long time and missed heroin and so he took a really big dose. His friends thought he should go to hospital, but his mum at first refused to take him to hospital because she didn't want a media circus or for him to go back to Rikers Island. We don't know what was running through his mind, but maybe he associated heroin with his punk heyday and his relationship with Nancy and all he wanted was to be with her.

After Sid Vicious died, he was cremated and his mother, Anne, asked Nancy's mother, Deborah, if he could be buried next to her, but she refused; it was a Jewish cemetery and Sid was a gentile. Anne drove to Philadelphia and scattered his ashes over Nancy's grave. There was no funeral because no funeral home in New York wanted to touch him because of his reputation.

There are a lot of questionable things and holes in this case. Why was Sid the only one arrested? Why did the police not question all the other people who were in Sid and Nancy's room on 11–12 October? It also doesn't help that in those days, they didn't have the forensic DNA technology we have now.

It makes sense why so many people don't trust the police. They don't always fully investigate and they're not always focused on getting the right person. They just want to make an arrest and put someone in jail; who cares if it's the wrong person? There's a reason why organisations like The Innocence Project exist. We also can't forget the racism and classism in the police and the respectability politics in the system. While Nancy was from a middle-class (you could say upper middle-class) background, she was deeply involved in the punk subculture, which was against the mainstream and to the establishment, punks (or anyone from an alternative subculture) don't look 'respectable'. Nancy's parents said that the police mocked their daughter right in front of them, which was incredibly unprofessional. So it's not exactly surprising that the police may not have done the best investigation; they probably just saw her as a 'whore' not deserving of respect. The media also painted a one-dimensional caricature of Nancy, which was hurtful to her and her family. Sid, on the other hand, was a working-class foreigner also involved in the punk subculture, he had a reputation for violence and wasn't 'respectable'.

CHAPTER 21

Keith Moon (1970)

Note: The reason I listed Keith Moon and Les McKeown at the end of this section is because while they both accidentally ran people over with a car, they were not convicted murderers. These were both accidents. Still, I find this worth talking about in a book about classic rock and true crime.

ABOUT KEITH MOON

The Who are easily one of the most important classic rock bands, period. Not just one of one of the most important British Invasion groups. Since we already talked about Roger Daltrey and The Who's history in chapter 4, we'll just talk about Keith Moon. Now, Keith Moon's reputation was for being a partier, but there was much more to him than that. He wasn't just Moon the Loon, he was one of rock and roll's greatest drummers. A superstar. Not a garden variety drummer who kept the beat, but one who stole the show and drove the band along. Gone too soon. Tony Fletcher, author of *Dear Boy: The Life of Keith Moon*, described him well, 'I like to think of him as a comet, blazing through and enlightening our earthly experience while burning himself out in the process.' He shone bright and there really was no substitute for him. There really was no Who without Keith Moon.

Keith Moon was born Keith John Moon on 23 August 1946 (although some records say 1947, but that's not true and it's common in show business for celebrities to lie about their age to seem younger) to working-class parents Alfred (Alf) and Kathleen (Kit) Moon and they couldn't have been more different from their son. They were quiet, peaceful, thrifty, modest, and didn't even drink. Alf served in WWII and afterwards worked various blue-collar jobs and Kit was a stay-at-home mother. Keith had a sister who was three years younger named Linda and another sister who was twelve years younger named Lesley, so he was the only boy in the Moon household.

Keith Moon was part of that rebellious baby boomer generation, rebelling against everything the older generation stood for: modesty, frugality, conformity. Instead, Keith showed off, made and spent lots of money, and stood out with his over-the-top persona and image. Even with all of that, he loved his parents and gave back to them by buying them their council home.

As a child, Keith was a hyper, silly, loveable prankster who loved music. He would sit next to an old record player for hours listening to jazz music. He was born to be a star because he loved being the centre of attention. In those days, psychology was rudimentary compared to the modern day and Keith might very well have had something like ADD/ADHD or, later on in life, depression, but in those days, you didn't go to therapy unless you had severe issues – it was stigmatised, and adults just thought hyperactivity was a phase.

In school, he had a reputation for being the class clown and for not caring about academics, so he did poorly in his eleven-plus exam and was put in a secondary modern school, which is where the poorest-performing students went, and those who went to those schools usually ended up in back-breaking blue-collar jobs.

Oddly enough, as outspoken and extroverted as he seemed, he was a bit of a loner, according to his mother.

Around the time Keith Moon sat his eleven-plus, rock and roll was starting to take over the airwaves, captivating the youth, and changing pop culture forever. Every week new rock songs would come out. Keith, like many kids his age, was spellbound and he'd play all the rock and roll hits on repeat. His other big interest at that time was comedy; he was a big fan of the radio show *The Goons*, and he would frequently imitate the characters of that show. His teachers didn't think much of him with his art teacher calling him 'retarded artistically, idiotic in other respects', his PE teacher saying he was 'keen at times but goonery [in reference to the radio show] seems to come before everything', and his music teacher saying he had 'great ability, but must guard against tendency to show off'. His strongest subject was English, where he got a B. He was a talented and charismatic boy, but school seemed to be the last place he wanted to be. Reading and sitting still in class didn't work for him, he was more the kind of person to be creative and do things hands on, like playing with home science kits and blowing the fuses at home, a precursor to him blowing up his drum kits and throwing cherry bombs in toilets. He ultimately left school at fourteen.

Music was an important outlet for him and when he was twelve, he picked up his first instrument, the bugle, which he played as part of the local Sea Cadet Corps. A strange choice for Keith considering his rebellious nature and that the Sea Cadets were to the Navy as the JROTC are to the military in the US. He also tried playing trumpet around that time, but he wasn't good at it, but he didn't care because he'd make a show of how bad he was.

Soon, he was assigned to play drums and that's where he found his niche. He loved the noise. Because there was no British rock and roll drummer to be a blueprint for Keith, he looked at jazz drummers, especially Gene Krupa, who was his idol. As for rock and roll, Keith really liked Carlo Little of Screaming Lord Sutch &

The Savages, who he saw live and took a few lessons from, boldly asking him for lessons after a gig. Later, he got into surf rock music and became fascinated with California.

Like a lot of the classic rock greats, he looked at classical training, reading music, and learning theory and thought, *Ain't nobody got time for that.* The rock and roll approach is DIY, self-taught, finding your own style, being a master of your craft, and shaping the history of the instrument you play. After leaving school, he got behind a drum set and played like a madman, hitting everything in sight; he had passion, but he just needed some polish and a drum kit of his own and one day he bought a blue Premier drum kit on hire purchase. His style was freestyle, wild, loud, and crazy. Not tight like Carlo Little, but that was the appeal. It was entertaining and different. Rob Lemon described him as being '… a real character. Madness bordering on genius.'

As a teenager, Keith played with different groups like The Escorts and Clyde Burns and The Beachcombers, and there's a funny story with the latter, who were a successful touring band. Keith was only sixteen and came along to the audition with his father and the band were all way older than him and sceptical of this teenage boy who claimed to be a good drummer, to the point where they turned him away. But Keith Moon didn't just have talent, he also had nerve, and he stood his ground and auditioned for them. And this quick learner blew them away with his drumming abilities, confidence, and knowledge of all the songs. Moonie would end up in the band that made him a household name in a similar way and it would only be a year and a half later. Oddly enough in his Beachcombers days, he didn't really drink and he didn't sleep around and it was only in 1964 that he started taking uppers. Far from the Moon the Loon we know and love. But he was very much a flamboyant, over-the-top showman and had the guts to steal the spotlight. He didn't just keep the beat, he also played drums along with the guitar riffs.

The Who, like The Beatles, had all the puzzle pieces of a great band, except a drummer; that would come last and complete the puzzle. They had gone through a bunch of drummers, but they didn't find one that was the right fit. The Who started off as an R&B-influenced rock band and their trademark was having a loud sound and a memorable stage act. Keith Moon was driven when it came to furthering his music career, prioritising it, while his Beachcombers bandmates were complacent, happy working comfortable day jobs and playing music as a side gig. In order to get better as a musician, you must fully dedicate yourself to it and it was time for Keith to spread his wings and move on to another band, one with ambitions and one that performed original songs, because that was the direction the music scene was moving towards.

Keith and The Beachcombers crossed paths with a young group from Acton/Ealing called The Detours (who would later be known as The Who), made up of three students from Acton County Grammar School: Roger Daltrey, John Entwistle, and Pete Townshend. The drummer, Doug Sandom, wasn't a good fit for the band with him being older, married, working a day job, and not being as ambitious as the rest of the group. The Who had a residency at the Oldfield and Keith Moon was a fan, appearing at their gigs. The legend goes that he told The Who that he could drum better than their drummer and played a few songs on stage with them and the gig was his; well, that's probably how a *Bohemian Rhapsody*-like biopic would tell it, but the reality was less sexy. On a quiet day, he asked the Oldfield manager, Louis Hunt, where The Who were and he told them where they rehearsed and he got the job.

The Beachcombers knew it was inevitable that Keith was going to move on to bigger and better things. Keith Moon was exactly the drummer The Who needed and from there, stardom was right around the corner and it was soon evident that The Who were one of rock and roll's best bands with each member being a revolutionary: Roger Daltrey for his voice and rock god stage presence, Pete Townshend for his songwriting and guitar showmanship, and the rhythm section of John Entwistle and Keith Moon: revolutionising the bass and drums and being among the best of all time in their instruments. Keith particularly revolutionised rock drumming by using a bigger drum kit than all the other rock drummers: two kick drums, at least three mounted toms and floor toms, and four crash cymbals – easily dwarfing the typical drum kit. Together they were one of rock and roll's best live acts. The other British Invasion groups may have been good, but no other band had Entwistle and Moon. Any band's rhythm sections that were on the same tier came out after The Who: Cream, Led Zeppelin, Yes, Rush, bands like that.

In 1964, The Who briefly changed their name to The High Numbers and had a mod image given to them by their young mod manager, Peter Meaden. The mod subculture was at its peak at the time and what better thing to market to these mod youth than some loud R&B-inspired rock and roll complete with smart pop-art-looking clothes and a memorable stage act full of character… and smashed guitars. As The High Numbers, they released two singles, 'I'm The Face' (based on Slim Harpo's 'Got Love if You Want It') and 'Zoot Suit' (based on The Showmen's 'Country Fool'). Meaden wrote the lyrics to both of those singles, which ended up flopping because they came across as contrived, even though the musicianship was great. But even as The High Numbers, they were still opening for some of the biggest acts in Britain and touring nationally.

Later in 1964, filmmakers Kit Lambert and Chris Stamp became the band's managers after buying Meaden out for £200 and renaming the band The Who, but they were fired a decade later for the usual, screwing around with The Who's money and being bad managers, causing rifts between band members.

As for the mod look and lifestyle, Keith very much liked it, considering he had an eye for fashion and was a party animal, taking pills and raving. He looked like a natural as a mod, it suited him that well. Soon, he quit his day job and became a full-time musician, with his weekly wages more than doubling. Even with this good news, his parents were naturally worried, thinking that rock and roll wasn't a sustainable and steady job like his day job was. Keith would go on to prove them wrong.

Like a lot of British rock bands, they started off playing R&B covers, but in order for a band to be great, they need to write their own songs. Pete Townshend stepped up to the plate and became the band's main songwriter, but like a lot of musicians, he took inspiration from what was around him. Although not performed by The Who, Pete Townshend's first composition, 'It Was You', was Beatle-esque; that's what people did in those days, emulate The Beatles. The Who's first hit, 'I Can't Explain', was inspired by The Kinks' 'All Day and All of the Night' – copying the great Ray Davies who wrote 'You Really Got Me' by copying 'Louie Louie'. Both bands' early singles were produced by Shel Talmy, an interesting connection.

By the time The Who released their debut album, *My Generation*, in 1965, they had quite a few original songs and listening to it, you already hear an amazing band that would only get better, easily one of the best debut albums in classic rock. 'I Can't Explain' was a top-ten hit and put The Who on the map, and from there they got a string of top-ten hits: 'Anyway, Anyhow, Anywhere', 'My Generation', 'Substitute', 'I'm a Boy', 'Happy Jack', 'Pictures of Lily', 'I Can See For Miles', and 'Pinball Wizard'.

The Who always moved forward and year after year, you saw an evolution. In 1966, they released a mini rock opera, 'A Quick One While He's Away', which was a precursor to the concept albums The Who were well known for: *The Who Sell Out, Tommy* – a full-blown rock opera, and *Quadrophenia* – another great rock opera. The Who just kept setting the bar higher and higher from the '60s to the early '70s. And with their incendiary live shows, with lots of action and explosions, they had to constantly up the ante and give the fans what they wanted and expected, even if it hurt them in the pocketbook. In fact, their first American tour left them about £50,000 in debt!

The Who are one of those bands that sound better live than in the studio. Just listen to *Live At Leeds* and you'll see what I mean. In 1967, The Who went to America for their first tour and that's when they got their reputation for being wild and crazy off stage. They were opening for Herman's Hermits and the tour was in the summer. Big things planned: Monterey Pop Festival (a big breakthrough for the band even if Jimi Hendrix upstaged them) and lots of dates across America, with one of these coinciding with Keith Moon's twenty-first birthday and what a party that would be and it would go down as one of the most notorious Keith Moon stories. Throughout the Herman's Hermits tour, there were drugs everywhere: acid, pills, and pot mostly. As you may already know, America's drinking age is twenty-one, so that's a big milestone birthday. Even then, Keith didn't have problems getting his hands on some booze thanks to room service and free stuff from the venues. The Who were playing a show in the working-class industrial city of Flint, Michigan. They had just flown in from Winnipeg and Keith Moon started the day drunk. The Who did the usual publicity stuff, interviews at radio stations and they played their show at a high school football stadium (at this time, The Who were still playing smaller venues) and it wasn't their best show because Keith was drunk, but Keith was still in good spirits because returning to the Holiday Inn, a 'happy birthday' message for him was on the marquee and it was time to par-tay! About thirty to forty people attended Keith's birthday party at the Flint Holiday Inn: radio station staff, promoters, some teenage fans who had won a competition, and of course members of The Who, The Blues Magoos, and Herman's Hermits. The party started off humble; what do you expect from a cheap hotel? A banquet hall full of birthday cakes for the Patent British Exploding Drummer. If you know the music video for 'Happy

Jack' with the cake flying everywhere and going in people's faces, let's just say the party was that on steroids. A food fight started with cake flying everywhere, then Keith's friends pantsed him and because he went commando, he was running through the hotel half naked, slipped, fell, and broke his front tooth. He was taken to an emergency dentist straight away, accompanied by John Entwistle and Karl Green (Herman's Hermits bassist and friend of Keith's). Keith was so inebriated that they couldn't give him anaesthesia, so he was naturally in a lot of pain. Meanwhile, the party turned into a riot, the hotel was totally destroyed (The Who had to pay the hotel a five-figure sum), and people sprayed fire extinguisher foam all over a bunch of cars, causing damage to the paint. Now that's what really happened. The tall tale that is well-known Who lore is that Keith Moon ran out of the hotel and drove a Lincoln Continental into the swimming pool, was arrested, and The Who were banned from Holiday Inns for life from that point – none of those three things happened. Like The Kinks' Pete Quaife, Keith Moon loved to tell an exaggerated, outlandish story as if it was the truth, but in Moonie's case, it became lore and it was all part of selling a fantasy. However, the Smothers Brothers performance was legendary, caught on camera, and showed the true extent of The Who's craziness: Keith Moon blew up his drums with extra explosives at the end of 'My Generation'. It was so explosive that the image went white, a few tufts of Pete Townshend's hair were on fire, Keith's arm was sliced by a cymbal, and John Entwistle clutched his bass for dear life. Off stage, Bette Davis fainted into Mickey Rooney's arms. Is causing an Old Hollywood star to faint because of your music not something to brag about?

Why did Keith Moon act the way he did, destroying hotel rooms and taking lots of drugs? Because The Who were successful and constantly on the road and staying in lodging that had strict rules, Keith felt the need to rebel against that because rock and roll was supposed to mean freedom and he hated being limited and told what to do. As for the drugs, there were a lot of problems behind the scenes and his personal life and being around a lot of drinkers and pill poppers, he tried to keep up with them, but it harmed his health even before his late twenties, with him blacking out and acting paranoid.

When he wasn't destroying hotel rooms, he was finally coming out of his shell and befriending fellow rock stars such as The Beatles, Bruce Johnston of The Beach Boys, Mark Volman of The Turtles, Vivian Stanshall and 'Legs' Larry Smith of Bonzo Dog Doo-Dah Band, Alice Cooper, Harry Nilsson, Marc Bolan, and Jimmy Page, among others. In The Who, he got along well with John Entwistle.

Meanwhile in Keith's personal life, he got his girlfriend, Kim Kerrigan, pregnant in late 1965. They got married on St Patrick's Day 1966, and their daughter Mandy was born on 12 July 1966. Kim was only seventeen when she gave birth, and she was horrified when she found out she was pregnant because she wasn't even an adult yet. Keith was very possessive of Kim. He demanded she quit modelling, and he would get angry if men even so much as complimented her or looked at her in a flirtatious way. He once told his sister Linda that he didn't marry Kim because she was pregnant, but rather he got Kim pregnant so he could marry her. Sometimes his anger would turn into violence, with Kim once hiding in the bathroom with Keith wielding a knife to try to cut the door down. While on tour, Keith would write to Kim and she'd write back to him, and he'd insist that he was behaving himself and not going out on the town, but we all know that was a lie. They might have looked like a cute young couple, but behind closed doors it was a nightmare and Keith lied to the music press about the wedding rumours because if he was married, it would hurt The Who's marketability. When you market a rock band as teen idols, you're selling this fantasy to the fans.

Keith's relationship with Kim was not the only turbulent thing going on in his life, as you'll see.

The '70s did not start well for Keith Moon, and unfortunately, he didn't survive the decade, and the reason for that was a night out gone wrong. First, though, we must go back to 1969. The Who ended the '60s on a high note, releasing *Tommy*, which many people consider the first rock opera (even though The Pretty Things' *S.F. Sorrow* came out before it), which went double platinum in the US. By the end of the decade, The Who had toured all over Europe, North America, and to Australia and New Zealand, making them proper jet-setters with passports full of stamps. That's a flex! What better way to round off the 1960s than to play Woodstock and be considered one of the best and most memorable performances of the festival? Imagine you're at Woodstock and Roger Daltrey starts singing 'See Me Feel Me' just as the sun is rising at about 6am that Sunday morning of 17 August; I can't imagine a more iconic sunrise than that! Weeks after that, The Who played the Isle of Wight Festival. Moonie being Moonie, he broke his feet just before it, but thanks to painkilling injections, he was a trooper and played a great show with The Who.

By the late '60s, his relationship with Kim was becoming more tumultuous. His violent side would come out more frequently because of his excessive drinking and he'd beat his wife, a huge contrast to the affable goofball he acted like when with his friends. Whenever she'd leave him, the charming Moonie would beg her to come back and she did and there would be that typical honeymoon phase and the cycle would continue until Kim left Keith for Small Faces keyboard player Ian McLagan. Keith, as you can imagine, was really upset about his former friend getting with his ex-wife and he threatened Kim and paid a threatening guy in the music industry £250 to break Ian's fingers. Thankfully, Pete Townshend found out about the scheme and paid that same person £250 to not break his fingers. That was nearly a Tonya Harding versus

Nancy Kerrigan situation (kind of a coincidence, since Kim's last name was Kerrigan!).

Besides that, though, career wise, The Who were on top of the world at the end of the '60s coming into the '70s. This was the golden age of their performances and creatively as a band. This was their peak, but not everything in life was happy. Behind the scenes was a freak accident that may not have taken Moonie's life, but in a way, you could say that it would.

Keith had close friends who weren't musicians: Pete 'Dougal' Butler, who worked as a roadie for The Who, and Neil Boland, his driver. Dougal Butler was a mod with a day job at HM Customs and Excise whose life changed when he met The Who and got a job for them as a roadie before being promoted to John Entwistle's assistant/driver and later Keith Moon's assistant/sidekick/best friend. Neil Boland was Irish and was around Keith's age. Just weeks before he died, on 15 December 1969, he accompanied Keith to John Lennon's War Is Over concert and there's a picture of John Lennon and friends all holding 'War Is Over' signs. It's a who's who of rock and roll: John & Yoko, George Harrison, Billy Preston, Alan White (who later would be in prog rock band Yes), Klaus Voormann, Eric Clapton, Jim Gordon (who we talked about in chapter 18), Delaney & Bonnie Bramlett, Bobby Keys, Jim Price, and Keith Moon with his friend Neil Boland (he's the guy with the short dark hair next to Keith).

A few days after New Year's, Keith Moon went to the Cranbourne Rooms adjacent to the humble, working-class Red Lion pub in Hatfield, just outside of London. The pub is in a grade II listed historic building that dates back to the late 18th century with extensions made in the 19th century and as recently as the mid-20th century. A bit unusual that he'd go there instead of somewhere in central London where you'd see more celebrities, but he was doing it as a favour to his neighbours whose son owned the pub and who wanted Keith Moon to appear there. Keith noticed that the venue was full of skinheads. Some of them were happy to see a Who member there, but others didn't like seeing someone who embodied rock and roll excess rubbing their wealth in their faces. The venue did not do the adequate preparation for a celebrity appearance. There was no VIP room where Keith and friends could retreat and get some privacy and there was very little security.

Keith naturally stood out like a sore thumb there with his fancy clothes, expensive Bentley, and ordering a brandy. The working-class patrons were not thrilled with this hot-shot nouveau-riche rock star rocking up to their hangout, so they got rowdy and intimidating towards him. The only other celebrities there were brothers Jimmy and Jack McCulloch, who were both in Thunderclap Newman, a group put together by Pete Townshend, who had had a hit with the protest song 'Something in the Air' a few months earlier. Eventually, Keith and his entourage had to leave the pub for their own safety and things got even worse to say the least. According to Tony Fletcher's book *Dear Moon*, they ran out of the door and into Keith's Bentley, and the McCulloch brothers got into their car. Keith, Kim, Larry Smith and his girlfriend Jean Battye and Neil were in the Bentley and about thirty patrons followed, surrounding the car, pelting stones and coins at it. When Neil got behind the driver's seat, the car was in drive and when he exited, he likely didn't put it in park and no one pushed on the brake. Neil often would help Keith get out of trouble and so he exited the luxurious vehicle and tried to mediate the situation and get Keith and his wife and friends to safety. Instead, things got even worse as the drunk troublemakers piled on top of the car, swarming like bees as Jack McCulloch put it, and Neil was trapped in that crowd as the car was moving forward. If Keith and Kim had stayed any longer, things could have got even more dangerous for them. As a last resort, Keith, who had no driving licence and was intoxicated, got behind the wheel of the car and Neil was in front of the car trying to get the rowdy teenagers out of the way. Some accounts say that Keith put his foot on the accelerator to escape, Larry tried to help Keith steer, the car leaped, and then he ran over Neil by accident because Neil was unlucky and ended up in front of the car. A hundred yards down the road, the passengers tried to get help and they were notified someone was under the car. Keith checked, and lo and behold, it was his friend and chauffeur, Neil Boland. Kim recalled in *Dear Boy* that under the car it was brains and Neil's head looked like an eggshell. A traumatising sight. Since everyone around there was drunk and there were a lot of people surrounding the car, there are other theories and people have different memories of what happened. There are theories that Keith Moon ran Neil Boland over on purpose (not likely) or that Kim was behind the wheel of the Bentley, and not Keith (Neil Boland's daughter, Michelle, believes Keith didn't run his friend over).

Of course, police and paramedics showed up and the passengers were taken to the police station and questioned. There was also a media circus around the accident because it involved the drummer of one of the biggest rock bands in the world. Keith was traumatised and distraught, blaming himself for what happened. His life would never be the same again. He couldn't live with it. John Entwistle told Tony Fletcher in *Dear Boy* that Keith blamed himself and knew that it was his actions that led to his friend's death. Groupie Pamela Des Barres told VH1 that Keith would often talk about how he ran over Neil and he'd cry and call himself a murderer; he was full of guilt. Neil Boland's family were devastated and pressed charges against the troublemaking skinheads and Keith Moon. According to Tony Fletcher's *Dear Boy*, Neil's family and his common-law wife blamed Keith Moon for making Neil work that day and accompany him to the pub, because had he stayed at home, he wouldn't have died. Keith Moon wanted to make it up to them and send money and look after them, but they rejected his offer. This devastated Keith even more and led to him turning to more drink to cope. He already had an unhealthy addiction and trauma worsened it. Keith's generous nature was genuine and in the '70s, he gave a bit of his fortune to his family, helping his sister purchase a house, paying for his parents' council home, and buying his father a brand-new Volkswagen. With friends, he was always generous and buying drinks for others and insisting he pay for himself. Keith didn't just go the extra mile with his music, he would do so for his friends too.

The Who being in their peak years, the show had to go on and two weeks later, Keith Moon was back on stage and on the road, playing drums for dates in France, Denmark, Germany, and the Netherlands. On Valentine's Day was the famous Leeds University concert, which was recorded for one of the best live albums of all time, *Live at Leeds*. Being the professional he was, he somehow got it together and gave some of his best performances, but off stage he was a wreck. Unfortunately, in those days, mental healthcare was not great and there wasn't enough emphasis on the importance of mental health and going to therapy for bereavement. But when you're a rock star, fans and your managers expect a constant stream of new music and tour dates. You can't stand still.

On 23 March, a remorseful Keith Moon pleaded guilty to all charges, drink driving and driving without a licence and insurance, and stated there were mitigating circumstances: he knew he'd be drinking that night so that was why he brought his chauffeur with him and he had no intention of driving at all and only did so to save himself and the other passengers. The judge cleared him of all charges and declared the death an accident. He told Moon in court, 'You had no choice but to act the way you did and no moral culpability is attached to you.'

After such a close call, you'd think Keith would have been careful and toned down the pranks, but he kept doing Moonie things. One of the most famous of them was dressing up as a Nazi (not out of bigotry, but rather edginess and shock value, as those were features common in '70s humour), taking photos and even going out to pubs dressed like that. By any era's standards, he crossed the line with his Nazi-themed pranking when he allegedly rode around the Jewish neighbourhood of Golders Green in London doing Nazi salutes. Not all his costumed antics were problematic; some more wholesome costumes he wore were those of a pirate or sailor. As well, he cross-dressed on many occasions. In 1971, Keith Moon bought a house called Tara (named after the mansion in *Gone With The Wind*) in Surrey from *The Italian Job* director Peter Collison for £65k pounds (which would be nearing a million pounds today). While living there, Keith threw many crazy parties and didn't slow down his party-animal lifestyle even if it wasn't good for his health. Eventually, it caught up with him and on the first date of the 1973 Quadrophenia US tour, he passed out twice on stage after taking horse tranquillisers washed down with brandy to calm his nerves. The first time, he was revived and came back after thirty minutes, but the second time, he was out. Pete Townshend asked drummer Artimus Pyle of Lynyrd Skynyrd, who were their opening act, to fill in for Moonie, but he didn't know the parts, so Pete asked the audience, emphasising that he needed someone who was good at drumming. A nineteen-year-old Iowan named Scot Halpin played the drums for the rest of the show. Talk about living the dream!

On a happier note, Keith Moon branched out into other creative fields, notably acting, and he was quite good at comedic movies. He appeared in Frank Zappa's *200 Motels* with Ringo Starr and Flo & Eddie; he acted in the nostalgic *That'll Be The Day* alongside other rock stars: David Essex, Ringo Starr, and Billy Fury; he appeared in *Son of Dracula* alongside friends Harry Nilsson and Ringo Starr and fellow musicians Peter Frampton, John Bonham, Leon Russell, and Klaus Voormann; he appeared in the *That'll Be The Day* sequel *Stardust* with fellow rock/pop stars David Essex, Adam Faith, Marty Wilde, Dave Edmunds, and Paul Nicholas; and played a gay fashion designer in *Sextette*, Mae West's last film; fellow musicians Ringo Starr, Alice Cooper, and Van McCoy were in the movie as well. Keith's most memorable performance was playing Uncle Ernie in the film adaptation of *Tommy*.

Year by year, the alcoholism and mental health struggles showed more and more on Keith and his once cute, youthful face looked tired and he had gained a considerable amount of weight because by the mid '70s, The Who didn't tour anymore, and Keith wasn't going to slow down his drinking or stop eating rich foods. During this time, he moved to LA like other British rockers and continued partying with his rock star friends and he bought a beach house in Trancas (near Malibu), where he was neighbours with the highest paid actor in the world, Steve McQueen (the two didn't get along).

By the late '70s, he looked much older than his age, which was only his early thirties, and he was starting to get seizures from drinking. People around Keith tried to help and encourage him to get professional help before it was too late. However, there were enablers around him who encouraged him to live up to the legend and keep pushing the envelope, Track Records employee Mark Timlin told Tony Fletcher in *Dear Boy* that he went to clinics and hospitals and to psychiatrists on multiple occasions and even went to AA meetings, but kicking an addiction isn't simple and the stays were typically short with him finding it hard to relate to others there. Plus, there were likely more issues deep down inside. In *Dear Boy*, it's speculated that Keith Moon could possibly have had undiagnosed ADHD or BPD (borderline personality disorder), explaining his hyperactivity and unstable relationships with others. Because of privacy laws, we'll never know if he was diagnosed with any mental illnesses, since he never disclosed it to anyone. Keith was self-aware though and, on those occasions, when he wasn't drunk, he admitted alcohol was his demon and was a crutch for him to hide his low self-esteem and feel less inhibited.

In 1976, The Who went on their last tour with Keith Moon, and it was necessary because the band were broke, partially because of Keith and John living opulent lifestyles (mansions, fancy cars, designer clothes, the whole lot) and partying a little too hard on tour. During that tour, The Who set a Guinness World Record for the loudest concert at 126 decibels (as loud as a clap of thunder), beating Deep Purple's record of 117 decibels in 1972. The following year, The Who didn't release anything and so Keith, with nothing to do, partied hard in LA and kept feeling the need to live up to the image of himself that he painted in his stories that he told in interviews with the media. But at some point, Keith wasn't his old self anymore. Mick Avory and Dave Davies of The Kinks saw him at the Hyatt and saw someone who was a shell of his former self, depressed and crying out for help, but had no idea how to get help. Eventually, his close friend Dougal Butler had enough and went back to England.

Keith Moon later came back to London and, like Sid Vicious, as discussed in the previous chapter, he was self-destructive but self-aware, he knew he needed help. Similarly, he didn't just drink and take drugs, he also self-harmed, slashing his wrists and needed to be hospitalised. His stamina and energy weren't the same and recording *Who Are You* was a challenge. It wasn't just Keith either. John and Pete were also drinking a lot; Pete injured his hand by punching a window, and Roger needed throat surgery. But Keith was in the worst condition and was the least consistent and it nearly got to the point where he was going to be fired, but deep down inside, The Who knew they wouldn't be the same without Moonie. The saddest irony is found on the *Who Are You* album cover; Keith is sitting on a chair that reads 'not to be taken away'. He was seated in the chair to hide his gut, which had grown a lot from years of alcohol abuse. The album was released just weeks before Keith Moon died.

At the time of his death, he was broke from living beyond his means and he couldn't buy another house, so he was living in rental homes, the last one being Harry Nilsson's Mayfair flat at 9 Curzon Place (a cursed flat to say the least because that's where Mama Cass died in 1974). The Who had a lot planned for the rest of the '70s: the release of their rockumentary *The Kids Are Alright* and a film adaptation of *Quadrophenia*, so Keith had a lot to live for. According to Tony Fletcher's *Dear Boy*, he told John Entwistle that he wanted to get back in shape so he could play concerts. Keith also had plans to write an autobiography that would have been called *The Moon Papers*. In the last months of his life, he tried to get sober, but would get really bad seizures from withdrawal and one night, when he had a fight with his girlfriend, Annette, he was so out of control that she called a doctor, who sedated Keith and prescribed him Heminevrin, a medication for treating alcohol withdrawal symptoms like seizures, insomnia, and psychosis, which is usually given to the patient short-term under direct supervision, such as in a hospital setting. Keith had a long-term habit of taking handfuls of pills, no surprise considering he was a part of the '60s raver scene (as pointed out by *The Who: Maximum R&B* author Richard Barnes in a documentary called *Keith Moon: The Final 24*) and giving him a big bottle of a hundred Heminevrin pills without checking him into hospital was especially dangerous, even deadly, especially when mixed with alcohol. And sadly, that's just what happened to Keith Moon.

Keith Moon spent his last day on Earth with his friend Paul McCartney, who was hosting a party in honour of one of his idols, Buddy Holly. In 1976, Paul bought the rights to Buddy Holly's back catalogue and *The Buddy Holly Story* was premiering that night, the day before what would have been Buddy Holly's forty-second birthday. Keith originally didn't want to attend the party because he was trying to get clean and a party where there's inevitably going to be an open bar and all-you-can-drink alcohol was tempting. Annette insisted he go since she really wanted to go too and so they went! Keith had a brilliant time at the party and wasn't acting like a drunk buffoon, but rather being funny, witty, and charismatic – the Keith everyone fell in love with. Most importantly, he seemed truly happy. However, he had a couple of drinks at the party and went home late at night. When he got home, he was hungry and asked Annette to make him some lamb and he fell asleep watching a movie, *The Abominable Dr Phibes*. Before falling asleep, he took his Heminevrin pills.

The next morning at about 7:30am, Keith Moon woke up crabby and hungry and demanded Annette make him some steak for breakfast. He swore at her and was upset with her. He took some more Heminevrin pills while Annette was in another room so she didn't see him overdosing. He went back to sleep and started snoring. Annette couldn't fall asleep because he snored so loudly, so she slept on the sofa and when she woke up to check on Keith, he wasn't breathing, and it was dead silent. Her worst fears were confirmed. He was dead. Soon after, The Who, their manager, and Keith's family found out the news. As you can expect, they were devastated and couldn't keep it together. They were in tears.

Harry Nilsson felt that his Curzon Place flat was cursed after two of his friends died at the age of thirty-two and so he sold it to Pete Townshend.

Afterwards, The Who continued recording with Kenney Jones, formerly of The Small Faces, on drums from 1978–1983. In the '90s, when The Who reunited, Ringo Starr's son Zak Starkey became The Who's drummer.

CHAPTER 22

Les McKeown (1975)

Boy bands have a long history and aren't just a recent phenomenon. Ever since teenagers became their own demographic with their own likes and their own tastes, record labels wanted to sell a product to them and so came the boy bands and girl groups, even though the term 'boy band' wasn't coined until the '80s. Some of them were manufactured, or rather casted, like The Monkees in the '60s or Menudo in the '80s, but even if they weren't cast like actors, the image and personas are manufactured and sold like a product. Other boy bands were genuine family bands like The Jackson 5 or The Osmonds. This isn't to say that these groups weren't talented in their own right. Definitely in the case of The Monkees, the members were talented actors and even knew how to play music and sing, but they felt stymied by their record label and managers because of how formulaic the music was, and they wanted to have a say and creative freedom. Because of disagreements, *The Monkees* TV series was cancelled early, and the band slowly began to disintegrate.

The Bay City Rollers were one of Scotland's biggest ever bands. What One Direction were in the 2010s, what NSYNC and The Backstreet Boys were in the '90s, that's what The Bay City Rollers were in the '70s. They were everywhere and they had an army of fans; those were the days of Rollermania. Love 'em or hate 'em, they had an impact and are a big part of '70s pop culture. As happy as the music is, there's a lot of sadness and tragedy behind the scenes.

Content Warning: Discussion of rape and child abuse.

ABOUT LES MCKEOWN

Les McKeown was born Leslie Richard McKeown on 12 November 1955 in a suburb of Edinburgh and grew up in a poor council estate called Broomhouse. He was the youngest of four children. His parents, Francis and Florence, were Irish and both worked in fashion with his deaf father being a tailor and his mother being a seamstress. He didn't have a lot of knowledge of his Irish roots, as his mother didn't talk about growing up there or why they came to Scotland, and they didn't have any contact with family in Ireland. Like a lot of British rock stars, he dropped out of school as a teenager because he had dreams of being a musician. He liked all kinds of music: blues, Motown, hard rock, but one of his biggest influences was David Bowie. When Les was a teenager, his older brother, Roni, took him to a Bowie concert and that changed everything for him and he wanted to be like Bowie, singing to audiences of thousands and being a superstar and so he borrowed £200 from his brother to buy a PA system to practise his singing.

He worked various odd jobs before the fame, including making tea for technicians at a recording studio, as a lab technician for a brewery, as an electrician's apprentice, and at a paper mill. While working a day job, he was in a band called Threshold, which he was in until he was recruited to join The Bay City Rollers as lead singer to replace Gordon 'Nobby' Clark, who sang on their 1971 top-ten hit, a cover of The Gentrys' 'Keep On Dancing'. Nobby Clark was growing tired of being in the band and refused to perform sometimes and that made the band's controlling manager Tam Paton start to look for a replacement. Paton was familiar with a group called Threshold who had a residency at the Americana Club in Edinburgh. They had more of a hard rock sound inspired by Free and Deep Purple. Tam Paton wanted to manage the band, but they didn't want to sell out and play pop music and cut their hair. Les on the other hand wanted to be famous and he went to Tam Paton's family home in Prestonpans to ask if he could be the singer of The Bay City Rollers. He had heard about Paton's alleged 'no girlfriends' rule and being a young, rebellious guy, he wasn't going to let anyone tell him what to do. The gutsy move paid off and he played a gig later that day. He was unprepared and had to sing songs he didn't know. What he didn't have in experience, he made up for with his charisma, spirit, and ambition. The ladies loved him, and he became the band's heartthrob. Sadly, for Nobby Clark, he was essentially sacked behind his back, and he had nothing to show for it because he wasn't paid the promised royalties. The rest of the band would get that same treatment too.

The Bay City Rollers were formed as The Ambassadors in 1964 by brothers Alan and Derek Longmuir, who soon after invited Derek's friend Gordon 'Nobby' Clark and another musician, Dave Pettigrew, to join the band. They were fascinated with The Beatles, Elvis, and American R&B music from Detroit such as Martha & The Vandellas and Mitch Ryder and the Detroit Wheels. Because they wanted to have an Americanised image, they changed their name to The Bay City Rollers after, according to legend, throwing a dart at a map and it landing near Bay City, Michigan. The other inspiration behind the band's name, according to founding member Alan Longmuir, were Mitch Ryder and the Detroit Wheels.

Every band needs a manager and former musician Tam Paton discovered the group because Alan Longmuir and his friends approached him at the Palais asking him to check out their band and Paton liked what he saw. This was a big deal for them because he was one of the most important behind-the-scenes figures in the music industry in Scotland. From there, Tam Paton took the group under his wing, and he would use his family's home as a rehearsal space and drive a lorry delivering potatoes to make money to support himself and the band. Before the international fame, Paton had his eyes all over Scotland and his goal was to get the Rollers to play every city and town in Scotland.

Like a lot of other gay men in the '60s and '70s (such as Brian Epstein, Joe Meek, Robert Stigwood, Bob Crewe, Kit Lambert, Tony Stratton-Smith, Ken Howard and Alan Blaikley, Simon Napier-Bell, Kit Lambert, and John Reid), he went behind the scenes in the music industry to make a living. However, Paton was accused of being a creep, a predator, and abusive towards The Bay City Rollers in multiple ways. Band members have called him controlling, forbidding them from drinking, having girlfriends or even hooking up with women so they could have a squeaky-clean marketable image and seem 'available' to the fans (sounds like that *South Park* episode with the Jonas Brothers and the purity rings) and be parent-approved, but he would give the band members amphetamines. When on tour, he'd make the band members share rooms and he'd book the cheapest possible hotels, usually a Holiday Inn, far away from the city centre, always keeping an eye on the band members. Far from a glitzy rock and roll lifestyle.

He would kick people out of the band on a whim and hire new members, making it very clear they could be replaced at any time, and this happened throughout the late '60s and the '70s. He was also a very big, intimidating guy. There were rumours that Tam Paton shot and killed a man or multiple men while serving in the Army in Cyprus.

He also wasn't the only shady person around the Bay City Rollers. Songwriter and producer Jonathan King produced their earliest single and first hit, a cover of The Gentrys' 'Keep On Dancing'. In 2001, King was convicted on four counts of indecent assault, one count of buggery, and one count of attempted buggery against five boys between the ages of fourteen and fifteen in 1987. In a separate trial that same year, he was acquitted of 22 similar charges. He was sentenced to seven years in prison, but was released on parole in 2005 after serving half his sentence. There was another trial in 2018, which resulted in him being acquitted of all charges. He has repeatedly proclaimed his innocence. Former BBC DJ Chris Denning worked for Bell Records as a promotions manager before moving to Jonathan King's UK Records and worked with the Rollers early on in their career. Denning was convicted for gross indecency and indecent assault in 1974 (but served no jail time for that) and was jailed multiple times from the '80s to the 2010s for child sexual abuse and producing and possessing child pornography. Paton, Denning, and King all frequented the Walton Hop teen disco in Walton-on-Thames in Surrey, just outside of London.

By the time The Bay City Rollers got signed and got their first hit, their style of poppy teenybopper music wasn't the coolest thing on the club scene (which at the time was heavy metal, hard rock, and prog rock), but the charts were a bit poppier with glam rock about to take over. There was a lot of competition in the early '70s because there was a lot of great music released during that time and The Bay City Rollers didn't get another domestic hit for three years. In the meantime, they feared becoming one-hit wonders.

While 'Mañana' wasn't a hit in the UK, it did well abroad and so they weren't dropped from their label and could still keep going as a band, even though it was an exhausting life travelling from Scotland to play dates in England – lots of hours of driving and many nights asleep in the back of the van. They were determined to succeed and so the line-up changed with Eric Faulkner, Stuart 'Woody' Wood, and Les McKeown joining the band and success became even closer. They switched from the once-successful Howard/Blaikley songwriting team to the Irish-Scottish Phil Coulter/Bill Martin songwriting/production team, famous for writing 1967 Eurovision-winner 'Puppet On A String', performed by Sandie Shaw. Coulter and Martin aimed to be Bell Records' equivalent of rival label RAK's Nicky Chinn/Mike Chapman songwriting team. Chinn and Chapman wrote hits for glam rockers The Sweet (not signed to RAK though), Suzi Quatro, and Mud. Coulter and Martin wrote some of The Bay City Rollers biggest hits such as 'Remember (Sha-La-La-La)' (number six in the UK), 'Shang-a-Lang' (number two in the UK), 'Summerlove Sensation' (number three in the UK), and 'Saturday Night' (number one in the US). Sound wise, they took a page out of Phil Spector and Joe Meek's playbooks and used session musicians (except for the vocals) and produced the songs to have a big sound. Coulter thought of The Crystals' 'Da Doo Ron Ron' as the blueprint for a good pop song and wanted to create his own version of that. But it wasn't long before the band had had enough of Coulter and Martin because they wanted to have more control over their music.

Only one thing was missing: a distinctive look and brand for the band. While MTV was a decade away, image was still important in music of the '60s and '70s and it was all part of the brand and marketing. Bands need to have a brand and a memorable image, and that's more important than being skilled musicians, especially in the pop world where it's about creating simple, catchy music to appeal to the masses. Newcomer guitarist/bassist Eric Faulkner was really inspired by glam rockers Slade and their loud dress sense – one of Noddy Holder's most iconic outfits was tartan patterned. The other group that influenced the Rollers' dress sense were Bilbo Baggins, another group Tam Paton managed. The members of Bilbo Baggins would wear tartan jackets, striped socks, wide trousers, and clothes with the band members' names on them. A very youthful aesthetic and one that the kids could easily copy and afford – no glittery outfits needed. This appealed to the young audience and made the band relatable. This look evolved into the signature Bay City Roller look that the fans imitated: tartan-trimmed shirts (often slightly unbuttoned) and cropped, flared trousers and the then-trendy platform shoes. A dated look by our standards, but one that's recognisably Scotland in the '70s.

At the height of the band's fame, they had a TV show called *Shang-a-Lang*, they had their own magazine that sold tens of thousands of copies a month, they had a mail order clothing business so fans could get clothes and accessories like the Rollers, they had merchandising deals with Woolworth's and C&A, and they would get thousands of fan letters a day. In fact, on Eric Faulkner's birthday, he received 25,000 letters and 5,000 parcels and it took multiple vans to deliver all of them. Fans would scream so loudly at concerts that one could barely make out what they were playing. At times, the Rollers had to stop playing because the crowds would surge towards the stage and people were getting crushed. The band wouldn't have many days off. Les McKeown said in the BBC *Rollermania* documentary that the band were on the road for three years and his mum counted that he was back home for only six days during that time.

With the band ascending up the British charts in 1974 with 'Remember', 'Shang-a-Lang', 'Summerlove Sensation', and 'All of Me Loves All of You' and reaching the top in 1975 with 'Bye Bye Baby' (a Frankie Valli and the Four Seasons cover) and 'Give a Little Love', there was only one thing left to do: take America by storm. Bell Records were owned by Columbia Pictures Industries and shut down in 1974, so that meant they needed to sign to a new label. Former President of Columbia Records, also known as 'The Man with the Golden Ears', Clive Davis, founded Arista Records and of the Bell Records artists, he signed just three: The Bay City Rollers, Barry Manilow, and Melissa Manchester. Davis wasn't sure about The Bay City Rollers at first because he wanted to have more serious bands on his label and he was sceptical they'd have success in America because other glam rock contemporaries like T. Rex and Slade didn't have much, if any, success in America. However, other big people in the music industry in America were curious and wanted to know what the latest teen sensation in the UK were all about and so concert promoter Sid Bernstein (who essentially brought The Beatles to America, promoting their famous Shea Stadium concert), music publicist Carol Klenfner, and a bunch of American journalists went to Glasgow to see what the hype was all about and they were blown away: streets packed full of screaming (and sometimes even fainting) tweenagers and teenagers taking over the city centre, reminiscent of Beatlemania just a decade before.

When Carol Klenfner, Danny Fields (Ramones manager and writer for *16 Magazine*) and other journalists saw the band, they knew they could appeal to young Americans and so Klenfner convinced Clive Davis that they could make a lot of money distributing The Bay City Rollers' records in America. When he looked at their UK hit singles, he didn't see hit potential in 'Bye Bye Baby', which he thought was an inferior cover, and thought even less of 'Give a Little Love'. But there was one more obscure song that made Clive Davis's ears perk up, 'Saturday Night'. The band and Tam Paton were confused. They didn't like the song and it had been a total flop when it was released as a single in the UK. Davis heard an infectious, catchy cheerleader-like chant that the fans could sing along to at concerts and that would get stuck in your head. And so, they created a plan for importing Rollermania to America: beam a performance in London via satellite to American homes to prime the fans, then fly the group over to America for TV appearances and concerts. 'Saturday Night' reached the top of the charts on 3 January 1976.

Sadly, though, the fame in the US didn't last as long as they thought it would, because disco was about to take over and usually the fame of a teen idol is short-lived because their target demographic grows up and moves on. Plus, there was some turbulence around this time with Alan Longmuir leaving the band for a while because of his age and being tired of Tam Paton's controlling behaviour. His two replacements, Ian Mitchell and Pat McGlynn, stayed in the band for only about six months each.

But one of the biggest controversies in the Bay City Rollers was a car accident Les McKeown was involved in, which ended up taking the life of an elderly woman. But that wasn't Les's only controversy. Too many added up and it hurt The Bay City Rollers' career.

THE ACCIDENTS, SCANDALS, AND LIFE AFTER THEM

It's a rite of passage for a young adult to get their driving licence and Les McKeown had just passed his driving test in 1974. What do you do when you are an A-list pop star with cash to burn? You buy a car and flex. So, Les bought a Ford Mustang. He'd always brag about how fast it could go and that's a problem when you're a new driver, young and thinking you're invincible, and with winding, curvy, twisty roads common in Scotland – definitely not novice-friendly! With Les being on the road and hardly ever at home, he wasn't an experienced driver.

On 28 May 1975, the Bay City Rollers played a concert at Great Yarmouth, a seaside resort town in Norfolk, England and the band had the following day off. Les decided to come back to his hometown of Edinburgh to spend a little time with family and friends before it was back on the road again to play more concerts. On 29 May, he, a girlfriend, and his brother got in the Mustang and drove to Edinburgh Airport. On the way there, they drove on the long Corstorphine Road which takes you from the city centre to the airport. Near this tricky bend, an elderly woman tried to cross the road and suddenly here comes Les's car going as fast as sixty or seventy miles per hour, according to accounts from the *Sun* newspaper and witnesses, respectively. So anywhere from ten to thirty miles per hour over the speed limit, which ranges from thirty to fifty miles per hour on that road. Les claimed that he was driving at forty miles per hour when he hit the elderly woman (later revealed to be his neighbour), whom he claimed was in two minds about whether to cross the road or not, so he beat the horn and tried to swerve, but hit her and crashed into a brick wall. All the passengers in the car were uninjured. McKeown was charged with causing death by dangerous driving. The woman's name was Euphemia Clunie and she died, aged seventy-six.

Definitely not safe driving and I can only imagine Les was in a hurry to get to the airport and fly to the next concert; lots of pressure. Still, not acceptable and not an excuse, as he could have chosen to take a taxi to the airport or left home earlier so he didn't have to speed to make his flight. News spread across the country to Bristol and The Bay City Rollers had to cancel their concert. Fans eager to see their favourites heard the news on the radio and cried and screamed. News of the car accident made the front page of the tabloids, a PR disaster for the Scottish boy band.

Svengali manager Tam Paton insisted that the tour must still go on and the following day, Les rejoined the Bay City Rollers to play a concert in Southampton and after that, two big, long-awaited shows at the Hammersmith Odeon. No break, no consideration for Les's feelings and the trauma. Les was really young when the car accident happened, only nineteen years old, and the guilt from running over an elderly woman, facing a trial, and possibly jail time was a lot for him to bear. It's likely that the logic would have been to keep the concerts going so it would take attention away from the tragedy that had happened. At that point, The Bay City Rollers had not made it to America yet, but thankfully for The Rollers, the world wasn't as globalised then as it is now.

Les's mental health really took a downturn after the accident. Similar to Keith Moon, he started taking harder drugs at higher frequencies and drank even more. Of the accident, he wrote in his book, *Shang-a-Lang*, 'I was nineteen years old, I'd just killed someone, and it seemed like everyone around me was pretending it hadn't happened or it didn't matter.'

Not only was Les hurting himself, but he also hurt others and there were other incidents after the car accident. One of them happened just days later. While playing a concert in Oxford on 2 June, a bunch of teenage fangirls stormed the stage and Les was accused of starting a riot at the concert. Les was feeling a lot of emotions, as it wasn't long after the car accident: anger, frustration, rage, and sadness. He lost control and beat up a photographer named Steve Hartley. Les beat Hartley up with his microphone stand and was arrested on assault charges and of course there was a court date for that. Les didn't just have one court date ahead of him in November, he had two court dates. On top of his pop star duties, that's a lot for a nineteen-year-old to handle, so no wonder he fell into a bad spiral and turned to drugs and drinking heavily. He lived even wilder and was the one band member who truly got away with having lots of sex and he loved to have quickies in lifts and hotel rooms because of the rush. It was like an escape from the traumas connected to being a Bay City Roller. In interviews, Les McKeown claimed he was raped by Tam Paton at just nineteen years old. He said that he was drugged with Quaaludes, a popular drug in the '70s. In 2009, he told his wife, Keiko, that when he was raped, he realised he was bisexual, describing his identity in the '70s and '80s as being a 'secret bisexual', and even during his marriage, which lasted until his death in 2021, he cheated on his wife with both male and female lovers.

Eventually, though, the truth started to come out about Les's legal problems. After an Australian visit (that Les and Derek were not part of), they played some dates in mainland Europe. A young American journalist named Cameron Crowe (he would go on to write *Fast Times at Ridgemont High* and *Almost Famous*; he also directed the latter) interviewed manager Tam Paton and co-manager Barry Perkins. He'd done his research on the band and heard about injuries at their concerts and Les McKeown's car accident, so he asked questions about that. Luckily for The Bay City Rollers, when they made their American debut in late 1975, their clean-cut straight-edge image was still intact and they were still able to go to America and get visas just fine, unlike The Sex

Pistols, who had to have their record label beg the government to grant the band visas so they could tour.

On 12 November, Les McKeown was fined £1,100 for the assault on a paparazzo in Oxford and given a suspended sentence of three months. On 18 November, the trial for the car accident that caused Euphemia Clunie's death began. As you can expect, there was a media circus around that with teenage fangirls attending the trial and standing outside the courthouse. In the end, he was found guilty of a lesser charge, driving recklessly. He was fined £100, and his driving licence was suspended for a year. No jail time, he left a free man (well, if you can count being in The Bay City Rollers as being free), albeit one who wasn't supposed to drive for a year, and went straight back to work, miming the Faulkner-Wood original 'Money Honey' on *Top of the Pops*. But that wasn't the end of Les's legal troubles. Not even a month after the trial ended, he got in trouble again.

On 18 December, just as 'Saturday Night' was climbing up the charts in America, Les threw a house party and since The Rollers were at the peak of their fame, there were overzealous fans hanging around their houses hoping to catch a glimpse of their idols or maybe even be invited in. A fifteen-year-old girl named Margaret Ness was one of those fangirls, and while she was sitting on a low wall outside the house, she was shot in the forehead with an air rifle. She had to go to hospital afterwards to get stitches and the police arrived on the scene. As Les McKeown was the owner of the home and the air rifle, he was charged with recklessly discharging a loaded firearm. The Bay City Rollers PR team had another disaster in 1975 and had to work overtime to protect the band's reputation. You could say one time is an accident and twice is coincidence, but three times… that's a pattern.

The Bay City Rollers would often do collaborations with companies and appear in advertisements, notably for Cadbury's Curly Wurly bars, endorsing products, but with their lead singer/face of the band finding himself in trouble and allegedly showing violent tendencies, a Bay City Rollers endorsement or collaboration would hurt the company and their image. The Bay City Rollers' PR agent, Alan Walsh, claimed the shooting of Margaret Ness was an accident, but British Caledonian Airways saw it as the straw that broke the camel's back and pulled out of an endorsement deal where they'd give The Bay City Rollers their own plane with tartan livery and flight attendants decked out in their special seven-colour tartan. To save face, Tam Paton had the band do charity work, sending the band members to do some photo ops at a children's hospital visiting sick kids.

For Les, the possibility of a prison sentence was hanging over his head for months. With their first American chart hit on the horizon, there was no time to be idle, it was back to the old grind so they could capitalise on the success of 'Saturday Night'. While in America, the band took even more drugs to deal with the stress of fame. Tam Paton was always heavily focused on the band's look and image and he would often get on Eric's case about losing weight and on Les's case about fixing his crooked teeth. Les refused to get work done on his teeth, but even then, he was worried that he could be replaced at any time since Paton had a history of doing that with The Rollers. However, Les was allowed more freedom than the other band members since Tam would let certain things like having a girlfriend or having sex or drinking slide with Les, but not as much with the other band members. Still, Les described Tam as an intimidating bully, a 'control freak', and said his behaviour was abusive.

Good news for Les came in February 1976 when roadie Hilary Tipping provided an alibi for him. Police had questioned him because he was at the party, but they hadn't asked him if he was the one who pulled the trigger, so he told Les's lawyers that he had pulled the trigger while Les was taking a bath. This likely saved Les from going to prison. Finally, on 25 September, Les was found not guilty of firing an air rifle at Margaret Ness. Like the previous court dates, fans came along and cheered when Les walked out a free man.

It wasn't just Les who dealt with addiction and mental health problems; Alan Longmuir attempted suicide and Eric Faulkner overdosed on downers but survived. Ian Mitchell felt it was all too much and left the band after six months, later saying, 'I had to get out before I put my head in the gas oven.'

At the end of 1978, just before turning twenty-three, Les McKeown left The Bay City Rollers, an end of an era. His replacement was Duncan Faure of South African rock band Rabbitt (future Yes guitarist Trevor Rabin was also in that band). Not long after that, the group fired Tam Paton as their manager and dropped the 'Bay City' from their name, hoping to rebrand and market themselves in a more mature way with a new rock/new wave sound, but none of their singles or albums were commercial successes. After their 1981 album *Ricochet* flopped and the band weren't getting royalty cheques, The Rollers split. Faure went back to his native South Africa and the other band members went on to play reunion shows because they were also not as rich as they appeared to be and finances would be a problem for the band for decades. In a 1983 interview, when Les and Eric were asked about money, they made a tongue in cheek remark about their lawyers and accountants being rich, but said they were okay, but perhaps there's pressure in show business to keep up appearances and not lose face.

Fast-forward to the '90s and The Bay City Rollers took their label to court. They were owed millions and they were determined to finally get the money they had earned. Eric Faulkner hired lawyer Mark St John who had helped '60s band The Pretty Things get the rights to their music and unpaid royalties and who had worked with Led Zeppelin's manager Peter Grant. Mark St John knew this case was perfect for him as someone who sued record labels for a living and called himself 'the Robin Hood of Rock 'n' Roll' and estimated that Arista Records owed the Bay City Rollers £35 million for selling over 120 million albums worldwide, all their merchandising deals, and with interest the amount was estimated to be £200 million. One problem, though, in the initial suit: only the classic line-up of the Longmuir brothers, McKeown, Faulkner, and Wood, were included and when other former Rollers like original lead singer Nobby Clark, and guitarists Pat McGlynn and Ian Mitchell, found out about this lawsuit, they wanted a piece of the pie too, and rightfully so because they were also part of the band's success. After a very long battle, though, the Rollers ended up settling for only £3.5 million and after the lawyers took their cut, each band member only ended up with about £70,000. That's an amount of money that won't last long.

Les McKeown toured with his own band until the coronavirus pandemic. He died of natural causes on 20 April 2021.

REFERENCES

Chapter 1

Abrams, D., & Fisher, D. (2021). *Kennedy's Avenger: Assassination, Conspiracy, and the Forgotten Trial of Jack Ruby*. Harlequin.

Acuña, O. (n.d.). 10 of the Most Lethal CIA Interventions in Latin America. *Telesur.* https://www.telesurenglish.net/analysis/10-of-the-Most-Lethal-CIA-Interventions-in-Latin-America-20160608-0031.html

AP Archive. (2018, March 14). *Jack Ruby Convicted – 1964 | Today In History | 14 Mar 18* [Video]. YouTube. https://www.youtube.com/watch?v=iaQ6lTnJu4k

Appendix 16: *A Biography of Jack Ruby*. (2016, August 15). National Archives. https://www.archives.gov/research/jfk/warren-commission-report/appendix-16.html

Ask a Mortician. (2022, April 22). *Why JFK's casket stayed closed* [Video]. YouTube. https://www.youtube.com/watch?v=3Sh06VUiXaA

Bloodletters & Badmen. (2015, November 24). *Jack Ruby, the Mob & the JFK assassination* [Video]. YouTube. https://www.youtube.com/watch?v=Zts-aAHWIek

Breaking Points. (2022, December 21). *NEW CLUES On Oswald's CIA Link REVEALED In JFK Docs | Counter Points* [Video]. YouTube. https://www.youtube.com/watch?v=5cCwITXJ1vs

Breaking Points. (2023, January 8). *(FULL) JFK Docs: CIA CAUGHT changing Oswald story | Breaking points* [Video]. YouTube. https://www.youtube.com/watch?v=09K8UTm7MWo

Capshaw, R. (2018, December 3). *Inside Jack Ruby's Jewish Paranoia.*

Tablet Magazine. https://www.tabletmag.com/sections/news/articles/inside-jack-rubys-jewish-paranoia

Curmudgeon, V. a. P. B. C. C. (2020, March 14). *March 14, 1964 Skyline Lounge.* Today in History. https://todayinhistory.blog/2020/03/14/march-14-1964-skyline-lounge/

Dannen, F. (1991). *Hit men: Power Brokers and Fast Money Inside the Music Business.* Vintage.

Darcy. (2022, August 29). Richard Manuel: Life in The Band | Revised 2023 | Revised 2023. *Rocksoffmag.* https://www.rocksoffmag.com/richard-manuel/

Doerschuk, R. (1999, December 7). *Rick Danko – The Last Interview.* http://theband.hiof.no/articles/rd_120799.html

Fox News. (2022, December 16). *Tucker Carlson: We were shocked to learn this* [Video]. YouTube. https://www.youtube.com/watch?v=PAiRmhXvJHs

Garth Hudson – Biography page. (2022, March 9). Garth Hudson. https://web.archive.org/web/20220705190924/https://www.garthhudson.com/biography/

Goldman, R. (2013, November 18). The Top 5 John F. Kennedy Assassination conspiracy theories. *ABC News.* https://abcnews.go.com/US/top-john-kennedy-assassination-conspiracy-theories/story?id=20614951

Grim, R. (2022, December 23). Lee Harvey Oswald, the CIA, and LSD: New clues in newly declassified documents. *The Intercept.* https://theintercept.com/2022/12/19/lee-harvey-oswald-cia-lsd-jfk/

Harris, C. (2016). *The Band: Pioneers of Americana Music.* Rowman & Littlefield Publishers.

Hedegaard, E. (2019, November 9). Rolling Stone. *Rolling Stone.* https://www.rollingstone.com/feature/the-last-confession-of-e-howard-hunt-76611/5/

Helm, L., & Davis, S. (2013). *This wheel's on fire: Levon Helm and the Story of the Band.*

Knoedelseder, W. K., Jr. (2019, March 10). Morris Levy Gets 10-Year Sentence : Roulette Records chief fined $200,000 in extortion case – Los Angeles Times. *Los Angeles Times.* https://www.latimes.com/archives/la-xpm-1988-10-29-fi-215-story.html

Maher, H. (2013, November 20). Why Lee Harvey Oswald fled to the Soviet Union. *The Atlantic.* https://www.theatlantic.com/international/archive/2013/11/why-lee-harvey-oswald-fled-to-the-soviet-union/281662/

Michael Franzese. (2020, October 2). *Mafias Involvement in the Music Industry | Morris Levy with Michael Franzese* [Video]. YouTube. https://www.youtube.com/watch?v=1AmP9hj71i8

Morrison, D. (2022a, March 2). Deep in the Heart of a Lonely Kid. *Medium.* https://medium.com/@delveintodanko/deep-in-the-heart-of-a-lonely-kid-a2b0eb5af32e

Morrison, D. (2022b, March 2). Farther On Up the Road. *Medium.* https://medium.com/@delveintodanko/farther-on-up-the-road-a4b02b4594df

Nygaard King, B. (2008, January 29). *Ronnie Hawkins.* The Canadian Encyclopedia. https://www.thecanadianencyclopedia.ca/en/article/ronnie-hawkins

Q with Tom Power. (2016, December 15). *Robbie Robertson Talks About Jack Ruby, Robbing A Poker Game And His New Memoir* [Video]. YouTube. https://www.youtube.com/watch?v=KkkoBJI-8Ko

Robertson, R. (2016). *Testimony.* Random House.

Roos, D. (2021). Before JFK, Lee Harvey Oswald tried to assassinate a former army general. *HISTORY.* https://www.history.com/news/lee-harvey-oswald-other-target

Ruby As a Young Man. (n.d.). https://www.jfk-assassination.net/ruby2.htm

Ruby's Childhood. (n.d.). https://www.jfk-assassination.net/ruby1.htm

Schneider, J. (2009). *Whispering Pines : The Northern Roots of American music From Hank Snow to The Band.* ECW Press.

Schultz, C. (2013, October 4). Before JFK, Lee Harvey Oswald tried to kill an army major general. *Smithsonian Magazine.* https://www.smithsonianmag.com/smart-news/before-jfk-lee-harvey-oswald-tried-to-kill-an-army-major-general-609517/

Scorsese, M. (Director). (1978, April 26). *The Last Waltz* [Video]. United Artists.

Scribner, H. (2022, December 6). *70% of voters want JFK assassination records release, poll shows.* Axios. https://www.axios.com/2022/12/06/jfk-assassination-records-cia-poll

Strombo (2013, November 21). *Robbie Robertson on Playing Jack Ruby's Nightclub: 'You Could Smell Danger In The Air'* [Video]. YouTube. https://www.youtube.com/watch?v=C4-F6GaqnD8

Times, N. Y. (1977, March 31). Professor, 65, who killed himself may have been Oswald confidant. *The New York Times.* https://

www.nytimes.com/1977/03/31/archives/professor-65-who-killed-himself-may-have-been-oswald-confidant.html

Times, N. Y. (1990, May 23). Morris Levy Is Dead; Power in Recording And Club Owner, 62. *The New York Times*. http://www.nytimes.com/1990/05/23/obituaries/morris-levy-is-dead-power-in-recording-and-club-owner-62.html

Titus, J. (2016). Wikileaks: CIA In Japan, LSD At Atsugi, Nagell And Oswald | Covert Book Report. *Covert Book Report | Tell the Truth and Run – George Seldes*. https://www.covertbookreport.com/wikileaks-cia-in-japan-lsd-at-atsusgi-nagell-and-oswald/

Warren Commission Report: Chapter 1. (2018, October 29). National Archives. https://www.archives.gov/research/jfk/warren-commission-report/chapter-1

Chapter 2

A British-invasion time line. (1997, December). AMERICAN HERITAGE. https://www.americanheritage.com/british-invasion-time-line

Crime Museum, LLC. (2021, August 13). *H.H. Holmes – Crime Museum*. Crime Museum. https://www.crimemuseum.org/crime-library/serial-killers/hh-holmes/

Davies, D. (1997). *Kink: An Autobiography*. Hyperion.

Davies, D. (2022). *Living On A Thin Line*. Hachette UK.

Davies, R. (1994). *X-Ray: The Unauthorized Autobiography*. Abrams.

Davies, R. (2013). *Americana: The Kinks, the Road and the Perfect Riff*. Random House.

Ellul, J. (2021, April 11). *K2 — The Kinks*. http://bandlogojukebox.com/blog/2021/4/3/k2-the-kinks-2t44e [dead link]

George, C. (1994, August 27). The Kitchen Sink Kink. https://kindakinks.net/misc/articles/indepen.html

Gewen, B. (2017, July 9). *Ray Davies, rock poet?* ArtsBeat. https://artsbeat.blogs.nytimes.com/2008/03/05/ray-davies-rock-poet/

Illinois Welcomes The Kinks! June 20–23, 1965. (2020, June 18). https://www.downstatesounds.com/2020/06/illinois-welcomes-kinks-june-20-23-1965.html

Jovanovic, R. (2013). *God Save The Kinks: A Biography*. Aurum.

Linedecker, C. L. (2013). *The man who killed boys: The John Wayne Gacy, Jr. Story*. St. Martin's Paperbacks.

Rogan, J. (2015). *Ray Davies: A Complicated Life*. Random House.

Ruggiero, B. (2014). Kinks Bio Shows Davies Brothers Brawl So Hard. *The Village Voice*. https://www.villagevoice.com/2014/07/24/kinks-bio-shows-davies-brothers-brawl-so-hard/

Savage, M. (2017, April 23). To Ray Davies, America is a 'beautiful but dangerous' place. *BBC News*. https://www.bbc.com/news/amp/entertainment-arts-39665367

Seaburn, P. (2017, March 30). *The Kinks' Dave Davies Had UFO and Alien Encounters*. https://web.archive.org/web/20170413021615/https://mysteriousuniverse.org/2017/03/the-kinks-dave-davies-had-ufo-and-alien-encounters/

Staff, B. C. B. (2023, June 23). *June 23, '65: Kinks promoted by John Wayne Gacy – Best Classic Bands*. Best Classic Bands. https://bestclassicbands.com/kinks-john-wayne-gacy-6-23-155/

Taysom, J. (2020, May 28). This is why The Kinks were banned from the United States. *Far Out Magazine*. https://faroutmagazine.co.uk/the-kinks-ray-davies-banned-from-usa-america/

Chapter 3

Barrett, D. (2009, July 26). *Letters shed new light on Kray twins scandal*. Telegraph. https://web.archive.org/web/20100313005219/http://www.telegraph.co.uk:80/news/newstopics/politics/lawandorder/5907125/Letters-shed-new-light-on-Kray-twins-scandal.html

BBC ON THIS DAY | 4 | 1969: Kray twins guilty of McVitie murder. (n.d.). http://news.bbc.co.uk/onthisday/hi/dates/stories/march/4/newsid_2515000/2515103.stm

Campbell, D. (2017, November 29). The selling of the Krays: how two mediocre criminals created their own legend. *The Guardian*. https://www.theguardian.com/uk-news/2015/sep/03/the-selling-of-the-krays-how-two-mediocre-criminals-created-their-own-legendlegends

Daltrey, R. (2018). *Thanks a lot Mr Kibblewhite: My Story*. Henry Holt and Company.

Davies, D. (1998). *Kink: An Autobiography*. Hyperion.

History of the Metropolitan Police : The Kray twins – jailed in 1969. (n.d.). https://web.archive.org/web/20130223114637/http://www.met.police.uk/history/krays.htm

'I made the Krays famous' – *photographer, David Bailey*. (2014, February 4). [Video]. BBC News. https://www.bbc.com/news/av/

entertainment-arts-26030503

Kemp, G. (2009). *I know this much: from Soho to Spandau.* HarperCollins UK.

Kemp, M. (2000). True: The Autobiography of Martin Kemp. Orion Publishing Company.

Kray, K. (2019). *The Twins – men of violence.*

Kray, R., & Dinenage, F. (1994). *My Story.* Macmillan Children's Books.

Mikkelson, B. (2012). Etymology of blackmail. *Snopes.* https://www.snopes.com/fact-check/blackmail/

Myall, S. (2015, August 31). How were Frank Sinatra and Morrissey mixed up with the Krays? *Mirror.* https://www.mirror.co.uk/news/uk-news/9-things-you-never-knew-6357210

NME. (2009). Ray Davies: 'The Kray twins wanted to manage The Kinks' *NME.* https://www.nme.com/news/music/the-kinks-39-1309143

Pearson, J. (2015). *The profession of violence: The Rise and Fall of the Kray Twins.* William Collins.

Rogovoy, S. (2018). The secret Jewish history of Roger Daltrey. *The Forward.* https://forward.com/culture/music/415570/the-secret-jewish-history-of-roger-daltrey/

What was National Service? (n.d.). National Army Museum. https://www.nam.ac.uk/explore/what-was-national-service

Chapter 4

Artsrunik, V. (n.d.). *JohnMcVicar.com.* https://web.archive.org/web/20080207073911/http://www.johnmcvicar.com/biog.htm

BBC News. (2010, October 19). Kray twins and Sir Elton John memorabilia sold. *BBC News.* https://www.bbc.com/news/uk-england-sussex-11575064

Beaumont-Thomas, B. (2020, November 6). Cliff Richard becomes first artist to reach UK Top 5 across eight decades. *The Guardian.* https://www.theguardian.com/music/2020/nov/06/cliff-richard-first-artist-top-five-eight-decades-music-the-air-that-i-breathe

Bellotti, A. (2022, August 8). *Kray twins' debauched legend – from EastEnders pals to scandalous sex secret.* Mirror. https://www.mirror.co.uk/news/uk-news/kray-twins-debauched-legend-knockout-24109313

Campbell, D. (2022, September 28). John McVicar obituary. *The Guardian.* https://www.theguardian.com/uk-news/2022/sep/26/john-mcvicar-obituary

Daltrey, R. (2018). *Thanks a lot Mr Kibblewhite: My Story.* Henry Holt

Fletcher, T. (2010). *Dear Boy: The Life of Keith Moon*. Omnibus Press.

Glacken, B. B. (1999, December 13). Cliff: Sexy, violent and naughty. *The Irish Times*. https://www.irishtimes.com/culture/cliff-sexy-violent-and-naughty-1.260680

Hughes, R. (2018, May 6). Cliff Richard kidnap plotted by Kray twins reveals former gangland boss. *Express.co.uk*. https://www.express.co.uk/celebrity-news/955876/cliff-richard-young-singer-kray-twins-gangster-kidnapping-london-crime

Jackson, C. (2016, October 21). *Aberfan: The mistake that cost a village its children*. BBC News. https://www.bbc.co.uk/news/resources/idt-150d11df-c541-44a9-9332-560a19828c47

Janes, D. (2015). Kray Twins: The Killer Truth Behind the Criminal Legends. *The Line Up*. https://the-line-up.com/kray-twins

Kray, R., & Dinenage, F. (1994). *My story*. Macmillan Children's Books.

Repsch, J. (2000). *The legendary Joe Meek: The Telstar Man*.

Simpson, D. (2017, May 31). Who's back. *The Guardian*. https://www.theguardian.com/music/2005/jan/28/petetownshend.popandrock

Sunder, K. (2021, January 18). Cliff Richard is one, so is Ben Kingsley: Anglo-Indians were known for fun and fusion food, but their communities are slowly fading. *South China Morning Post*. https://www.scmp.com/lifestyle/family-relationships/article/3117731/cliff-richard-one-so-ben-kingsley-anglo-indians-were

Turner, D. (2022). Smoke, the. *Nostalgia Central – the Way Things Used to Be*. https://nostalgiacentral.com/music/artists-l-to-z/artists-s/smoke/

Chapter 5

Abigail Folger | Charles Manson family and Sharon Tate–LaBianca murders | *Cielodrive.com*. (n.d.). https://www.cielodrive.com/abigail-folger.php

Beachcombing. (2016, September 29). *Bottomless Pit in the Californian Desert – Beachcombing's Bizarre History Blog*. Beachcombing's Bizarre History Blog. https://www.strangehistory.net/2016/09/05/bottomless-pit-californian-desert/

Blanco, J. I. (n.d.). *Steve Grogan | Murderpedia, the encyclopedia of murderers*. https://murderpedia.org/male.G/g/grogan-steve-dennis.htm

Brooks Poston | Charles Manson Family and Sharon Tate–LaBianca

Murders | *Cielodrive.com.* (n.d.). https://www.cielodrive.com/
brooks-poston.php

Bugliosi, V., & Gentry, C. (2014). *Helter Skelter: The True Story of the Manson Murders.* Random House.

Bustamante, M. (2019, November 26). *Infamous story of the Beach Boys and Murderous Manic: Charles Manson – StMU History Media.* https://
web.archive.org/web/20210423165144/https://stmuhistorymedia.
org/infamous-story-of-the-beach-boys-and-murderous-manic-
charles-manson/

Chappell, B. (2023, July 12). A former Manson Family member is
free, after her parole was reversed 5 times. *NPR.* https://www.npr.
org/2023/07/12/1187225790/leslie-van-houten-manson-murder-
freed-prison-parole

Cobb, J. C. (2018, April 4). Even though he is revered today, MLK
was widely disliked by the American public when he was killed.
Smithsonian Magazine. https://www.smithsonianmag.com/history/
why-martin-luther-king-had-75-percent-disapproval-rating-year-
he-died-180968664/

Definition of helter-skelter. (n.d.). In *Merriam-Webster Dictionary.*
https://www.merriam-webster.com/dictionary/helter-skelter

DeLong, W. (2019). Tex Watson: From Nice Texas Boy To Manson
Family Murderer. *All That's Interesting.* https://allthatsinteresting.
com/tex-watson

*Donald 'Shorty' Shea | Charles Manson family and Sharon Tate–LaBianca
murders | Cielodrive.com.* (n.d.). https://www.cielodrive.com/
donald-shea.php

Editor At Surfertoday.com & Editor at SurferToday.com. (2023). Dennis
Wilson: the only surfer in The Beach Boys. *Surfertoday.* https://
www.surfertoday.com/surfing/dennis-wilson-the-only-surfer-in-the-
beach-boys

Felton, D., & Dalton, D. (1970, June 25). *Charles Manson: The Incredible
Story of the Most Dangerous Man Alive.* Rolling Stone. https://web.
archive.org/web/20210107031625/https://www.rollingstone.com/
culture/culture-news/charles-manson-the-incredible-story-of-the-
most-dangerous-man-alive-85235/

Genetically Modified Skeptic. (2018, November 17). *How quacks and cults
recruit followers.* YouTube. https://youtube.com/watch?v=qMpP_
WqdpLQ

Genetically Modified Skeptic. (2019, April 30). *The Skeptik's guide*

to starting a cult [Video]. YouTube. https://www.youtube.com/
watch?v=Ij88on7Us8k

Griffiths, D. (1968, December 21). Dennis Wilson – 'I live with 17 girls'
Record Mirror. http://www.smileysmile.net/uncanny/index.php/
dennis-wilson-i-live-with-17-girls

Guinn, J. (2014). *Manson: The Life and Times of Charles Manson.* Simon
and Schuster.

Inmate Charles Manson Dies of Natural Causes. (2017, November 19).
California Department of Corrections and Rehabilitation. https://
web.archive.org/web/20171120064948/https://news.cdcr.ca.gov/
news-releases/2017/11/19/inmate-charles-manson-dies-of-natural-
causes/

Jackson, C. (2021, August 17). What is redlining? *The New York Times.*
https://www.nytimes.com/2021/08/17/realestate/what-is-redlining.
html

james doakes. (2012, October 28). *Paul Watkins CNN interview* [Video].
YouTube. https://www.youtube.com/watch?v=rzpLyB8IE0M

*Jay Sebring | Charles Manson family and Sharon Tate–LaBianca murders |
Cielodrive.com.* (n.d.). https://www.cielodrive.com/jay-sebring.php

Lansing, H. A. (2022, May 10). The Only Manson Family Killer
to be Paroled – H. Allegra Lansing – Medium. *Medium.* https://
themansonfamily-mtts.medium.com/the-only-manson-family-
killer-to-be-paroled-6cd33ca0b07e

Leaf, D. (1978). *The Beach Boys and the California Myth.*

Lester, P. (2020). Pet Sounds: The story of how the Beach Boys helped
inspire progressive rock. *Louder.* https://www.loudersound.com/
features/pet-sounds-the-story-of-how-the-beach-boys-went-proto-
prog

Love, M., & Hirsch, J. S. (2017). *Good vibrations: My Life as a Beach Boy.*
Blue Rider Press.

Manson Family Utopia. (2022, September 26). *Manson Documentary
Film 1973 original* [Video]. YouTube. https://www.youtube.com/
watch?v=EctcD91kcBA

Margaritoff, M. (2019). Leona 'Candy' Stevens: The Wife Who Lied
For Charles Manson. *All That's Interesting.* https://allthatsinteresting.
com/leona-candy-stevens

Margaritoff, M. (2021). Leslie Van Houten: From Homecoming
Queen To Manson Family Murderess. *All That's Interesting.* https://
allthatsinteresting.com/leslie-van-houten

Romano, A. (2023, July 12). The Manson Family murders and Helter Skelter, explained. *Vox*. https://www.vox.com/2019/8/7/20695284/charles-manson-family-what-is-helter-skelter-explained

Runtagh, J. (2019, March 21). The 'Once upon a Time in Hollywood' trailer makes a chilling secret reference to Charles Manson. *Peoplemag*. https://people.com/music/once-upon-a-time-in-hollywood-trailer-chilling-musical-secret/

Sanders, E. (2002). *The Family*. Da Capo Press.

Sanders, L. (2017, November 20). Charles Manson is dead: What was his 'Helter Skelter' race war plan? *Newsweek*. https://www.newsweek.com/charles-manson-what-was-helter-skelter-race-war-plan-716625

Schaal, E. (2019). The Classic Beach Boys Album Paul McCartney Said Inspired Sgt. Pepper. *Showbiz Cheat Sheet*. https://www.cheatsheet.com/entertainment/the-classic-beach-boys-album-paul-mccartney-said-inspired-sgt-peppers.html/

Sederstrom, J. (2023, May 23). Who did Roman Polanski first suspect murdered his wife Sharon Tate? *Oxygen Official Site*. https://www.oxygen.com/true-crime-buzz/who-did-roman-polanski-first-suspect-killed-wife-sharon-tate

Spahn Ranch Search Warrant. (2019). *CharlesManson.com*. https://www.charlesmanson.com/vicinity-crimes/spahn-ranch/spahn-ranch-search-warrant/

Steven Parent | Charles Manson family and Sharon Tate–LaBianca murders | Cielodrive.com. (n.d.). *https://www.cielodrive.com/steven-parent.php*

Sullivan, P. (2018, June 25). Rolling Stone. *Rolling Stone*. https://www.rollingstone.com/music/music-news/gram-parsons-the-mysterious-death-and-aftermath-204652/

The Associated Press. (2011, January 20). Manson follower Patricia Krenwinkel, who was arrested in Mobile, faces parole hearing. *Al*. https://www.al.com/wire/2011/01/manson_follower_alabama_krenwinkel.html

Van Matre, B. L. (1991, October 13). CHILD OF ABUSE. *Chicago Tribune*. https://www.chicagotribune.com/news/ct-xpm-1991-10-13-9104020625-story.html

Wilson, B. (2016). *I am Brian Wilson: The genius behind the Beach Boys*. Hachette UK.

Wojciech Frykowski | Charles Manson Family and Sharon Tate–LaBianca murders | Cielodrive.com. (n.d.). https://www.cielodrive.com/wojciech-frykowski.php

Yee, G. (2022, May 26). Manson follower Patricia Krenwinkel approved for parole – Los Angeles Times. *Los Angeles Times*. https://www.latimes.com/california/story/2022-05-26/manson-follower-patricia-krenwinkel-approved-for-parole

Chapter 6

Boot Leg. (2018, September 2). *Sonny Ochs speaks at the 1976 Phil Ochs Memorial celebration* [Video]. YouTube. https://www.youtube.com/watch?v=OMHY2u3f0aI

Bowser, K. (Director). (2011, January 5). *Phil Ochs: There But For Fortune* [Video].

Breshears, J. (2014). *Phil Ochs*. The Areopagus. https://www.theareopagus.org/blog/wp-content/uploads/2014/07/Phil-Ochs-Background-Biography.pdf

Burns, A. (2005, October 21). *AmericanHeritage.com / Events*. https://web.archive.org/web/20051219220648/http://www.americanheritage.com/articles/web/20051021-pentagon-vietnam-protest-washington-dc-lyndon-johnson-jerry-rubin-david-dellinger-allen-ginsberg-yippie-robert-mcnamara.shtml

Crowe, C. (2023, April 6). Rolling Stone. *Rolling Stone*. https://www.rollingstone.com/music/music-news/neil-young-the-rolling-stone-interview-123513/

Davidson, S. (2011, February 19). Friday Film: Phil Ochs finally gets his biopic. *The Forward*. https://forward.com/schmooze/135541/friday-film-phil-ochs-finally-gets-his-biopic/

DeCurtis, A. (2009, August 8). Peace, love and Charlie Manson. *The New York Times*. https://www.nytimes.com/2009/08/02/weekinreview/02decurtis.html

Ed Sanders Collection | Library. (n.d.). https://library.stlawu.edu/collection/ed-sanders-collection

Eliot, M. (1995). *Death of a rebel*. Carol Publishing Corporation.

Guinn, J. (2014). *Manson: The Life and Times of Charles Manson*. Simon and Schuster.

January 7, 1966 – New York City, NY – Carnegie Hall. (2016, March 22). Celebrating Phil Ochs. https://celebratingphilochs.com/january-7-1966-new-york-city-ny-carnegie-hall/

Jolly, N., & Jolly, N. (2018). Charles Manson and Mamas and the Papas: Manson and the musical world, part three. *The Brag*. https://thebrag.com/charles-manson-mamas-papas/

Love, M., & Hirsch, J. S. (2017). *Good vibrations: My Life as a Beach Boy*. Blue Rider Press.

McDonough, J. (2013). *Shakey: Neil Young's Biography*. Random House.

McNeil, L. (2014, April 29). Dirty Water: The Story of the Standells. *Vice*. https://www.vice.com/en/article/yvq34y/dirty-water-the-story-of-the-standells

Moon, A. (2023, June 23). *Interview: Tony Valentino of The Standells*. The Diversity of Classic Rock. https://crazyonclassicrock.com/2023/05/24/interview-tony-valentino-of-the-standells/

Moore, N., & Kelly, D. (2016). Celebrities Connected To Charles Manson. *Grunge*. https://www.grunge.com/34378/celebrities-connected-charles-manson/

Olofsson, H. (2020). Gene Clark – The Byrd And The Best (Part 2 of 6). *PopDiggers*. https://popdiggers.com/gene-clark-the-byrd-and-the-best-part-2/

Peace Eye Bookstore. (2018, September 5). The Downtown Pop Underground. https://dsps.lib.uiowa.edu/downtownpopunderground/place/peace-eye-bookstore/

Poetry Foundation. (n.d.). *Ed Sanders | Poetry Foundation*. https://www.poetryfoundation.org/poets/ed-sanders

Sanchez, J. (2020, March 26). Phil Ochs: the doomed folk singer who woke up from the American dream. *The Guardian*. https://www.theguardian.com/music/2020/mar/26/phil-ochs-the-doomed-folk-singer-who-woke-up-from-the-american-dream

Sanders, E. (2002). *The Family*. Da Capo Press.

Schumacher, M. (2018). *There But for Fortune: The Life of Phil Ochs*. U of Minnesota Press.

Standells. (2017, April 8). Remember Gordon McLendon? 50 years ago today: Influential radio programmer and group station owner Gordon McLendon decided in the spring of 1967… Facebook. *https://www.facebook.com/Standells/posts/10155251022019312/*

Stanley, T. (2017, November 21). Charles Manson was the sum of the Sixties and all its excess. *The Telegraph*. https://www.telegraph.co.uk/news/2017/11/21/charles-manson-sum-sixties-excess/

Sweeney, C. (2016, May 15). 50 years of 'Dirty Water' by the Standells. *Boston Magazine*. https://www.bostonmagazine.com/arts-entertainment/2016/05/15/50-years-dirty-water-the-standells/

Terrence Melcher testimony. (2018, July 19). CharlesManson.com. https://www.charlesmanson.com/testimony/terrence-melcher/

The aftermath. (n.d.). Crime + Investigation UK. https://www.crimeandinvestigation.co.uk/crime-files/charles-manson/aftermath

The Fugs History Continued. (n.d.). The Fugs. http://www.thefugs.com/history3.html

The History of the Fugs Continued. (n.d.). The Fugs. https://www.thefugs.com/history2.html

The Mamas & the Papas: inside the band's love quadrangle, drug problems and hit songs. (2023, May 9). *Biography*. https://www.biography.com/news/the-mamas-and-the-papas-origins

Young, N. (2012). *Waging heavy peace: A Hippie Dream*. Penguin UK.

Chapter 7

Allans Films. (2022, February 25). *Meredith Hunter: A Black Man with a Gun (Submitted version)* [Video]. YouTube. https://www.youtube.com/watch?v=EsjGhHiF4Vk

Altamont Rock Festival: '60s Abruptly End. (2010, March). *Livermore History*. https://web.archive.org/web/20111226045553/http://www.livermorehistory.com/Newsletters/2010_03-04_MarApr.pdf

Andrews, S. (2018). The End of the Hippies: Chaos and Violence at the 1969 Altamont Music Festival. *Thevintagenews*. https://www.thevintagenews.com/2018/08/21/altamont-festival/

Austerlitz, S. (2018a). *Just a shot away: Peace, Love, and Tragedy with the Rolling Stones at Altamont*. Thomas Dunne Books.

Austerlitz, S. (2018b, August 3). Just a shot away: Peace, love, and tragedy with the Rolling Stones at Altamont. *Vulture*. https://www.vulture.com/2018/08/peace-love-and-tragedy-with-the-rolling-stones-at-altamont.html

Austerlitz, S. (2020, July 19). Rolling Stone. *Rolling Stone*. https://www.rollingstone.com/feature/remembering-meredith-hunter-the-fan-killed-at-altamont-630260/

Bangs, L., Brown, R., Burks, J., Egan, S., Goodwin, M., Link, G., Marcus, G., Morthland, J., Schoenfeld, E., Thomas, P., & Winner, L. (1970, January 21). Rolling Stone. *Rolling Stone*. https://www.rollingstone.com/feature/the-rolling-stones-disaster-at-altamont-let-it-bleed-71299/

Browne, D. (2012, May 23). Rolling Stone. *Rolling Stone*. https://www.rollingstone.com/music/music-news/grace-slicks-festival-memories-fearing-orgies-and-getting-lit-71111/

Craig, P. (1969, December 8). Out Of Sight, Man!

300,000 At Bash! *Google News.* https://news.google.com/newspapers?id=kXwzAAAAIBAJ&sjid=4DIHAAAAIBAJ&pg=4739%2C6027593

Davies, D. (2021, June 2). Historian Uncovers The Racist Roots Of The 2nd Amendment. *NPR.* https://www.npr.org/2021/06/02/1002107670/historian- uncovers-the-racist-roots-of-the-2nd-amendment

Dowd, K. (2019, December 5). 'If Jesus had been there, he would have been crucified': 50 years ago, terror and death at Altamont. *SFGate.* https://www.sfgate.com/bayarea/article/altamont-free-concert-rolling-stones-14879702.php

Eden, R. (2008, March 2). Hells Angels plotted to kill Mick Jagger. *The Telegraph.* https://www.telegraph.co.uk/news/uknews/1580456/Hells-Angels-plotted-to-kill-Mick-Jagger.html

Ferranti, S. (2018, July 3). The Grim Story of Hells Angels Killing a Black Teen at a Rolling Stones Concert. *Vice.* https://www.vice.com/en/article/bj39dm/the-grim-story-of-hells-angels-killing-a-black-teen-at-a-rolling-stones-concert

Frere-Jones, S. (2019, March 28). The chaos of Altamont and the murder of Meredith Hunter. *The New Yorker.* https://www.newyorker.com/culture/cultural-comment/the-chaos-of-altamont-and-the-murder-of-meredith-hunter

Gleiberman, O. (2022, February 24). Altamont at 45: The most dangerous rock concert. *BBC Culture.* https://www.bbc.com/culture/article/20141205-did-altamont-end-the-60s

Golsen, T. (2022, May 29). Watch Crosby, Stills, and Nash play 'Suite: Judy Blue Eyes.' *Far Out Magazine.* https://faroutmagazine.co.uk/watch-crosby-stills-and-nash-play-suite-judy-blue-eyes-at-woodstock/

Lewis, S. (2023, February 20). *Put the Boot In: Flying Burrito Brothers Live at Altamont Speedway 1969.* Talk From the Rock Room. https://www.talkfromtherockroom.com/2023/02/put-boot-in-flying-burrito-brothers.html

Maysles, A., Maysles, D., & Zwerin, C. (Directors). (1970, December 6). *Gimme Shelter* [Video]. Maysles Films.

Metzger, R. (2010, December 13). Who was Meredith Hunter, the young man stabbed to death at Altamont? *Dangerous Minds.* https://dangerousminds.net/comments/ who_was_meredith_hunter_the_young_man_stabbed_to_death_at_altamont

Moehlis, J. (2010, April 25). *Interview: Paul Kantner.* Music-Illuminati.

http://music-illuminati.com/interview-paul-kantner/

National News Briefs – UPI Archives. (1985, April 10). *UPI.* https://www.upi.com/Archives/1985/04/10/National-News-Briefs/3657481957200/

Parker, L. (2019, July 23). Bill Wyman remembers 'absolutely brilliant' Rolling Stones bandmate Brian Jones, 50 years later. *Yahoo! Entertainment.* https://www.yahoo.com/entertainment/bill-wyman-remembers-late-rolling-stones-bandmate-brian-jones-50-years-later-absolutely-brilliant-193632827.html

Ruggiero, B. (2016, August 24). *Inside Altamont: New book looks back at Rock's 'Darkest Day.'* Houston Press. https://web.archive.org/web/20220928120454/https://www.houstonpress.com/music/inside-altamont-new-book-looks-back-at-rocks-darkest-day-8690359

RustedTelevisione. (2022, December 20). David Crosby on… the chaos at Altamont (1969) [Video]. YouTube. https://www.youtube.com/watch?v=abN92Kyj3Tc

Selvin, J. (2016a). *Altamont: The Rolling Stones, the Hells Angels, and the Inside Story of Rock's Darkest Day.* HarperCollins.

Selvin, J. (2016b, October 4). Rolling Stones' gig at Altamont has darker past in revealing new details. *Mail Online.* https://www.dailymail.co.uk/news/article-3750676/The-dark-truth-Jagger-Altamont.html

Staff. (2019, December 6). The Rolling Stones & the Altamont Free Concert, 50 years on. *Far Out Magazine.* https://faroutmagazine.co.uk/the-rolling-stones-altamont-free-concert-1969/

Sullivan, P. (1973, October 25). Gram Parsons: The Mysterious Death – and Aftermath. *Rolling Stone.* https://www.rollingstone.com/music/music-news/gram-parsons-the-mysterious-death-and-aftermath-204652/

White, D. (2012, February 10). R.I.P. Altamont Raceway. *SFGate.* https://www.sfgate.com/sports/article/R-I-P-Altamont-Raceway-3231903.php

Yusko, D. (2020, April 17). The short life and tragic death of Meredith Hunter – Dennis Yusko – Medium. *Medium.* https://medium.com/@day4343/the-short-life-and-tragic-death-of-meredith-hunter-fb6eee23b5ad

Chapter 8

BBC News. (2019, March 13). California death penalty: Governor

Gavin Newsom halts executions. BBC News. https://www.bbc.co.uk/news/world-us-canada-47549422

BIOGRAPHY: BOBBY BEAUSOLEIL. (n.d.). http://bobbybeausoleil.com/biography.html

Bobby Beausoleil arrest Report – California Highway Patrol – August 6, 1969. (n.d.). http://www.cielodrive.com/bobby-beausoleil-arrest-report-08-06-69.php

Breznikar, K. (2012, July 27). Bobby BeauSoleil interview (The Orkustra) – It's Psychedelic Baby Magazine. *It's Psychedelic Baby Magazine.* https://www.psychedelicbabymag.com/2014/07/bobby-beausoleil-interview-orkustra.html

Carlson, A., & Pelisek, C. (2017, November 21). Relative of First Manson 'Family' Victim Speaks Out After Cult Leader's Death: 'About Time' *Peoplemag.* https://people.com/crime/gary-hinman-family-charles-manson-death/

Gary Hinman | Charles Manson family and Sharon Tate–LaBianca murders | *Cielodrive.com.* (n.d.). http://www.cielodrive.com/gary-hinman.php

Hattenstone, S. (2022, October 19). Kenneth Anger: 'No, I am not a Satanist.' *The Guardian.* https://www.theguardian.com/film/2010/mar/10/kenneth-anger-interview

Hoskyns, B. (2001). *Arthur Lee: Alone Again Or.* Canongate Books Limited.

Sanders, E. (2002). *The Family.* Da Capo Press.

Serena, K. (2019). Gary Hinman: the first Manson family murder victim. *All That's Interesting.* https://allthatsinteresting.com/gary-hinman

Zappa, F., & Occhiogrosso, P. (1989). *Real Frank Zappa Book.* Simon and Schuster.

Chapter 9

ABC News. (2020a, February 1). Life with Bundy 120/20 1 PART 4 [Video]. YouTube. https://www.youtube.com/watch?v=rqDYIfsnd2Y

ABC News. (2020b, February 1). Life with Bundy 120/20 1 PART 5 [Video]. YouTube. https://www.youtube.com/watch?v=ogapLWfUQ5E

Atkinson, J. (2019, October 1). Debbie Harry's Memoir Face It: 17 Amazing Anecdotes. Gigwise. https://web.archive.org/web/20230129204331/https://gigwise.com/features/3361726/debbie-harrys-memoir-face-it-17-amazing-anecdotes

Audioburst. (2016, July 12). Debbie Harry On The Night She Possibly

Hitched A Ride With Ted Bundy [Video]. YouTube. https://www.youtube.com/watch?v=hCT5gvr_Mo4

Bailey Sarian. (2020, March 30). 1 Of Americas Most Notorious, Ted Bundy – Mystery & Makeup | Bailey Sarian [Video]. YouTube. https://www.youtube.com/watch?v=ySOKrCusEjw

Brown, N. (2020, September 22). How Ted Bundy managed to escape prison more than once. *NZ Herald.* https://www.nzherald.co.nz/world/how-ted-bundy-managed-to-escape-prison-more-than-once/37QKUMRPPITUV37N6KRT7UTM4M/

Casuso, B. J. (1989, January 24). Bundy Blames Pornography. *Chicago Tribune.* https://www.chicagotribune.com/news/ct-xpm-1989-01-24-8902270928-story.html

Cimino, A. (2019). *Ted Bundy: America's Most Evil Serial Killer.* Arcturus Editions.

Cloudylime. (2021, March 16). Ted Bundy last interview [Video]. YouTube. https://www.youtube.com/watch?v=sCUQLPOjvxs

Debbie Harry and Chris Stein: Blonde on Blonde. (2006, July 13). *The Independent.* https://web.archive.org/web/20090526093231/http://www.independent.co.uk/news/people/profiles/debbie-harry-and-chris-stein-blonde-on-blonde-407773.html

Gillibrand, A. (2019, May 30). Debbie Harry claims she survived Ted Bundy – he smelt 'incredibly bad.' *Metro.* https://metro.co.uk/2019/05/30/debbie-harry-claims-survived-ted-bundy-getting-car-smelt-incredibly-bad-9743128/

Green, P. (2019, October 1). Debbie Harry: 'Sex is what makes everything happen.' *The Irish Times.* https://www.irishtimes.com/culture/music/debbie-harry-sex-is-what-makes-everything-happen-1.4035186

Harry, D. (2019). *Face it.* HarperCollins.

How Blondie's Debbie Harry escaped serial killer Ted Bundy. (2021, March 18). *Far Out Magazine.* https://faroutmagazine.co.uk/debbie-harry-blondie-escaped-ted-bundy-killer/

Independent.ie. (2014, August 29). Blonde beauty: Debbie Harry talks looks, music, and lacking that maternal instinct ahead of the Picnic tonight. *Independent.ie.* https://www.independent.ie/entertainment/music/blonde-beauty-debbie-harry-talks-looks-music-and-lacking-that-maternal-instinct-ahead-of-the-picnic-tonight/30538928.html

Kendall, E. (2020). *The Phantom Prince: My Life with Ted Bundy, Updated and Expanded Edition.* Abrams.

Laytham, E. (2019, June 14). 'Evil, walking amongst us.' UK psychology professor studying Ted Bundy 3 decades later. *Lexington Herald Leader*. https://www.kentucky.com/news/local/crime/article231306373. html?_ga=2.249913295.897975615.1566239692-1726379062.1564160452

Lohr, D. (2017, December 7). DNA Evidence Fails To Link Ted Bundy To Ann Marie Burr. *HuffPost*. https://www.huffpost.com/entry/ann-marie-burr-ted-bundy_n_996660

Meet Elizabeth Kloepfer, Ted Bundy's former girlfriend. (2023, June 15). *Biography*. https://www.biography.com/crime/ted-bundy-elizabeth-kloepfer

Messy Messages. (2022, October 12). TED BUNDY AS A CHILD TO BECOMING A MONSTER [Video]. YouTube. https://www.youtube.com/watch?v=25_vttWYatY

Morris, R. (2020, May 5). Ann Marie Burr, 8, disappears from her Tacoma home on August 31, 1961. HistoryLink. https://historylink.org/File/21027

Piccotti, T. (2023, August 30). Inside Ted Bundy's troubled and disturbing childhood. *Biography*. https://www.biography.com/crime/ted-bundy-childhood

Rosewood, J. (2018, September 20). 9 early warning signs of a serial killer. *Insider*. https://www.insider.com/warning-signs-of-serial-killers-2018-5

Rule, A. (2018). *The stranger beside me: The Shocking Inside Story of Serial Killer Ted Bundy*. Gallery Books.

Sederstrom, J. (2019, August 20). What was Ted Bundy's childhood like? *Oxygen True Crime*. https://www.oxygen.com/martinis-murder/what-was-ted-bundys-childhood-like

Simpson, D. (2022, March 4). Blondie's Debbie Harry: 'It wasn't a great idea to be as reckless as I was.' *The Guardian*. https://www.theguardian.com/culture/2022/mar/03/blondies-debbie-harry-it-wasnt-a-great-idea-to-be-as-reckless-as-i-was

Taylor, T. (2018). Obvious History: Did Debbie Harry have a near-fatal brush with Ted Bundy? *Interview Magazine*. https://www.interviewmagazine.com/culture/obvious-history-debbie-harry-near-fatal-brush-ted-bundy

The Stillettos. (n.d.). [Video]. Sceneroller. https://www.sceneroller.com/bands/stillettos

Tron, G. (2020, November 20). What Did A Doctor Learn About Ted Bundy That Made Her Think He Isn't 'Pure Evil'? *Oxygen True*

Crime. https://www.oxygen.com/true-crime-buzz/crazy-not-insane-what-ted-bundy-secret-did-dorothy-lewis-learn

Wolf, E. (2022, June 28). 10 Facts About Blondie's Debbie Harry. *Mental Floss*. https://www.mentalfloss.com/article/597936/blondie-debbie-harry-facts

Chapter 10

ABC News. (2019, April 30). Two former Manson followers discuss how cult family, 1969 murders changed their lives [Video]. YouTube. https://www.youtube.com/watch?v=UHCeX27buug

ATWA Earth. (n.d.). ATWA: Air Trees Water Animals. http://www.atwaearth.com/index.html

Barrell, T. (2014). *RIFFS AND LEGENDS* – Tony Barrell. Tony Barrell. https://www.tonybarrell.com/riffs-and-legends/

Bravin, J. (2013). *Squeaky: The Life and Times of Lynette Alice Fromme*. St. Martin's Press.

Climate change history. (2017, October 6). *HISTORY*. https://www.history.com/topics/natural-disasters-and-environment/history-of-climate-change

CNN. (2015, September 22). Why she tried to kill the president [Video]. YouTube. https://www.youtube.com/watch?v=y4k4WF72dqk

Davis, S. (1985, July 4). Power, Mystery And The Hammer Of The Gods: Led Zeppelin : Rolling Stone. *Rolling Stone*. https://web.archive.org/web/20080128165609/http://www.rollingstone.com/artists/ledzeppelin/articles/story/17537975/power_mystery_and_the_hammer_of_the_gods

Davis, S. (2008). *Hammer of the Gods: The Led Zeppelin Saga*. It Books.

Duke, L. (2006, December 31). Caught in Fate's trajectory, along with Gerald Ford. *Washington Post*. https://www.washingtonpost.com/wp-dyn/content/article/2006/12/30/AR2006123000160.html

Ezard, J. (2002, November 5). Lonnie Donegan, sultan of skiffle, dies at 71. *The Guardian*. https://www.theguardian.com/uk/2002/nov/05/arts.artsnews

Herman, S. (1987, December 24). 'Squeaky' Fromme Missing from Prison. *Associated Press*. https://web.archive.org/web/20221128192132/https://apnews.com/article/1e5e5c15acfb01de03b79a767e534d97

Naughton, J. M. (1975, September 6). TWO FEET AWAY. *The New York Times*. https://www.nytimes.com/1975/09/06/archives/front-page-1-no-title-ford-safe-as-guard-seizes-a-gun-woman-pointed.

html

Salewicz, C. (2019). *Jimmy Page: The Definitive Biography*. Da Capo Press.

Sanders, E. (2002). *The Family*. Da Capo Press.

Schulps, D. (1977). Jimmy Page: The Trouser Press Interview – TeachRock. TeachRock. https://teachrock.org/article/jimmy-page-the-trouser-press-interview/

thechurchofrock. (2018, October 15). Lynette 'Squeaky' Fromme interview 10/14/18 with Rev Derek Moody and Sister Tracy [Video]. YouTube. https://www.youtube.com/watch?v=Jo5eydVrMS0

thechurchofrock. (2019, February 11). Lynette 'Squeaky' Fromme interview 2/10/19 with Rev. Moody and Sister Tracy [Video]. YouTube. https://www.youtube.com/watch?v=YKPR8tfevxo

Times, N. Y. (1975a, August 8). Smog Widespread In Rural Areas, Too, A U.S. Study Finds. *The New York Times*. https://www.nytimes.com/1975/08/08/archives/smog-widespread-in-rural-areas-too-a-us-study-finds.html

Times, N. Y. (1975b, December 18). Miss Fromme gets life in Ford Attack. *The New York Times*. https://www.nytimes.com/1975/12/18/archives/miss-fromme-gets-life-in-ford-attack-rehabilitation-doubted-by.html

Walters, D. (2011, June 2). Brown's gaffe recalls 1975 Ford assassination attempt. *Sacramento Bee*. https://web.archive.org/web/20121125073402/http://blogs.sacbee.com/capitolalertlatest/2011/06/jerry-brown-gerald-ford-assassination.html

Yang, A. (2019, May 1). Former Manson follower says despite murders, she still loves him: 'I don't think you fall out of love.' *ABC News*. https://abcnews.go.com/US/manson-follower-murders-loves-dont-fall-love/story?id=62708850

Chapter 11

Bonham, M. (2015). *John Bonham: The Powerhouse behind Led Zeppelin*. Oldcastle Books Ltd.

Cartwright, G. (2021, August 12). Bowie, bed-hopping and the blues: the wild times of Dana Gillespie. *The Guardian*. https://www.theguardian.com/music/2021/aug/12/bowie-bed-hopping-and-the-blues-the-wild-times-of-dana-gillespie

Clements, T. (2005, August 1). Aged 14, and already a harder man than most. *The Telegraph.* https://www.telegraph.co.uk/culture/books/3645442/Aged-14-and-already-a-harder-man-than-most.html

Davis, S. (2008). *Hammer of the Gods: The Led Zeppelin Saga.* It Books.

Donovan, C. (2021, February 2). *Bowie Buddie Dana Gillespie Ain't No Man, PopMatters.* PopMatters. https://www.popmatters.com/dana-gillespie-2650015130.html

Hoare, P. (1993, November 6). Obituary: John Bindon | The Independent. *The Independent.* https://www.independent.co.uk/news/people/obituary-john-bindon-1502412.html

Jovanović, M. (2020, January 9). Robert Plant Looks Back on His Son Dying at Age 5 & How It Affected Led Zeppelin. *Ultimate Guitar.* https://www.ultimate-guitar.com/news/general_music_news/robert_plant_looks_back_on_his_son_dying_at_age_5__how_it_affected_led_zeppelin.html

Led Zeppelin | Official Website Auditorium Arena – December 26, 1968. (n.d.). Led Zeppelin | Official Website – Official Website. https://www.ledzeppelin.com/show/auditorium-arena-december-26-1968

Led Zeppelin | Official website Tampa Stadium – May 5, 1973. (n.d.). Led Zeppelin | Official Website – Official Website. https://www.ledzeppelin.com/show/tampa-stadium-may-5-1973

Legge, C. (2021, March 26). Thug on and off the screen. PressReader. https://www.pressreader.com/uk/daily-mail/20210326/282905208336374

Lochrie, C. (2022, February 16). On this day: Led Zeppelin embark on their only Australia tour in 1972. *Tone Deaf.* https://tonedeaf.thebrag.com/led-zeppelin-australia-tour/

Miller, F. (2019, October 16). Princess Margaret romance: Queen's sister's whirlwind 'affair' with London gangster. *Express.co.uk.* https://www.express.co.uk/news/royal/1191738/princess-margaret-love-affair-john-bindon-mustique-royal-family-news

Miserandino, D. (2000, November 29). Led Zeppelin: John talks about his musical career with Led Zeppelin, before and after. *The Celebrity Cafe.* https://web.archive.org/web/20150512202604/http://thecelebritycafe.com/interviews/john_paul_jones.html

Robert Plant talked about the death of his son Karac in a clip from his upcoming TV interview. (2018, March 6). Led Zeppelin News. https://ledzepnews.com/2018/03/06/robert-plant-talked-about-the-death-of-his-son-karac-in-a-clip-from-the-big-interview-dan-rather/

Spitz, B. (2021). *Led Zeppelin: The Biography*. Penguin.

Starkey, A. (2022, January 7). When backstage Led Zeppelin violence erupted with John Bonham. *Far Out Magazine*. https://faroutmagazine.co.uk/oakland-incident-led-zeppelin-violence-john-bonham-peter-grant/

Wall, M. (2010). *When giants walked the Earth: A Biography Of Led Zeppelin*. Hachette UK.

Williamson, N. (2007). *The rough guide to Led Zeppelin*. Rough Guides UK.

Wootton, K. (Director). (2002, July 1). *John Bindon*. ITV Studios.

Yesterday's Papers. (2021, October 18). John Paul Jones | The Session Man (1966) [Video]. YouTube. https://www.youtube.com/watch?v=toxUbNqFcjs

Chapter 12

Alain From France. (2009, December 4). MARK OF DEVO interview 1982 [Video]. YouTube. https://www.youtube.com/watch?v=d0T0JJvhwUw

Brathwaite, L. F. (2013, January 14). WATCH: Jodie Foster 'Comes Out' During Acceptance Speech At 2013 Golden Globes – Queerty. *Queerty*. https://www.queerty.com/jodie-foster-comes-out-2013-golden-globes-20130114

CBS News. (2011, March 27). Ronald Reagan's close call [Video]. YouTube. https://www.youtube.com/watch?v=2Wr-4gNTWs4

Davis, P. (2016, July 27). *JOHN HINCKLEY – Books By Patti Davis*. Books by Patti Davis. https://booksbypattidavis.com/john-hinckley/#more-1164

DevoBook.com: 1973 Sextet DEVO. (n.d.). https://web.archive.org/web/20110814135057/http://devobook.com/sextet.html

Discovery UK. (2010, December 13). Reagan assassination attempt [Video]. YouTube. https://www.youtube.com/watch?v=N1Jid5uRFo4

Domanick, A. (2018, August 29). The Truth About Devo, America's Most Misunderstood Band. *Vice*. https://www.vice.com/en/article/43p97n/devo-mark-mothersbaugh-gerald-casale-anniversary-interview-2018

Goldberg, M. (1981, December 10). Rolling Stone. *Rolling Stone*. https://www.rollingstone.com/music/music-news/devo-sixties-idealists-or-nazis-and-clowns-119053/

Hauser, C. (2021, September 27). John Hinckley Jr. to Be Unconditionally Released in June. *The New York Times.* https://www.nytimes.com/2021/09/27/us/john-hinckley-reagan-assassination-attempt-release.html

Hermann, P., & Ruane, M. E. (2023, April 15). Medical examiner rules James Brady's death a homicide. *Washington Post.* https://www.washingtonpost.com/local/crime/james-bradys-death-ruled-homicide-by-dc-medical-examiner/2014/08/08/686de224-1f41-11e4-82f9-2cd6fa8da5c4_story.html?wpisrc=al_national

Hinckley, J. (2021a, October 29). I am a singer/songwriter but I am also an Outsider Artist. I paint abstracts, folk art, portraits and expressionism. Twitter. https://twitter.com/JohnHinckley20/status/1454122827213418504

Hinckley, J. (2021b, October 31). I believe in Peace, Love and Understanding. That's what my songs are about. If you're looking for negativity, go elsewhere. https://twitter.com/JohnHinckley20/status/1454793976188448768

Hooton, C. (2016, May 20). Jodie Foster details how 'uncomfortable' it was playing a prostitute aged 12 in Taxi Driver. *The Independent.* https://web.archive.org/web/20190226052352/https://www.independent.co.uk/arts-entertainment/films/news/jodie-foster-details-how-uncomfortable-it-was-playing-a-prostitute-aged-12-in-taxi-driver-a7040016.html

I Desire by Devo | Song Stories | Rolling Stone. (n.d.). *Rolling Stone.* https://web.archive.org/web/20140329043423/http://www.rollingstone.com/music/song-stories/i-desire-devo

Kretsch, R. (2016, April 7). IT'S ALL DEVO! New video from devolution's mutant mastermind Gerald Casale—a DM premiere. *DangerousMinds.* https://dangerousminds.net/comments/its_all_devo_new_video_from_devolutions_mutant_mastermind_gerald

Levenson, M. (2020, October 29). John Hinckley can publicly display his artwork, judge rules. *The New York Times.* https://www.nytimes.com/2020/10/29/us/john-hinckley-art.html

Linder, D. O. (n.d.-a). Hinckley's New Year's Eve 1981 monologue. https://famous-trials.com/johnhinckley/541-hinckleymono

Linder, D. O. (n.d.-b). Items found in searches conducted of Hinckley's wallet and hotel room. https://famous-trials.com/johnhinckley/542-hinckleysearch

Linder, D. O. (n.d.-c). JOHN W. HINCKLEY, JR. https://famous-trials.com/johnhinckley/523-hinckley

Linder, D. O. (n.d.-d). *Taxi driver*. https://famous-trials.com/johnhinckley/535-taxidriver

MacFarlane, S. (2018, May 10). Officials failed to assess potential risk posed by Freed Reagan shooter John Hinckley. *NBC4 Washington*. https://www.nbcwashington.com/news/local/officials-failed-to-conduct-risk-assessment-of-freed-reagan-shooter-john-hinckley/2028507/

Murphy, T. (2011, July 26). Devo's Gerald Casale: 'We're the predators that nobody can stop.' *Westword*. http://www.westword.com/music/devos-gerald-casale-were-the-predators-that-nobody-can-stop-5113527

Newport, F., Jones, J., & Saad, L. (2004, June 7). Ronald Reagan From the People's Perspective: A Gallup poll review. *Gallup.com*. https://news.gallup.com/poll/11887/Ronald-Reagan-From-Peoples-Perspective-Gallup-Poll-Review.aspx

NME. (2009, March 20). *SXSW – Devo* [Video]. YouTube. https://www.youtube.com/watch?v=FTSAVVCdr14

Pollard, A. (2021, March 31). Jodie Foster and the stalker who shot the president 'to win her heart.' *The Independent*. https://www.independent.co.uk/arts-entertainment/films/features/jodie-foster-john-hinckley-jr-shooting-b1824353.html

Schneider, M. (2015, January 29). The song co-written by DEVO and John Hinckley Jr., Ronald Reagan's failed assassin. *DangerousMinds*. https://dangerousminds.net/comments/the_song_co-written_by_devo_and_john_hinckley_jr

Slisco, A. (2021, October 27). DEVO responds to John Hinckley, Would-Be Reagan Assassin, over song royalties. *Newsweek*. https://www.newsweek.com/devo-responds-john-hinckley-would-reagan-assassin-over-song-royalties-1642869

Sommer, T. (2018, May 4). How the Kent State massacre helped give birth to punk rock. *Washington Post*. https://www.washingtonpost.com/outlook/how-the-kent-state-massacre-changed-music/2018/05/03/b45ca462-4cb6-11e8-b725-92c89fe3ca4c_story.html

The Associated Press. (2018, November 17). Judge rules would-be Reagan assassin John Hinckley can move out of his mother's house. *NBC News*. https://www.nbcnews.com/news/us-news/judge-rules-would-be-reagan-assassin-john-hinckley-can-move-n937471

TODAY. (2021, September 28). Ronald Reagan's daughter slams John

Hinckley Jr.'s coming release [Video]. YouTube. https://www.youtube.com/watch?v=xn2-9NoPDXk

Volokh, E. (2021, October 24). 'Hinckley won't face murder charge in death of James Brady, prosecutors say.' *Washington Post*. http://www.washingtonpost.com/news/volokh-conspiracy/wp/2015/01/02/hinckley-wont-face-murder-charge-in-death-of-james-brady-prosecutors-say/

Warnock, K. (1991, August 1). *The KZEW Story*. 98FM KZEW; *D Magazine*. https://web.archive.org/web/20190811202906/http://thezoofile.com/The_KZEW_Story.html

Wray, D. D. (2023, August 19). 'We were once paid $50 to quit': new wave heroes Devo on boos, Bowie and retiring after 50 years. The Guardian. https://www.theguardian.com/music/2023/aug/19/devo-band-interview-mark-mothersbaugh-gerald-casale

Chapter 13

Bear, C. (2008, May 12). American Indian boarding schools haunt many. *NPR*. https://www.npr.org/templates/story/story.php?storyId=16516865

Brooks, B. (2021, June 22). Native Americans decry unmarked graves, untold history of boarding schools. *Reuters*. https://www.reuters.com/world/us/native-americans-decry-unmarked-graves-untold-history-boarding-schools-2021-06-22/

COOLEY, DONNELL CLYDE 'SPADE' (1910–1969). (n.d.). https://web.archive.org/web/20141102135928/http://digital.library.okstate.edu/encyclopedia/entries/C/CO049.html

Guardian Staff and Agencies. (2021, June 22). US to investigate 'unspoken traumas' of Native American boarding schools. *The Guardian*. https://www.theguardian.com/us-news/2021/jun/22/us-investigation-native-american-boarding-schools

Kearns, B. (2018, September 12). The Wife & Death Of Spade Cooley, Hollywood's King Of Western Swing. *PleaseKillMe*. https://pleasekillme.com/wife-death-spade-cooley/

Tony D'Astoli. (2014, December 6). SPADE COOLEY 1 [Video]. YouTube. https://www.youtube.com/watch?v=1tHmhEaZZtM

Chapter 14

Field, K. (2018). Fever and Fate – Kim Field. *Kim Field*. https://www.kimfield.com/blog/2018/11/15/fever-and-fate

John, 'Little Willie' – Encyclopedia of Arkansas. (2023, June 16). Encyclopedia of Arkansas. https://encyclopediaofarkansas.net/entries/little-willie-john-322/

Little Willie John is arrested for murder after performing at Seattle. (n.d.). *HistoryLink.* https://www.historylink.org/File/8414

Whitall, S. (2011). *Fever: Little Willie John's Fast Life, Mysterious Death, and The Birth of Soul: The Authorised Biography.* Titan Books.

Chapter 15

Bennett, W. (2020). Welcome to Meeksville: the incredible world of Joe Meek. *Traxploitation.* https://web.archive.org/web/20200821145029/https://traxploitation.co.uk/joemeek

Bevan, N. (2009, July 12). Tom Jones' former bandmate recalls gun terror from legendary producer. Wales Online. https://www.walesonline.co.uk/news/wales-news/tom-jones-former-bandmate-recalls-2093911

Burgess, S. (2018, August 14). Chopped up and placed in suitcases: Mystery of teen's 1967 murder. *Sky News.* https://news.sky.com/story/chopped-up-and-placed-in-suitcases-mystery-of-teens-1967-murder-11463539

Buzzer365. (2019, November 29). *Patrick Pink talking about Joe Meek's last hours* [Video]. YouTube. https://www.youtube.com/watch?v=NoiKuMNKY_w

Farber, J. (2021, February 2). The Velvet Mafia: the gay men who helped shape music in the 60s. *The Guardian.* https://www.theguardian.com/music/2021/feb/02/the-velvet-mafia-the-gay-men-who-helped-shape-music-in-the-60s

Humphrey Lyttleton: Bad Penny Blues (1956). (2013, December 19). Atuneadayblogdotcom. https://atuneadayblogdotcom.wordpress.com/2013/12/18/humphrey-lyttleton-bad-penny-blues-1956/

Repsch, J. (2000). *The legendary Joe Meek: The Telstar Man.*

Sky News. (2018, August 14). Chopped up and placed in suitcases: Mystery of teen's 1967 murder. *Sky News.* https://news.sky.com/story/chopped-up-and-placed-in-suitcases-mystery-of-teens-1967-murder-11463539

Chapter 16

DiegoMJHDBrasil. (2011, October 29). Santana – Smooth Criminal Live At San Quentin State Prison 1988 [Video]. YouTube. https://

www.youtube.com/watch?v=AKUCfrHBnEo

Fong-Torres, B. (1972, December 7). Rolling Stone. *Rolling Stone*. https://www.rollingstone.com/music/music-news/the-resurrection-of-santana-228986/

Greene, A. (2020, May 28). Rolling Stone. *Rolling Stone*. https://www.rollingstone.com/music/music-news/santana-on-reuniting-classic-lineup-how-to-fight-trump-238504/

Katsilometes, J. (2014, January 22). Who owns this lake? Carlos Santana has the answer. *Las Vegas Sun*. https://lasvegassun.com/blogs/kats-report/2014/jan/22/who-owns-lake-carlos-santana-has-answer/

KRON 4. (2013a, December 21). Carlos Santana reunites with homeless ex bandmate in Oakland [Video]. YouTube. https://www.youtube.com/watch?v=s2rVpnWnRUU

KRON 4. (2013b, December 22). KRON 4's Stanley Roberts and Carlos Santana on CNN [Video]. YouTube. https://www.youtube.com/watch?v=MKa5UsDz5kQ

KRON 4. (2014, January 9). Santana bandmate Marcus Malone interview raw [Video]. YouTube. https://www.youtube.com/watch?v=RYIFGqVU8lU

Marcus Malone obituary – Oakland, CA. (n.d.). Dignity Memorial. https://www.dignitymemorial.com/obituaries/oakland-ca/marcus-malone-10404363

Marcus 'The Magnificent' Malone. (2014, July 15). Good day fb friends and family… Since Carlos and I have reunited, I've had so many inquiries as to what's next?… Facebook. https://www.facebook.com/Marcusleemalone/posts/259974194200319

Marcus 'The Magnificent' Malone. (2016, June 22). Hi fb friends, family and fans of Marcus 'The Magnificent' Malone. On 6/18/16 Marcus was involved in a freak accident… Facebook. https://www.facebook.com/Marcusleemalone/posts/523608411170228

Santana, C., Kahn, A., & Miller, H. (2014). *The universal tone*. Hachette UK.

Santana Plans Recording with Homeless Ex-Bandmate. (2013, December 23). KRON4. https://web.archive.org/web/20131225061243/http://news.kron4.com/news/santana-plans-recording-with-homeless-ex-bandmate/

Chapter 17

Chammah, M. (2016, May 12). Tower of Power Star to funkifize a California prison. The Marshall Project. https://www.themarshallproject.org/2016/05/11/tower-of-power-star-to-funkify-a-california-prison

Daniels, G. (2012, August 13). Rick Stevens, early Tower of Power lead singer, has been released on parole. This Black Sista's Memorial Page. https://thisblksistaspage.wordpress.com/2012/08/12/rick-stevens-early-tower-of-power-lead-singer-has-been-released-on-parole/

Freedman, R. (2013, January 18). Prison behind him, former Tower of Power singer set to perform Thursday. *The Mercury News.* https://www.mercurynews.com/2013/01/18/prison-behind-him-former-tower-of-power-singer-set-to-perform-thursday/

Genzlinger, N. (2017, September 8). Rick Stevens, Funk-Soul singer convicted of murder, dies at 77. *The New York Times.* https://www.nytimes.com/2017/09/08/arts/music/rick-stevens-dead-tower-of-power-singer-convicted-of-murder.html

Herhold, S. (2017, September 11). Rick Stevens: Tower of Power singer's redemption in prison. *The Mercury News.* https://www.mercurynews.com/2017/09/10/rick-stevens-tower-of-power-singers-redemption-in-prison/

Rick Stevens Official Website biography. (n.d.). https://web.archive.org/web/20150218100218/http://rickstevensmusic.com/Biography.html

Schuppe, J. (2016, May 12). After 36 years in prison, Tower of Power's Rick Stevens returns to sing. *NBC News.* https://www.nbcnews.com/news/us-news/after-36-years-prison-tower-power-s-rick-stevens-returns-n573001

Selvin, J. (2013, January 29). Singer Rick Stevens embraces 2nd chance. *SFGate.* https://www.sfgate.com/music/article/singer-rick-stevens-embraces-2nd-chance-4229673.php

St. Clair, K. (2002, January 30). Free Rick Stevens. *East Bay Express | Oakland, Berkeley & Alameda.* https://eastbayexpress.com/free-rick-stevens-1/

Story Connection TV. (2015, November 19). Story Connection: Rick Stevens pt 1 [Video]. YouTube. https://www.youtube.com/watch?v=4wRPNkEjOaU

Tellez, M. (2013, March 29). Ex-Tower of Power singer: Prison helped me grow up. *NBC Bay Area.* https://www.nbcbayarea.com/news/local/ex-tower-of-power-singer-prison-helped-me-grow-up/1938809/

Chapter 18

Aswad, J. (2023, March 16). Jim Gordon, Drummer for Eric Clapton and 'Layla' Co-Writer Who Was Convicted of Murder, Dies at 77. *Variety*. https://variety.com/2023/music/news/jim-gordon-drummer-layla-cowriter-dead-1235555775/

Booe, M. (1994, July 3). BANG THE DRUM SLOWLY. *Washington Post*. https://www.washingtonpost.com/archive/lifestyle/1994/07/03/bang-the-drum-slowly/18987952-f600-4120-88f3-8f7920e63e3e/

Flanary, P. (2023, March 16). Billboard. *Billboard*. https://www.billboard.com/articles/news/8408395/jim-gordon-drummer-denied-parole-layla-songwriter

Hartman, K. (2012). *The wrecking crew: The Inside Story of Rock and Roll's Best-Kept Secret*. Macmillan.

Olson, D. E. (2018, June 20). Psychedelic drugs could treat depression, and other mental illnesses. University of California. https://www.universityofcalifornia.edu/news/psychedelic-drugs-could-treat-depression-and-other-mental-illnesses

Rehfeld, B. (1985, June 6). Rolling Stone. *Rolling Stone*. https://www.rollingstone.com/music/music-news/when-the-voices-took-over-52761/

Robinson, J. (2011, March 16). The curse of the Dominos. *The Telegraph*. http://www.telegraph.co.uk/culture/music/rockandpopfeatures/8386038/The-curse-of-the-Dominos.html

Chapter 19

Brown, M. (2012). *Tearing Down The Wall of Sound: The Rise And Fall of Phil Spector*. A&C Black.

California Convictions. (2021a, January 18). Phil Spector Stole $20 From Me In Prison [Video]. YouTube. https://www.youtube.com/watch?v=SGV29B5LHYw

California Convictions. (2021b, January 22). Phil Spector's prison visiting room antics [Video]. YouTube. https://www.youtube.com/watch?v=xVNtKGQhA5E

California Convictions. (2021c, January 25). I Refused To Be Phil Spector's Prison Bodyguard [Video]. YouTube. https://www.youtube.com/watch?v=E6oSJqUemsk

California Convictions. (2021d, May 28). He stole Phil Spector's $300 shoes in prison [Video]. YouTube. https://www.youtube.com/watch?v=ZPCWbUhZHDo

Delbyck, C. (2021, January 18). Ronnie Spector Reacts To 'Lousy Husband' Phil Spector's Death. *HuffPost*. https://www.huffpost.com/entry/ronnie-spector-reacts-to-lousy-husband-phil-spectors-death_n_6004a465c5b697df1a069fd1

DeMain, B. (2011, August 1). 5 Artists reportedly held at gunpoint by Phil Spector | Mental floss. *Mental Floss*. https://www.mentalfloss.com/article/28392/5-artists-reportedly-held-gunpoint-phil-spector

Doyle, J. (n.d.). *Ronettes lawsuit | The Pop History Dig*. https://www.pophistorydig.com/topics/tag/ronettes-lawsuit/

Grimes, W. (2021, January 22). Phil Spector, famed music producer and convicted murderer, dies at 81. *The New York Times*. https://www.nytimes.com/2021/01/17/arts/music/phil-spector-dead.html

Harris, K. (2021, January 17). Rolling Stone. *Rolling Stone*. https://www.rollingstone.com/music/music-news/phil-spector-dead-obit-67459/

Hood, B. (2018, November 28). Ronnie Spector says Phil Spector adopted twins without telling her. *Page Six*. https://pagesix.com/2018/11/28/ronnie-spector-says-phil-spector-adopted-twins-without-telling-her/

Kemp, S. (2021, October 1). The moment Phil Spector held a gun to Leonard Cohen's head. *Far Out Magazine*. https://faroutmagazine.co.uk/phil-spector-held-gun-to-leonard-cohen-head/

Kubernik, H. (2019, November 15). Phil Spector, the musical legacy: Part three. *Goldmine Magazine: Record Collector & Music Memorabilia*. https://www.goldminemag.com/articles/phil-spector-the-musical-legacy-part-three

Marre, J. (Director). (2007, October 16). *Phil Spector's Demons*.

Mercer, D. (2023, January 8). The murderer and musical 'genius': How Phil Spector killed actress – and why daughter is 'trying to clear his name' *Sky News*. https://news.sky.com/story/the-murderer-and-musical-genius-how-phil-spector-killed-actress-8211-and-why-daughter-is-trying-to-clear-his-name-12741669

Michaels, S. (2009, July 28). Phil Spector's biggest fan: Charles Manson. *The Guardian*. https://www.theguardian.com/music/2009/jul/28/phil-spector-charles-manson

Phil Spector: Prosecution's motion to admit evidence of other crimes. (n.d.). https://sprocket-trials.blogspot.com/2008/08/phil-spector-prosecutions-motion-to.html

Ramone, D. D., & Kofman, V. (2016). *Lobotomy: Surviving the Ramones*. Da Capo Press.

Ramone, J. (2012). *Commando: The Autobiography of Johnny Ramone.* Abrams.

Reuters Staff. (2010, August 20). Phil Spector documentary gets OK from killer's son. U.S. https://www.reuters.com/article/us-spector-idUSTRE67J18320100820

Ribowsky, M. (2000). *He's a rebel: Phil Spector, Rock and Roll's Legendary Producer.* Rowman & Littlefield.

Spector, R., & Waldron, V. (2015). *Be my baby: How I Survived Mascara, Miniskirts, and Madness, Or My Life as a Fabulous Ronette [Deluxe Paperback with Color Photos].*

Timrots, A. D., & Rand, M. R. (1987). Violent crime by strangers and nonstrangers. U.S. Department of Justice Office of Justice Programs. https://www.ojp.gov/ncjrs/virtual-library/abstracts/violent-crime-strangers-and-nonstrangers

Wenn. (2023, September 6). Phil Spector's Son Is Homeless. *Contactmusic.com.* https://www.contactmusic.com/phil-spector/news/phil-spector.s-son-is-homeless

Chapter 20

Battersby, M. (2012, September 12). The Sex Pistols' 1977 Jubilee pageant | The Independent. *The Independent.* https://www.independent.co.uk/arts-entertainment/art/news/sex-pistols-1977-jubilee-pageant-8130561.html

BBC ON THIS DAY | 12 | 1978: Sex Pistol Vicious on murder charge. (n.d.). http://news.bbc.co.uk/onthisday/hi/dates/stories/october/12/newsid_2543000/2543439.stm

Browne, D. (2010, April 12). New York Dolls' Sylvain Sylvain Remembers Malcolm McLaren. *Rolling Stone.* https://www.rollingstone.com/music/music-news/new-york-dolls-sylvain-sylvain-remembers-malcolm-mclaren-78305/

Dig Gallery. (2010). Ramones: Interview With Eileen Polk of His Ramones Memories in 2011. http://www.ramonesheaven.com/inter/EileenPolkRamonesMemories2011.html

Indicted For Second Degree Murder. (n.d.). The Smoking Gun. http://www.thesmokinggun.com/file/indicted-second-degree-murder

Levine, N. (2013, November 9). John Lydon praises Mick Jagger for paying Sid Vicious's murder charge lawyers. *NME.* https://www.nme.com/news/music/sex-pistols-12-1237951

Lydon, J., & Zimmerman, K. (2008). *Rotten: No Irish, No Blacks, No*

Dogs. Macmillan.

Malraux, A., McNeil, L., & McCain, G. (2006). *Please kill me: The Uncensored Oral History of Punk*. Grove Press.

Michaels, S. (2009, February 6). Malcolm McLaren: Sid didn't kill Nancy. *The Guardian*. https://www.theguardian.com/music/2009/feb/06/malcolm-mclaren-sid-vicious

MTV. (2014, July 14). *Rock Stories* | 'Chrissie Hynde's Vicious Love' | MTV [Video]. YouTube. https://www.youtube.com/watch?v=PzgFOb9mtx4

Olson, M. (1977, July 23). Sex Pistols – Expressen July 23 1977. Summer of Hate. https://web.archive.org/web/20150705011021/http://www.acc.umu.se/~samhain/summerofhate/expressenjuly23.html

On This Day in 1977: Sid Vicious uses a bicycle chain very irresponsibly | Rhino. (2016, June 15). *Rhino.com*. https://www.rhino.com/article/on-this-day-in-1977-sid-vicious-uses-a-bicycle-chain-very-irresponsibly

Popcornflix. (2020, September 15). Sid Vicious: The Final 24 (Full Documentary) The Story of His Final 24 Hours [Video]. YouTube. https://www.youtube.com/watch?v=qfkywgPbbyw

Savage, J. (2002). *England's Dreaming, revised Edition: Anarchy, Sex Pistols, Punk Rock, and Beyond*. Macmillan.

Savage, J. (2009, January 18). Sid Vicious: Little boy lost. *The Guardian*. https://www.theguardian.com/music/2009/jan/18/sid-vicious-death-icon

Savage, J. (2012, May 29). The Sex Pistols' jubilee boat trip – a classic account. *The Guardian*. https://www.theguardian.com/music/2012/may/29/sex-pistols-jubilee-boat-trip

Sex Pistols' Sid Vicious on Trial for the Murder of Girlfriend. (n.d.). The Courtroom Sketches of Ida Libby Dengrove. https://web.archive.org/web/20220122025316/https://archives.law.virginia.edu/dengrove/writeup/sex-pistols%E2%80%99-sid-vicious-trial-murder-girlfriend

Sid Confesses To Cops. (n.d.). The Smoking Gun. http://www.thesmokinggun.com/file/sid-confesses-cops

Simmons, R. (2015, October 5). 10 Well-Known Songs Banned by the BBC (For Ridiculous Reasons), 1965–1977. *Rebeat Magazine*. http://www.rebeatmag.com/10-well-known-songs-banned-by-the-bbc-for-ridiculous-reasons-1965-1977/

Skafish, J. (2011, January 25). *Sid Vicious' last Hurrah… again – Official*

Skafish Blog. https://skafishblog.skafish.com/2011/01/25/sid-vicious%E2%80%99-last-hurrah-again/

Special to National Post. (2015, September 10). Chrissie Hynde: 'No one was particularly surprised' when Sid Vicious killed Nancy Spungen. *National post.* https://nationalpost.com/entertainment/books/chrissie-hynde-no-one-was-particularly-surprised-when-sid-vicious-killed-nancy-spungen

Spungen, D. (1996). *And I don't want to live this life: A Mother's Story of Her Daughter's Murder.* Ballantine Books.

SSidVicious. (2008, December 21). Sid Vicious Interview, after stabing [sic] Nancy [Video]. YouTube. https://www.youtube.com/watch?v=R2lilvnx4q0

Telegraph Reporters. (2016, June 23). It was Sid Vicious's mum who gave him fatal final dose of heroin says Sex Pistols photographer. *The Telegraph.* https://www.telegraph.co.uk/music/news/it-was-sid-viciouss-mum-who-gave-him-fatal-final-dose-of-heroin/

Temple, J. (Director). (2000, May 12). *The Filth and the Fury.* FilmFour.

Tippins, S. (2013, December 4). Sid and Nancy: The final hours. *Salon.* https://www.salon.com/2013/12/04/sid_and_nancy_the_final_hours/

Trista. (2018, October 16). 16 Truly Disturbing Moments That Made Punk Rocker Sid Vicious of the Sex Pistols Live Up to His Name. History Collection. https://historycollection.com/16-truly-disturbing-moments-that-made-punk-rocker-sid-vicious-of-the-sex-pistols-live-up-to-his-name/4/

Wakeman, J. (2017, October 12). Rolling Stone. *Rolling Stone.* https://www.rollingstone.com/culture/culture-news/flashback-nancy-spungen-found-dead-at-chelsea-hotel-118648/

Whatley, J. (2021). Sid Vicious: not that talented and probably a murderer. *Far Out Magazine.* https://faroutmagazine.co.uk/sid-vicious-not-that-talented-and-probably-a-murderer/

Chapter 21

15 December 1969: Plastic Ono Band live at Lyceum Ballroom, London | The Beatles Bible. (n.d.). *The Beatles Bible.* https://www.beatlesbible.com/1969/12/15/plastic-ono-band-live-lyceum-ballroom-london/

Caldwell, N. (2023). Steve McQueen: The life story you may not know. *Stacker.* https://stacker.com/stories/13316/steve-mcqueen-life-story-you-may-not-know

Chapman, R. (1998). Keith Moon: Patent British Exploding Drummer. https://web.archive.org/web/20210512070723/http://rob-chapman.com/pages/moon.html

Cow Palace, 1973: The Who's Keith Moon Passes Out From Drugs, And An Audience Member Fills In. (2019, November 20). *Groovy History.* https://groovyhistory.com/who-keith-moon-drummer-scot-halpin

Curzon Place. (n.d.). https://nilssonschmilsson.com/curzon-place-210601130345.html

familiar to billions. (2017, March 8). Keith moon puts to [sic] much gun powder in his drum kit and blows up in his face [Video]. YouTube. https://www.youtube.com/watch?v=gu42_-Dp4Tw

Fletcher, T. (2010). *Dear Boy: The Life of Keith Moon.* Omnibus Press.

Historic England. (n.d.). THE RED LION HOTEL, Hatfield – 1173348 | Historic England. https://historicengland.org.uk/listing/the-list/list-entry/1173348?section=official-listing

Keith Moon Gets Off Easy. (1970, April 30). *Rolling Stone.* https://www.rollingstone.com/music/music-news/keith-moon-gets-off-easy-102505/

Maxham, E. (2022). Paul McCartney Owns The Back Catalog Of This Rock Icon. *Grunge.* https://www.grunge.com/759502/paul-mccartney-owns-the-back-catalog-of-this-rock-icon/

pheniafilms. (2014, December 21). VH1 100 Shocking rock & Roll Moments KEITH MOON 5/2001 [Video]. YouTube. https://www.youtube.com/watch?v=iJ4uXmOXgzs

Piller, E. (2011, October 12). Eddie Piller talks Pete Meaden and Quadrophenia – Modculture. https://www.modculture.co.uk/feature-eddie-piller-talks-pete-meaden-and-quadrophenia/

Popcornflix. (2020, October 29). Keith Moon: The Final 24 (Full Documentary) [Video]. YouTube. https://www.youtube.com/watch?v=qxtp4xV1xMw

Rare Photographs From John & Yoko's 'Peace For Christmas' UNICEF Concert in December 1969 | *Vintage News Daily.* (2018, December 21). https://vintagenewsdaily.com/rare-photographs-from-john-yokos-peace-for-christmas-unicef-concert-in-december-1969/

Staff. (2020, September 2). Keith Moon once accidentally ran over and killed his driver. *Far Out Magazine.* https://faroutmagazine.co.uk/keith-moon-the-who-killed-driver-accident/

Staff. (2021, August 23). When The Who's Keith Moon drove a car into a swimming pool. *Far Out Magazine.* https://faroutmagazine.co.uk/

who-keith-moon-drove-a-car-into-a-swimming-pool/

Starkey, A. (2021, August 23). Remembering the madcap, tragic genius of Keith Moon. *Far Out Magazine*. https://faroutmagazine.co.uk/remembering-the-madcap-tragic-genius-of-keith-moon/

Taylor, R. (2014, July 18). *Keith Moon almost put an end to rocker Ian McLagan's career when he stole his woman*. Irish Mirror. https://www.irishmirror.ie/whats-on/music-nightlife-news/keith-moon-put-end-rocker-3880810

Taysom, J. (2020, August 12). Mama Cass and Keith Moon died in same 'cursed' apartment. *Far Out Magazine*. https://faroutmagazine.co.uk/mama-cass-keith-moon-death-the-who-mayfair/

Taysom, J. (2021, January 14). Keith Moon and Steve McQueen were once neighbours from hell. *Far Out Magazine*. https://faroutmagazine.co.uk/keith-moon-steve-mcqueen-neighours-from-hell/

The WHO: 50 years of Peace & Music. (n.d.). Bethel Woods Center for the Arts. https://www.bethelwoodscenter.org/blog/the-who

Townshend, P. (2012). *Who I Am*. HarperCollins Publishers.

Wawzenek, B. (2016, May 31). *How the Who Become the World's Loudest Band*. Ultimate Classic Rock. https://ultimateclassicrock.com/who-loudest-band/

Yaffe, A. (n.d.). Keith Moon Accidentally Killed a Man and Paid the Price. *Musicoholics*. https://web.archive.org/web/20210731082912/https://musicoholics.com/backstage-stories/keith-moon-accidentally-killed-a-man-and-paid-the-price/

Chapter 22

Andrew Harry Briggs. (2015, December 20). Rollermania: Britain's Biggest Ever Boy Band (The Story Of The Bay City Rollers) [Video]. YouTube. https://www.youtube.com/watch?v=W0YihqJxiz8

BelfastTelegraph.co.uk. (2015, May 25). Still on a roll: Former Bay City Roller Les McKeown. *BelfastTelegraph.co.uk*. https://www.belfasttelegraph.co.uk/life/features/still-on-a-roll-former-bay-city-roller-les-mckeown-31249499.html

Billboard. (n.d.). *Bay City Rollers | Biography, Music & News | Billboard*. https://www.billboard.com/artist/bay-city-rollers/chart-history/hsi/

Boy Bands Through The Years. (n.d.). https://web.archive.org/web/20200313063752/http://webpage.pace.edu/eh57156n/Boybandsthroughouttheyears.html

Brinsford, J. (2021, April 23). Bay City Rollers tragedies from Les McKeown's sudden death to original members. *Mirror*. https://www.mirror.co.uk/3am/celebrity-news/bay-city-rollers-tragedies-les-23966125

By The Newsroom. (2009, February 18). Bay City Roller Les McKeown's gay sex romps revealed to wife on TV. *The Scotsman*. https://www.scotsman.com/news/bay-city-roller-les-mckeowns-gay-sex-romps-revealed-wife-tv-2444163

By The Newsroom. (2016, October 15). Bay City Rollers legal battle reaches end of the road. *The Scotsman*. https://www.scotsman.com/whats-on/arts-and-entertainment/bay-city-rollers-legal-battle-reaches-end-road-865600

Davies, N. (1993, February 13). The dark side of the Bay City Rollers. https://www.nickdavies.net/1993/02/13/the-massacre-inside-the-bay-city-rollers/

jannylovesbcr. (2012, April 9). Eric Faulkner & Leslie McKeown (Bay City Rollers) – 1983 interview [Video]. YouTube. https://www.youtube.com/watch?v=66i7x7LQgzA

Jonathan King jailed for child sex abuse. (2001, November 21). *The Guardian*. https://www.theguardian.com/uk/2001/nov/21/childprotection.society

Maloney, A. (2021, April 23). How Les Mckeown overcame teen rape, a tragic accident at 19 and drug addiction which ended his Bay City… *The Sun*. https://www.thesun.co.uk/tvandshowbiz/14741937/les-mckeown-bay-city-rollers-killed-oap-rape/

Pazzanese, C. (2014, November 14). The man with the 'golden ear' *Harvard Gazette*. https://news.harvard.edu/gazette/story/2014/11/star-maker-lands-at-law-school/

Radio 1 DJ jailed for paedophilia claims offences were consensual. (2010, February 22). *The Telegraph*. https://www.telegraph.co.uk/news/uknews/crime/7291723/Radio-1-DJ-jailed-for-paedophilia-claims-offences-were-consensual.html

Ronson, J. (2017, December 1). The fall of a pop impresario. *The Guardian*. https://www.theguardian.com/lifeandstyle/2001/dec/01/weekend.jonronson

Ross, P. (2003, September). Les McKeown | Peter Ross. *Peter Ross*. https://peterross.scot/articles/les-mckeown/

Spence, S. (2016). *When the screaming stops: The Dark History of Pop's First Boy Bands.*

Telegraph Obituaries. (2021, April 22). Les McKeown, frontman of the Bay City Rollers, darlings of 1970s teenyboppers whose hits included Bye, Bye, Baby and Give a Little Love – obituary. *The Telegraph.* https://www.telegraph.co.uk/obituaries/2021/04/22/les-mckeown-frontman-bay-city-rollers-darlings-1970s-teenyboppers/

ACKNOWLEDGEMENTS

There are many people I want to thank for their support throughout my writing career.

Thank you to my parents for supporting my love of classic rock and all things '60s/'70s, taking me to record stores and vintage clothing stores, and telling me stories of the past like my dad's brief time as a DJ in the '70s. Once again, I couldn't have written this book without the influence of my dad, because every Friday night we'd watch true crime documentaries together when I was as young as eight or nine years old. Thanks, Dad for getting me into the 'based on a true story' genre of movies – those were an inspiration to me as a writer too. And thank you, Dad, for giving me feedback on my secondary school essays, which made me a better writer.

Thank you to my husband, Eoin, for believing in my writing and my mission with *The Diversity of Classic Rock* and now *Crime of the Century* and staying by my side even when the going got tough. Also, for tolerating my daily infodumps about classic rock. It's because of him that this book idea wasn't just relegated to a blog post on *The Diversity of Classic Rock*. If you enjoyed the book, thank Eoin too!

I also want to thank my grandmother, Maurine, for always being there for me. For the family who are sadly no longer with us, Grandpa Sol and Grandma Esperanza, I hope you're enjoying this book wherever you are.

A thank you also goes to two friends who passed away. A classmate from my Journalism MA at the University of Limerick, Cillian, who played a song by Charles Manson when I guested on his radio show. That was the day that I learnt that Charles Manson had a connection to classic rock and was an early inspiration for me to write this book. I may have only known Cillian for a short time, but he really made an impact on me. I also want to remember an early supporter and friend of the blog, Matt, a writer from New Jersey. He always believed in my work and we'd often talk about classic rock.

I also want to thank two of my friends, Paul and Nick, who both encouraged me to follow my dream to write a book. When Paul told me about his journey in writing a book, it inspired me and I wanted to do the same. You both have been inspirations to me.

Another thank you to my two close friends who both enjoy true crime and classic rock, Amanda and Kate. You were among the first people I told about this project and your enthusiasm for the project motivated me to keep going even when I was going through difficult times.

Another thank you to Patrick and Jeffrey, who have been generous patrons to the blog.

And, of course, a thank you to every *Diversity of Classic Rock* fan for all the support over the years.

ABOUT THE AUTHOR

Angie Moon is a writer and classic rock historian based in England. She started *The Diversity of Classic Rock* in 2015 as a project during her undergraduate studies and has continued writing blog posts for it ever since. While in university, she had her own classic rock radio show called Crazy on Classic Rock. She graduated with an MA in Journalism from the University of Limerick in 2018. Besides classic rock and writing, Angie loves collecting vintage clothing, collecting vinyl records, photography, travelling, and spending time with her cat, Bowie.

You can find *The Diversity of Classic Rock* on
crazyonclassicrock.com

You can follow Angie on social media too:
Facebook: facebook.com/angiemoonclassicrock
Twitter: twitter.com/theangiemoon
Instagram: instagram.com/angiemichellemoon

Printed in the USA
CPSIA information can be obtained
at www.ICGtesting.com
LVHW070824220324
775209LV00020B/44/J

9 781805 143925